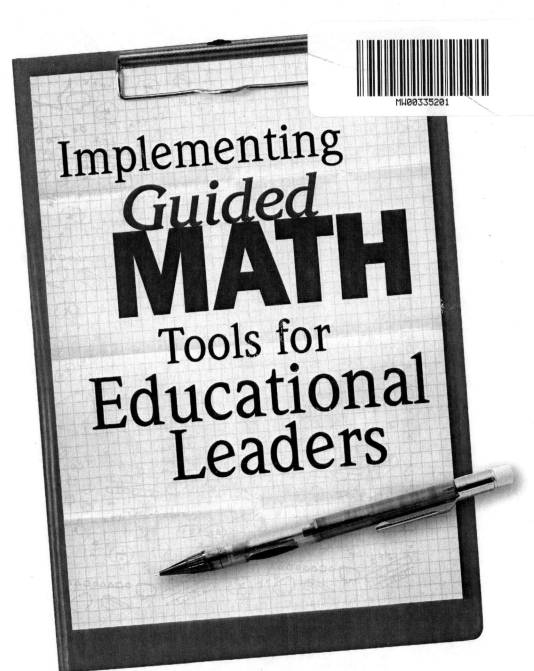

Implementing *Guided* MATH
Tools for Educational Leaders

Author
Laney Sammons, M.L.S.
Foreword
Mary Esther Reynosa, M.A.Ed

SHELL EDUCATION

Publishing Credits

Corinne Burton, M.A.Ed., *Publisher*; Kimberly Stockton, M.S.Ed., *Vice President of Education*; Conni Medina, M.A.Ed., *Managing Editor*; Sara Johnson, M.S.Ed., *Content Director*; Paula Makridis, M.A.Ed., *Editor*; Kyleena Harper, *Assistant Editor*; Marissa Dunham, *Editorial Assistant*; Grace Alba Le, *Multimedia Designer*; Robin Erickson, *Multimedia Designer*; Kevin Pham, *Production Artist*

Shell Education

5301 Oceanus Drive
Huntington Beach, CA 92649-1030
http://www.shelleducation.com

ISBN 978-1-4258-1512-7

© 2016 Shell Educational Publishing, Inc.

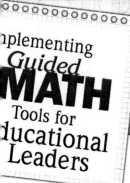

Table of Contents

4 ◆

Foreword

One District's Guided Math Journey

My journey into the world of Guided Math was a B.R.I.T.E. beginning that started over eight years ago. As an Instructional Specialist for Elementary Mathematics for Northside ISD in San Antonio, Texas, I had a strong team of Instructional Support Teachers who shared my goal of making our students mathematically proficient. The U.C.A.R.E. model we used to understand the components from the research of Adding it Up: Helping Children Learn Mathematics (2001) showed that our teachers were doing great in teaching for (U) Understanding and (C) Computation, but were not as effective with (A) Analysis, (R) Reasoning, and especially, (E) Engagement. Using the research from the Institute of Educational Services (IES), we had been targeting spiral review as part of our district's Math Action Wall time initiative. This was the first 20 minutes of instruction, similar to Calendar Math, when our students were engaged in some interactive and prescriptive review. But for the rest of the 90-minute math block, our teachers taught through whole-group instruction and pulled a small group of students as needed for extra help. In visiting classrooms where students appeared to be learning, I realized that something was still missing from their instruction. Our students were not doing enough analyzing and reasoning through problem solving, and they did not seem fully engaged and excited about what they were learning. They were developing mathematical capability but not proficiency.

In 2007, one of my Instructional Support Teachers discovered some ideas for math stations online. She then created the acronym B.R.I.T.E., for math stations for our district, where B stood for Basic Facts, R for Review, I for Instruction with teacher, T for Tools and Technology, and E for Estimation and Problem Solving. The stations were field tested and district-wide training sessions were held for teachers, who left with materials ready to use in their classrooms. Although the reviews from teachers were always positive, the whole idea of math stations was not strong enough to become a district-wide initiative. Some teachers felt forced to use the B.R.I.T.E. acronym, although we stressed that they could create their own acronym. Most of the teachers just did not understand the effectiveness of the stations and the importance of creating purposeful and meaningful independent learning experiences for their students.

When Laney Sammons' book, Guided Math: A Framework for Mathematics Instruction, was published in 2010, I was very impressed with the connection she made to Guided Reading. This was just the connection needed to make this a district-wide initiative. It was well known that teachers were comfortable teaching in this reading format, so why couldn't they transfer it to mathematics? This was the missing link that could help make our students mathematically proficient by giving them an environment of numeracy, and Guided Math workstations would make their instruction more differentiated and engaging. The spiral review, that I knew was effective in building long-term retention of concepts, would come alive through interactive stations focusing on review of previously mastered concepts and computational fluency. The problem-solving stations including mathematical investigations would involve the students in reasoning and analyzing that were so important in developing their mathematical proficiency. It was a framework that I knew would maximize student engagement!

In an effort to make this a district-wide initiative, I started my own implementation plan in 2010. I purchased Laney's book for all campus math leaders and led a book study throughout the year. I also offered a session for all elementary school administrators on Guided Math and provided them with a copy of the book. I stressed that they use the book as part of a book study with their teachers. Some administrators requested training from my department, which was very well received. The sessions were usually 3–6 hours in length for either K–2 or 3–5 teachers, and they ended with "Make and Take" time. We always emphasized that the training was just the beginning. We worked with the campus math leader to ensure that team planning would continue to involve planning for Guided Math workstations. My department worked with administrators and created a checklist of "look-fors" that we used for classroom visits, and we took pictures of best practices that we shared with grade-level teams. It was an ongoing process that continued throughout that first year and the years to come.

In 2011, a few campuses partnered to bring Laney Sammons to their campus for professional development. It was a 6-hour session that was well worth the time of the teachers and administrators. Bringing the campuses together was a springboard that led their math leaders into a deeper understanding and implementation of Guided Math. The session ultimately led to many other campuses adopting Guided Math with one campus even volunteering to be a model school for other campuses to visit. Along the way, I used every opportunity to share the good news of Guided Math best practices to administrators at our Curriculum Updates. By 2014, we had many other campuses that had made the journey and were going into their second or third year of implementation. As part of my support at certain campuses, I organized campus visits and conferences for the teachers to learn about the framework from each other.

In spring of 2015, my math department started looking specifically at lessons learned from our journey through Guided Math. We noted what was effective in our district's implementation and what needed improvement. We learned that our journey had evolved in a positive manner from stations that at one time only targeted basic facts to now targeting important focal point areas, such as problem solving, engaging games for computational fluency, and the use of technology. Also, most classrooms had management charts that were effectively used in assigning students to stations.

However, as we listened to the instruction in the teachers' Guided Math groups and as we rotated to the varied math workstations, we noticed that there was not enough differentiation. We also observed that at most workstations students were not being held accountable with a recording sheet or a math journal entry. Differentiation and accountability became our focus as we provided professional development for campuses. We made sure to collaborate with the campus math leaders so that they could work with their teachers on these issues. We also made sure to find different resources for math workstations either online or from different companies. Shell Education has some great resources for math games that were lifesavers in this process! And again, as better examples of differentiation and accountability occurred, we compiled best practices to share with administrators and other teachers who began this journey.

Each year more schools have joined the bandwagon of Guided Math in Northside ISD, which consists of 75 schools and continues to grow. This is a journey that will continue to evolve for many years to come. For those of you who are just now starting the journey, Laney Sammons' new book, *Implementing Guided Math: Tools for Educational Leaders*, provides some specific guidelines and plans for implementation. From the specific role of Math Coaches, to a yearlong plan for Professional Learning Communities, to the varied classroom visit checklists and self-assessments, this is a book that I needed in my initial journey. The implementation plan in this book will fit any district's individual needs. Although our district has already started the implementation process, it is never too late to try some of the outstanding ideas this book has to offer. It will be the next book study for my math leaders!

—Mary Esther Reynosa, M.A.Ed.
Instructional Specialist for Elementary Mathematics,
Northside ISD: San Antonio, Texas
Macmillan McGraw-Hill Mathematics Textbook Author

Acknowledgments

Over the past few years, I have been fortunate to work with schools and school districts throughout the United States and Canada training teachers to use the Guided Math framework. Repeatedly, educational leaders have sought advice about how they can most effectively support the implementation of Guided Math. In this book, I am sharing what I have learned from working with many dedicated educators who have been involved in that effort. I hope the book will give education leaders, whether they are central office staff, principals, assistant principals, coaches, math specialists, or teacher leaders, some guidance for supporting teachers as they begin using Guided Math in their classrooms.

My thanks go to Ed Varjassy, Curriculum Coordinator, and the math coaches from the Chinook School Division in Saskatchewan, Canada, for including me in their multi-year Guided Math implementation plan and for allowing me to share their work with the readers of this book. I also especially wish to thank Catiia Greene, Title I Coordinator in Virginia, for allowing me to include the comprehensive implementation plan she developed for her district. In addition, I thank all of the educators with whom I have worked over the years for sharing their ideas about and their experiences with Guided Math. I feel privileged in being able to share the ideas of these many dedicated professionals as I continue to work with both teachers who already use Guided Math in their classrooms and those who are just learning about the framework.

As always, I thank Shell Education and its editors for making this book possible. Sara Johnson has been steadfast in encouraging me to write about my ideas and then editing my work. I value our relationship that has grown over the past seven years—even as her family has grown. Thank you, Sara!

And last, but certainly not least, thank you to my family who so patiently support me through my days of writing—especially when it seems the book will never be finished. My love to you all, especially to my husband Jack, who has by far endured the most!

Introduction

In 2000, the National Commission on Mathematics and Science Teaching for the 21st century reported that "In the United States there is one dominant instructional technique employed by classroom mathematics teachers to the virtual exclusion of other, more effective methods" (20). Any educator, as well as almost anyone who has been a part of mathematics education as a student, can most likely accurately describe the instructional technique that the report was referencing: whole-group, direct instruction. When working with teachers around the country, I often ask them to describe the math instruction they received as students. The following descriptions are common: large group, teacher-led, paper and pencil, from the book, boring, drill and kill, don't ask why, emphasis on computation, and only one right answer. It is amazing how consistent the responses are from teachers who have been educated in very different school environments in localities across the country.

According to Balka, Hull, and Miles, "The traditional instructional pattern of lecture, then demonstration, followed by independent student practice on worksheets has not changed in many, many years" (2010, 29). In fact, "Materials and instructional techniques that differ from this approach are often disregarded without fair analysis" (2010, 29). Why have instructional techniques for mathematics stagnated?

Instinctively, we know that teachers tend to teach the way they were taught, even when their experiences as students were not positive—just as people tend to parent their children in the same ways their parents parented them. New teachers may find reassurance in replicating the teaching methods with which they are most familiar. Over time, these methods become habitual. Even as they acquire more experience, many teachers continue to employ these teaching techniques. Changes in the status quo may feel threatening, especially with the pressures of teacher accountability based on high-stakes testing results. In addition, because the traditional method is so ubiquitous, teachers who recognize the benefits of more effective methods of instruction too often find themselves working in isolation—resented by teachers who view these teachers' efforts to change as tacit criticism of their own teaching.

Research tells us that increases in student learning are directly linked to the strategic instructional choices made by teachers (Marzano 2003). Not every teaching method is effective for all situations or for all learners. But, when teachers have a "repertoire of strategies from which they can select a suitable one for a given purpose" (Danielson 2007, 24), and they make considered and purposeful decisions when choosing teaching strategies, student learning should increase. According to Danielson (2007), "Selecting instructional approaches rests absolutely with a teacher; this decision is a critical element of professionalism" (24). Implicit in Danielson's framework for teaching is the assumption that instructional decisions must be purposeful and made by teachers.

With this in mind, many schools and school districts include in their improvement efforts, measures aimed at increasing the instructional strategies that teachers have available to them, supporting teachers' efforts to move away from the traditional instructional practices, and encouraging teachers to both individually and in collaboration with other teachers reflect on the effectiveness of their mathematics instruction. "When teachers are supported and encouraged to inquire deeply about their teaching, are trusted to do this work with integrity, and are seen as sources of knowledge and expertise, they can make meaningful changes to their instruction" (Van Tassel 2014, 78).

The Guided Math Framework

To help teachers build capacity by expanding their repertoire of instructional strategies, many education leaders may consider the implementation of Guided Math (Sammons 2010, 2013).

This framework offers a wide selection of instructional strategies from which teachers can choose—all of which engage students in challenging mathematical instruction. The flexibility of the framework permits teachers to adapt it to align with their own teaching styles and to meet the needs of their students. When implemented, Guided Math instruction may vary from week to week and from classroom to classroom (Sammons 2013).

Creating a Classroom Environment of Numeracy

Essential in a Guided Math classroom is the establishment of a classroom environment of numeracy. It should be obvious upon entering the classroom that mathematics is being taught and learned there. For a math-rich setting, teachers display math word walls, mathematical work by students, math-related literature, math anchor charts, and references to real-life mathematical application. Manipulatives and instruments of measure are readily available and used frequently. In addition, care is taken to nurture a community of young mathematicians in which math talk abounds. Within this kind of environment, in which students are immersed in math, students come to appreciate its importance in their lives and to enjoy the challenge of becoming mathematicians in their own right.

Math Warm-Ups

While setting a mathematical tone for the day, Math Warm-Ups at the beginning of a day or a class period also provide valuable ongoing mathematical practice for students. Calendar board activities and Math Stretches may serve as brief warm-ups for students. Warm-ups also provide opportunities for students to learn about current event connections to mathematics and to assume classroom responsibilities that reinforce mathematical skills.

Whole-Class Instruction

This more traditional instructional mode is an option for teachers to deliver mini lessons, conduct math-related read-alouds, and model mathematical thinking. They are also valuable for Math Huddle discussions as follow-ups to Math Stretch tasks. Additionally, this format can be used for review, class mathematical games, and activating strategies. Working together in these ways is important in establishing a sense of mathematical community.

Small-Group Instruction

At the heart of the framework is small-group instruction with groups in which the composition is fluid and based upon previously identified, specific instructional needs. These small-group lessons allow teachers to more easily differentiate instruction and to help students develop proficiency in the mathematical practices as described by the Common Core State Standards for Mathematics (NGA and CCSSO 2010) and the National Council of Teachers of Mathematics (NCTM) Process Standards (2000).

In addition, the intimate nature of small-group lessons enables teachers to maximize student engagement (both hands-on and minds-on), to conduct ongoing informal formative assessment, and to closely monitor understanding as students work. Because teachers are able to respond immediately when misconceptions are observed or move forward with greater challenges when understanding is evident, instruction is more efficient than traditional whole-class lessons. In spite of the fact that these lessons are usually much shorter in duration, greater student understanding of concepts and skills is achieved.

Math Workshop

During Math Workshop, students work independently on math workstation tasks that provide practice of previously mastered concepts and skills, promote computational fluency, or challenge students to engage in mathematical investigations. Playing math games is a common component of Math Workshop, but not the only option. Paper and pencil tasks may be included, as well as tasks that require documenting mathematical thinking in math journals. Students learn to assume the responsibility for working independently during Math Workshop. This allows teachers to teach small-group lessons and conduct conferences with individual students.

Math Conferences

These one-on-one conversations between a teacher and a student are important assessment and teaching tools. Students explain their mathematical thinking related to the work at hand while teachers ask clarifying questions, assess student understanding, and determine the students' next steps in learning. Specific, targeted, and brief teaching points are delivered during these conversations. Students practice mathematical communication skills as they are encouraged to self-assess their progress toward their own mathematical learning goals.

Assessment

Essential to the Guided Math framework is balanced and timely assessment, especially formative assessment. Knowing students' learning needs allows teachers to plan lessons so that students receive "just right" instruction. That may require instruction that fills gaps in knowledge and skills for some students or provides additional challenges for others. Only by knowing specific needs when learning is occurring can teachers maximize their effectiveness. Figure I.1 provides a brief overview of the components of the Guided Math framework.

Figure I.1 Guided Math Menu of Instruction

Daily: Classroom Environment of Numeracy
In the classroom environment, students are immersed in math. The classroom contains evidence of real-life math tasks, data analysis, math word walls, instruments of measurement, mathematical communication, class-created math anchor charts, graphic organizers, calendars, and authentic problem-solving challenges.
Daily: Math Warm-Ups
This daily appetizer prepares students for the "Your Choice" entrees with Math Stretches, calendar activities, problems of the day, math-related classroom responsibilities, data work, incredible equations, reviews of skills to be maintained, and previews of skills to come.
Your Choice: Whole-Class Instruction
This is an excellent teaching strategy to use when students are working at the same level of achievement, to introduce lessons with an activating strategy, for teacher modeling and think-alouds, for read-alouds of math-related literature, to review previously mastered skills, as preparation for work in cooperative groups, for paper and pencil assessments, or for Math Huddles.
Your Choice: Small-Group Instruction
Students are instructed in small groups whose composition changes based on their needs. The individualized preparation for these groups offers tantalizing opportunities to introduce new concepts, practice new skills, work with manipulatives, provide intensive and targeted instruction to struggling learners, introduce activities that will later become part of Math Workshop, conduct informal assessments, and re-teach based on student needs.
Your Choice: Math Workshop
This is independent work by students either individually, in pairs, or in cooperative groups. The work may be follow-up from whole class or small group instruction, ongoing practice of previously mastered skills, investigations, math games, math journals, or interdisciplinary work.
Daily: Conferences
To enhance learning, teachers confer individually with students, informally assessing understanding, providing opportunities for one-on-one mathematical communication, and determining teaching points for individual students as well as for the class.
Daily: Assessment
A generous helping of assessment *for* learning to inform instruction with a dollop of assessment *of* learning to top off each unit is essential to determine instruction needs of each student.

(Sammons 2010)

Meeting Student Needs in Mathematics

One of the most challenging tasks teachers face is how to best address the wide range of learning needs typical in a classroom of students—those that need additional challenges as well as those that may be struggling. The differences in background knowledge and previous mathematical experiences of students that teachers encounter in their classes make this undertaking difficult. Teachers must not only accurately assess the needs and strengths of their students, but also plan ways to meet those needs. Because of the extent of the variations in student needs, whole-class instruction is rarely able to address them effectively. With that instructional approach, "Too often we begin our instruction aiming toward the middle and praying for ricochet. We hope the knowledge we impart to the center will bounce around until everyone gets it" (Taylor-Cox 2008, 1). But, sadly, that is not often the case.

Balka, Hull, and Miles (2010) offer the sage advice "Classroom teachers need to employ instructional methods that increase the likelihood of success for *every* student" (48). Furthermore, Pink (quoted in Azzam 2014) calls on teachers to provide Goldilocks tasks for students. "[Tasks] that are not too difficult and not too easy. If a task is too easy, people—whether they're children or adults—will get bored. If it's too hard, they'll get anxious or frustrated. You want that sweet spot, where something is within our range of challenge—not too easy, not too hard, but just challenging enough that we're engaged and being pushed to a slightly higher level" (15). That kind of instruction is needed in our classrooms, but it is too seldom found. Using the Guided Math framework, however, teachers assess the needs of their students, group them based on current identified needs, and then deliver instruction targeted precisely to address those needs. Indeed, they are able to provide Goldilocks lessons for their mathematics learners.

Promoting Mathematical Proficiency

Although there are some who still consider procedural fluency to be the hallmark of mathematical proficiency, recent mathematics standards call for much more—and rightly so. The National Research Council (NRC) in their publication *Adding It Up: Helping Children Learn Mathematics* (2001, 116) delineated five components of mathematical proficiency:

- ✎ conceptual understanding
- ✎ procedural fluency
- ✎ strategic competence
- ✎ adaptive reasoning
- ✎ productive disposition

Procedural fluency is a part, but only a part, of what it means to be mathematically proficient. This broader view of mathematical proficiency is also reflected in the NCTM's *Principles and Standards for School Mathematics* (2000) and the Common Core State Standards for Mathematics (NGA and CCSSO 2010). Not only do both of these sets of standards specify the content knowledge students should acquire, but they also place a strong emphasis on the acquisition of mathematical practice skills by students.

For many years, the NCTM mathematical standards (2000) have included these process standards:

- ✎ problem solving
- ✎ reasoning and proof
- ✎ communication
- ✎ connections
- ✎ representation

More recently, the Common Core State Standards for Mathematics set forth eight Standards for Mathematical Practice to be taught from kindergarten through high school and connected to the content standards during instruction (NGA and CCSSO 2010, 6–8).

1. Make sense of problems and persevere in solving them.

2. Reason abstractly and quantitatively.

3. Construct viable arguments and critique the reasoning of others.

4. Model with mathematics.

5. Use appropriate tools strategically.

6. Attend to precision.

7. Look for and make use of structure.

8. Look for and express regularity in repeated reasoning.

To become proficient in these practices, students need active engagement in learning and constructing mathematical meaning. "Engagement means that students participate: talk, record information, share thoughts and ideas, speculate, justify, and make sense of what they are doing" (Balka, Hull, and Miles 2010, 128). This type of engagement only exists when teachers "assign challenging work and regularly check in with students as they work, making sure they have the right supports, the skills to grow intellectually, and the confidence that with effort they can reach their goals" (Quate and McDermott 2014, 62).

Teaching and learning in this type of learning environment may take more time initially because students need time to explore concepts rather than just be told about them. Since students' understanding of mathematics depends largely on their experience constructing meaning, "they must do much of the intellectual work themselves" (Danielson 2007, 16). As a result, student learning tends to be more comprehensive and permanent. For this to occur, teachers must break away from the traditional instructional pattern of "This is what we are going to learn about today. This is how to do it. Now you try." and instead become facilitators in the learning process. This role is more challenging and is even more critical to learning than the traditional role of teachers.

Teachers may find it stressful to relinquish well-practiced methods of instruction that instinctively "feel right" to them to implement those that they believe to be more effective. Over time, though, as they observe the positive impact on student learning, these teachers become more confident—focusing more of their teaching "on designing activities and assignments… that engage students in constructing important knowledge" (Danielson 2007, 17). This shift only occurs when teachers have instructional strategies available to them that will allow this method of teaching.

Although the entire Guided Math framework supports this kind of instructional change, its most valuable component for teachers may be small-group instruction. Within this instructional setting, students are encouraged to explore concepts and share their thinking about mathematics with both their fellow students and their teachers. Teachers assign problems, observe students as they work, pose challenging questions, hold students responsible for justifying their work, and generally create a climate that "fuels the passion" of students by making sure they "feel intellectually challenged" (Quate and McDermott 2014, 62). In other words, students not only act as, but truly become mathematicians.

Supporting Guided Math Implementation

As with much innovation in education, effective leadership plays a significant role in supporting the implementation of the Guided Math framework. Whether the leadership comes from central office administrators, principals, coaches, or from lead teachers, educational leaders pave the way for collaboration, reflective practices, and new ideas. In working with schools and districts, I have discovered that there are many ways in which this can happen—some more effective than others. With this book, I hope to share some of the approaches that work.

As the author of *Guided Math: A Framework for Mathematics Instruction*, I have given much thought to how teachers can maximize students' mathematical learning—for all their students, with all their diverse learning needs. As a classroom teacher, I implemented the Guided Math framework. As an instructional coach, I worked with education leaders to support teachers as they implemented it in their classrooms. From these experiences and from my consulting work with schools and school districts across the United States and Canada, I have had an opportunity to see what works and how teachers can best be supported in their implementation efforts. As with the framework itself, there is no one right way to do this. Each school and district has unique needs, priorities, and resources. With this book, I hope to provide education leaders with a variety of approaches that they can adapt to make their own as they assist teachers in their efforts to adopt the Guided Math instructional structure.

The formation of Professional Learning Communities is one aspect of implementation efforts that appears to consistently bring about lasting change. As Schmoker (2006) writes, "Professional Learning Communities have emerged as arguably the best, most agreed upon means by which to continuously improve instruction and student performance" (Kindle Locations 1569–1571). The last section of this book includes a yearlong plan for Professional Learning Communities focused on the implementation of the Guided Math framework.

One caveat for education leaders to consider: successful change emerges from shared vision. It is not enough for a leader to decide that Guided Math must be implemented. Kaser et al. caution, "A leader's role in leading a change effort is to help people connect the desired change to their own personal visions and to make sure these personal visions are aligned with the organization's overall vision" (2013, 61). Even if it appears that the implementation of Guided Math will move a school toward meeting its goals, "best practices are doomed to failure when administrators [or other education leaders] pressure teachers to quickly implement them without taking time to embed them in what they already do" (Van Tassel 2014, 78).

This book begins with a look at the characteristics of effective education leadership in mathematics at both district and school level. How can leaders create an environment in which educators are open to change, working in harmony to bring about agreed upon school improvement? Focusing on the need to empower members of the education community, to collaboratively examine current strengths and needs, and to build a shared vision is paramount in effective math leadership. Furthermore, once a vision is shaped, how can leaders support the desired change efforts? And then, more specifically, how can leaders encourage or even mandate the implementation of Guided Math? **Part I** examines these issues.

The focus of **Part II** turns to the role of mathematics coaches. What exactly is math coaching? How can coaches support change initiatives? What are their roles in providing professional development? What kinds of learning activities for teachers will make the implementation of Guided Math more successful? From there, the book describes ways in which coaches working one-on-one with teachers can best assist and encourage them as they make changes in their instructional math methods.

Part III provides an overview of Professional Learning Communities and the role of teacher leaders in instigating change in mathematics. How can administrators and coaches establish a climate in which teachers have the opportunity and the desire to collaborate to effect change? What are Professional Learning Communities in mathematics? What are the roles of teachers as members of these collaborative study groups? And, finally, a year-long plan for Professional Learning Communities designed to support the implementation of the Guided Math framework is suggested—with the understanding that it can be adapted as needed.

Chapter 1

What Is Effective Math Educational Leadership?

All of us have had personal experiences with leadership, either as leaders or working with leaders, or both—often with varying degrees of success. These experiences shape our attitudes toward and expectations for those in leadership positions. If teachers were queried about the characteristics of an effective leader, there would probably be some common themes, but also much disagreement. Some teachers prefer leaders who pretty much leave them alone to educate students while taking care of the many administrative functions required for a school district or an individual school to function smoothly. Others favor leaders who have common visions of what constitutes quality education and then work closely with them to promote those visions. Some teachers prefer to know in detail exactly what the leader's expectations are, while others flourish in settings where they are given little specific guidance and, instead, are expected to rely on their own professional judgment. Indeed, in any school setting, there will be disagreement as to the effectiveness of their current school leaders and the reasons why these leaders are deemed to be effective or not. Precisely because of these differences in perspective, the research into what constitutes effective leadership has been extensive and often conflicting.

Kruse (2013, para. 17) defines leadership as "a process of social influence, which maximizes the efforts of others, towards the achievement of a goal." He points out the key elements of this definition from which aspiring mathematics leaders can learn:

> ✎ **Leadership stems from the *social* influence of an individual, not from authority or power.** An individual's influence arises from the respect of others, not just from his or her seniority or hierarchy in an organization. Leaders *prove* themselves worthy of

the task of leading in the eyes of those with whom they work. This respect cannot be artificially bestowed by others or seized by an individual without the buy-in of those with whom he or she works.

- **Leadership requires the involvement of others.** A leader cannot lead without those who willingly follow. Someone who works alone to accomplish a goal cannot be considered a leader. Likewise, just having others who are compelled to follow orders does not qualify as true leadership. The *others* must trust the leader's judgment and believe that it is in the best interests of their shared visions or goals to follow his or her lead.

- **Leadership does not require particular personality traits, attributes, or even a title.** In fact, there are many different styles and paths employed by effective leaders. Because of this, leadership may seem difficult to define. Those desiring to build leadership skills can learn much from observing strong leaders. What works for these leaders? Will these techniques work for me? How can I adapt what these leaders are doing well to enhance my leadership capabilities?

- **Leadership requires working to attain *a goal*.** It is not social influence without an intended outcome. Leaders help others identify shared goals and also create the motivation and empowerment of others needed to reach those goals.

- **Leadership emphasizes the *maximizing* of other's efforts, not just working to achieve a goal.** In a business or, indeed, any kind of organization, this translates into inspiring employee engagement. Drucker (1954, Kindle Location 2862) writes that "leadership is not magnetic personality, that can just as well be demagoguery. It is not 'making friends and influencing people,' that is salesmanship. Leadership is lifting a person's vision to higher sights, the raising of a person's performance to a higher standard, the building of a personality beyond its normal limitations." Leaders must be able to motivate their followers to their peak performance, to create a working environment in which followers have what they need to succeed, and to effectively organize efforts of others to attain shared goals as efficiently as possible.

Those who wish to hone their leadership abilities should seek to learn what has worked well for others and then choose what aspects of those behaviors they can adapt and make their own. A wealth of research on leadership is available in journals, books, and online for aspiring leaders. But, perhaps, one of the most valuable methods of learning more about leadership is by simply observing leaders in action. What is it that earns the respect and following of others? What brings out the best in those with whom the leader works?

Leadership in Education

Much has been written about leadership, especially in the field of business. Indeed, educators can learn from and adapt successful business models to meet the unique needs of learning institutions. While the insight into leadership gained from research on effective business leadership offers math leaders some guidance as to best practices, it has its limitations. Obviously, there are many similar features, but also some fundamental differences. The preeminent leadership and management expert Peter Drucker (1954, Kindle Location 244) in describing business leadership stated, "It can only justify its existence and authority by the economic results it produces." Mathematics educational leadership, however, justifies its existence and authority on the quality of education its students receive.

This major difference in the ultimate aim of business enterprises and educational institutions results in quite a shift in perspective. The bottom line for schools is not economic performance. Instead, the bottom line for educational institutions is the academic performance of young learners. Unlike businesses, where "every act, every decision, every deliberation of management has as its first dimension an economic dimension" (Drucker 1954, Kindle Locations 264–265), every act, every decision, every deliberation of educational leadership has as its first dimension the academic achievement of its students. For example, education leaders would not consider barring students with special needs because of the detrimental effect on a school's rating of the mathematical achievement of their students, but instead would provide the extra resources these students require.

The importance of effective leadership in education cannot be overstated. According to Leithwood et al. (2004, 5), "Leadership is second only to classroom instruction among all school related factors that contribute to what students learn at school." It sets the tone for the school districts, schools, and learning communities. From their own professional experiences, most veteran teachers will readily vouch as to the enormous influence leaders have—either positive or negative—on their teaching and on the learning of their students. To exert a strong positive influence in schools, education leaders must perform a multitude of roles well. Many of these roles are intertwined.

In education, as in many other fields, leadership roles are not limited to only certain positions. While district level staff and principals are most frequently recognized as education leaders, the importance of the leadership capacity of instructional coaches and teachers cannot be overstated. In this book, the term *education leader* has a very broad definition. It includes central office staff, school administrators, academic coaches, math specialists, and teacher leaders.

The sections that follow describe the many functions and responsibilities of education leaders. Throughout the book, the importance of these various functions in promoting the implementation of Guided Math will be explored. While an effective education leader exhibits strength in all of these leadership functions, some of them are more important in supporting the implementation of Guided Math than others. To most effectively lead educators in implementing the Guided Math framework, it is helpful to identify the various leadership functions and how they impact its implementation.

Managerial Leadership

Managing leaders exercise the organization skills necessary to keep schools running smoothly. Fullan emphasizes the importance of these skills stating, "leading the development of a culture of professional capital requires strong managerial skills" (2014, 56). Managerial tasks include planning budgets that support the needs of teachers and students, as well as making personnel decisions. Moreover, all members of school communities rely on the managerial abilities of their leaders to provide school environments that are safe and conducive to learning.

A smoothly operating school is the foundation that supports successful implementation of other leadership functions. When teachers have schedules that work, the supplies they need, and the expectation of consistency in school procedures, they can participate more fully as a member of a school's professional community. It frees them to engage in a process of studying, planning, doing, reflecting, modifying, and planning once again—the ongoing cycle of self-reflective and self-motivated professional development aimed at enhancing instruction and maximizing student learning.

Yet this type of leadership, although imperative for successful schools, is inadequate in and of itself. "Managers need to plan, measure, monitor, coordinate, solve, hire, fire, and so many other things. Typically, managers manage *things*. Leaders lead people" (Kruse 2013, para. 5). It is this quality— the ability to lead people—that true leaders consistently demonstrate.

Relationship-Building Leadership

Relationship-building leaders are well aware of how crucial positive relationships are to any learning community. Developing these relationships requires education leaders to reach out to others by establishing personal bonds of many kinds. When interacting with staff members or colleagues, these leaders are caring and respectful. They recognize people's accomplishments and work closely with them to solve problems that may arise. They support people's efforts to improve their teaching performance.

Students, as the most important members of the learning community, deserve special attention from education leaders. So, these leaders make special efforts to speak to students and find ways to acknowledge student achievements.

To further build relationships, these leaders are also highly visible to parents and interact freely and regularly with them—not waiting until a problem occurs to interact with them.

Community Liaison Leadership

Community liaison leaders strive to build high regard for the educational institutions within the local community. They proactively represent individual classrooms, schools, and school districts in a positive light during their day-to-day dealings with community members. By making themselves available when community members have questions and by encouraging community participation in school activities, they build trust in the school system.

Curriculum Leadership

As *curriculum leaders*, it is essential that leaders not only know the curriculum, but also guarantee that it is taught *and* learned (Marzano 2003). To ensure that the mathematics curriculum is effectively taught by teachers and learned by students, education leaders themselves must have a deep understanding of its content. Only through thorough understanding and careful monitoring can the curriculum be guaranteed and can leaders be assured that students are successfully learning it.

The close attention to curricular content and requirements by those in leadership positions sends a clear message to the learning community of how important this knowledge is to all involved in the education of students. In this way, curriculum leaders set an example for others to follow.

Also, in this capacity, educational leaders make frequent classroom visits to ensure that what is being taught accurately aligns with the curriculum. They encourage all members of the professional community to engage in reflection and self-assessment regarding how well their instruction reflects the required curriculum. With this process, curriculum leaders are able to identify and support teachers who need or desire additional content training. This is particularly important in mathematics leadership with the implementation of new, more rigorous mathematics standards. Teachers are delving more deeply into the content in order to help their students master these new standards.

Instruction Leadership

Instruction leaders ensure high levels of both teaching and learning. To positively impact instruction, strong leaders continue to learn about effective instructional strategies and provide ongoing opportunities for teachers to learn together, try new instructional methods, and then reflect collaboratively on their teaching practices. These leaders clearly articulate instructional expectations so that teachers understand them. And finally, they consistently monitor classroom instruction to be sure these expectations are met.

Educational leaders who make time for informal classroom visits with context-specific feedback encourage teachers to grow and develop professionally (Zepeda 2005). Furthermore, when leaders work closely with teachers to gauge student achievement and to collaboratively identify instructional strategies with the greatest positive (or sometimes negative) impact on learning, it encourages teachers to discard those that are proven to be ineffective and to maintain or try new instructional techniques that research suggests are successful. By encouraging teachers to reflect and assess their own teaching, these leaders promote the implementation of best instructional practices. Perhaps the most positive consequence of this instructional focus by leaders is the nurturing of a spirit of inquiry among teachers and leaders—epitomized by professional growth and personal fulfillment. In this aspect, the role of being an instructional math leader is closely interwoven with the coaching function of educational leaders.

Team-Building Leadership

Team-building leaders strive to establish an environment of trust and a shared sense of direction. Today's schools are mini communities, composed not only of teachers, but also a myriad of support staff working to educate students. Success is dependent on the entire staff pulling together in one direction with focused and shared goals.

Establishing a climate of collaboration is imperative. Through close collaboration, focused conversations, and guided reflection, individuals with vastly different approaches to teaching and learning can identify shared values and goals. During this collaborative process, team-building leaders encourage the emergence of other leaders within the group and willingly distribute the leadership load. All in all, the team-building process creates a sense of shared responsibility for meeting shared goals that community members work together to achieve.

Motivating Leadership

It might seem obvious, but *motivating leaders* must "have time and [the] skills to motivate…" (Kirtman 2013, 8). Motivation is essential in moving staff members to become committed to working toward shared goals. Consider the enormous difference between simple compliance and true engagement. According to Pink (quoted in Azzam 2014, 14), "With compliant behavior, you're doing what someone told you to do the way they told you to do it. There's nothing wrong with that, but it's different from engagement. With engagement, you're doing something because *you* truly want to do it, because you see the virtues of doing it."

Encouraging teachers to reflect on why they first decided to become teachers and on the impact they have on young learners inspires the kind of emotional engagement that takes teaching to a higher level. Motivation also increases when educators explicitly identify their common beliefs and passions and then work together as a community in their pursuit.

Furthermore, educational leaders motivate members of the learning community by calling upon their experience and expertise when making difficult decisions—particularly decisions that directly impact their work. Thus empowered, teachers and staff members more willingly assume greater responsibilities. Along with empowering teachers and other staff, leaders increase motivation when both ongoing and extraordinary efforts of the education community are regularly recognized and acknowledged.

In contrast, when educational leaders lack the ability to motivate teachers, instruction typically becomes lackluster and rote. Teachers tend to work independently, rather than collaboratively. While some teachers continue to pursue their passion for teaching, these efforts are too often isolated, and sometimes even resented by others. The status quo remains unchallenged and fiercely defended. When attempting the implementation of new instructional strategies such as the Guided Math framework, this can be particularly detrimental.

Coaching Leadership

Some view *coaching leadership* "not as a subset of the field of management, but rather as the heart of management" (Evered and Selman 1989, 116). This perspective represents something of a paradigm shift. "The prevailing management paradigm focuses heavily on control, order, and compliance, with the consequence that people become objectified, measured, and expended. Coaching, on the other hand, focuses on discovering actions that enable and empower people to contribute more fully, productively, and with less alienation than the control model entails" (116). With the primary aim of education leaders being the creation of conditions under which students learn to their fullest potential, supporting and enhancing the ability of teachers and other school staff members are major areas of concern to education leaders.

Without a doubt, *all* teachers deserve the opportunity to be coached. Educators are beginning to recognize that coaching is more than just a way to support struggling teachers. The benefits of coaching have long been valued in athletics. Talented athletes work closely with their coaches to gain additional perspectives on their performance and how to improve it. Although not all schools or school districts have leaders specifically designated as coaches, effective mathematics leaders recognize this aspect of leadership as crucial to their success and will work with their faculties and staffs by coaching them in their professional growth.

In their roles as math coaches, leaders help teachers reflect on their teaching practices to identify strengths and needs based on shared curricular and instructional expectations. Frequent, non-evaluative classroom visits make the leader's classroom presence feel less threatening to teachers. Working in a coaching capacity, leaders send the message that they are partners in mathematics instruction with teachers—giving specific feedback, sometimes in areas designated by the teachers themselves. The collaborative nature established through the coaching function enables teachers to be more comfortable in asking for help when needed. Although some education leaders may not have the same expertise as instructional math coaches or the time to provide the assistance, they do their best to make it available. When leaders act as coaches, teachers feel supported in their efforts to grow professionally.

Promoting Change Leadership

Those who aspire to be *change leaders* often find that the process of change is not easy to bring about. First, desired changes must be identified. While it may be tempting for education leaders to unilaterally decide what changes should occur, strong change leaders invite the participation of others in this process. In many cases, the need for change becomes apparent as a consequence of examining data on student achievement—focusing on strengths and needs. By asking the tough questions that reveal not only problems, but also potential solutions, leaders are "helping people come to their own conclusions based on their experience" (Couros 2013, para. 7). When this happens, people feel an emotional connection and assume ownership in implementing desired changes.

Change also becomes more compelling when associated with personal moral imperatives (Reeves 2009, Kindle Locations 1142–1145)—in other words, when linked to issues people care about deeply. Kaser et al. (2013) likens the creation of a sense of urgency for change to an art form. Lowering the resistance of others is a balancing act of "increasing the tension of not supporting the change effort and reducing the tension related to trying it" (72). The motivation that results from people feeling a sense of urgency can be a powerful influence on the success or failure of improvement efforts.

Harvard Business School Professor John P. Kotter (2007) claims that it is necessary for 75 percent of an organization's management to be convinced that doing business as usual is unacceptable or there will be serious problems with change efforts later in the process. "Without motivation, people won't help, and the effort goes nowhere" (2).

Finding the perfect balance between the two is crucial. Since all "change is…loaded with uncertainty" (Fullan and Miles 1992, 749), establishing a supportive climate for those involved is paramount in bringing about transformational change. Leadership promotes change when it helps others work through its uncertainty—"sometimes by overcoming resistance, but mostly by reassuring the potential losers that there is something to gain" or "by helping the willing gain the grounded confidence that is essential to success" (Fullan 2014, 7). Leaders can reassure those who are uncertain about how changes will affect them and foresee personal loss as a result by making explicit what will be gained.

Capacity-Building Leadership

"Passion without skill is dangerous," warns Fullan (2014, 24). What happens once educators are motivated and become passionate about making changes in teaching and learning? Many times, efforts to build the capacity of educators to change require further knowledge and training. As Fullan wisely cautions, more than passion is needed—in fact, even with the best intentions, attempts to enhance learning can go astray if teachers lack the support and resources they need to develop new skill sets. Leaders shoulder the responsibility of building capacity for changes once desired changes are identified.

To successfully implement desired changes, educational leaders must consider the following: What types of resources, training, and/or coaching experiences are needed? Is funding needed to provide this support? If so, from where will the funding come? In addressing these questions, the interconnected nature of the leadership functions is obvious. Clearly the curriculum, instruction, coaching, and managerial function of leadership are interconnected and essential to build capacity to implement change.

While this leadership function has long been recognized as critical, there is growing awareness that the customary model of professional development is limited and often fails to build capacity. Too often, the professional development provided consists of a single day of training. Armed with new ideas for instruction, teachers return to their classrooms to implement them—or not. Only rarely is coaching or other ongoing, follow-up training provided. Not only that, but there is often no monitoring to verify that changes are being implemented, assess the quality of implementation, determine what additional support is needed, or measure the impact it has on student learning.

With more effective professional development, leaders provide ongoing support with site-based coaching, opportunities for teachers to engage in Professional Learning Communities, monitoring to ensure implementation, and periodic assessment of effectiveness.

Change-Monitoring Leadership

Change monitoring leaders believe not only in the importance of creating a consensus for change, providing the resources to bring it about, and making expectations for change explicit, but also in closely monitoring its implementation. After the change is identified and professional development provided, education leaders are responsible for checking to be sure that all members of the community are implementing the desired change.

With the implementation of Guided Math, there may be a number of reasons why it is not being fully implemented within a school or district. Some educators may not fully understand the expectations for change. Some may even believe that they are implementing it. Some may understand the expectations, but may still need more support before they can carry them out successfully. Others may be encountering difficulties with the change process. A few may disagree with the change and decide that they are unwilling to make it.

So, with monitoring, not only do leaders have to determine if the change is being implemented, but if not, they must discover why not to ensure that implementation does occur. Based on what they find during the monitoring process, educational leaders may need to do more work in building capacity to ensure that everyone understands the expectations for change and is capable of making them. Providing teachers specific, descriptive feedback in a non-threatening manner allows them to more clearly understand and meet the expectations for change. With some individuals, leaders may have to more firmly delineate their responsibilities for change.

Another valuable reason for monitoring implementation is to gauge the effectiveness of the planned changes. While there may have been strong justifications for a desired change at the outset, the results may not always be what were anticipated. In those instances, the implementation process should be examined to see if the change could be made more effective. It may be necessary to revise aspects of the change or to revisit altogether the decision to make the change.

An effective monitoring process is multifaceted. It may include classroom visits, collection and analysis of data, and solicitation of feedback from teachers as they self-assess their progress, their needs, and their view of what is working and what is not. Only when leaders care enough to check with those who are in the trenches implementing the change can the monitoring process be completely accurate.

Figure 1.1 provides a brief overview of the leadership functions and responsibilities of education leaders.

Figure 1.1 Leadership Functions and Responsibilities

Leadership Functions	Leaders' Responsibilities
Managerial	Ensure that the district, school, or classroom run smoothly. Manage budgeting and finances. Establish schedules and organizational structures. Manage personnel decisions. Provide sufficient supplies and resources. Create an environment that is safe and conducive to learning.
Relationship Building	Build a trusting and respectful relationship with staff members. Try to know the names and faces of students. Be highly visible and interact freely with students and parents. Recognize student achievements. Communicate regularly with parents. Be accessible for conferences.
Community Liaison	Positively represent the classroom, school, and/or district outside the school system. Be available when community members have questions. Include the community in school activities whenever possible. Recognize and give ample thanks to members of the community who volunteer or contribute.

Leadership Functions	Leaders' Responsibilities
Curriculum	Have an in-depth knowledge of the curriculum. Remain abreast of curriculum changes. Monitor what is being taught to ensure that it aligns with the required curriculum. Encourage reflection and self-assessment by all members of the professional community. Identify and support teachers who need or desire additional content training.
Instruction	Be knowledgeable about instructional best practices. Clearly articulate expectations for instruction. Monitor classroom instruction. Encourage reflection and self-assessment by all members of the professional community. Identify and support teachers who need or desire additional training in effective instructional strategies.
Team Building	Establish a climate of collaboration. Identify shared values through focused conversations and reflections with others. Share leadership with others. Create a sense of shared responsibility for meeting shared goals.
Motivating	Reaffirm the mission of educators and its importance to society. Empower teachers and all staff members. Provide recognition for the efforts of others. Involve teachers and other staff in the decision-making process—especially when it affects their work.

Leadership Functions	Leaders' Responsibilities
Coaching	Lead teachers to reflect and identify strengths and needs based on clear curricular and instructional expectations. Make frequent visits to all classrooms. Involve teachers in the process of identifying areas of need. Use observations to address areas identified by teachers as well as any other areas that merit attention. Confer with the teacher before and after a classroom visit. Offer support for areas identified as needs or areas in which the teacher wishes to grow.
Promoting Change	Work with education team to do the following: · Examine data documenting student achievement. · Identify strengths and needs. · Determine changes that will address needs. · Motivate team to implement change.
Capacity Building	Identify what resources, training, and/or coaching experiences are needed. Find funding for needs. Provide professional development and coaching—initial and ongoing.
Change Monitoring	Make expectations explicit. Visit classrooms frequently. Provide specific, descriptive feedback to teachers in a non-threatening manner. Solicit feedback from teachers on their assessment of progress, their needs, and their view of what is working and what is not.

Review & Reflect

1. In what ways are the functions of business leaders similar to those of math education leaders? In what important ways do they differ?

2. Reflect on your leadership experience. With which of the leadership functions and responsibilities are you most effective? How can you draw upon these leadership strengths to promote the implementation of Guided Math?

3. Which of the functions provide the greatest challenge for you? What can you do to become more effective in those areas as you lead the implementation of the Guided Math framework in your school or district?

Chapter 2

Creating a Professional Education Community to Support Guided Math

What is a professional education community? The Oxford Dictionaries defines a community as "a feeling of fellowship with others, as a result of sharing common attitudes, interests, and goals" (2015). Certainly, these elements characterize an educational professional community. But, that "feeling of fellowship" is only part of it. Newman (1994, 1), writing about school-wide professional communities, goes further, stating that the concept can be described as "school staff members taking collective responsibility for achieving a shared educational purpose and collaborating with one another to achieve that purpose." Perhaps the most comprehensive definition is a combination of the two. Community, then, is not only the feeling of fellowship resulting from common attitudes, interests, and goals, but also a sense of collective responsibility and collaboration in achieving those goals. To significantly impact the academic achievement of students, members of the community must *assume responsibility* to work together to achieve their goals. In schools where there is a strong professional community, "teachers work together more effectively, and put more effort into creating and sustaining opportunities for student learning" (Kruse, Louis, and Bryk 1994, 4). For the successful implementation of Guided Math, both of these aspects of a professional education community are essential. For schools striving to improve student achievement in mathematics, involving teachers and other staff members in Professional Learning Communities is a way to empower teachers, draw upon their expertise, and identify common goals.

Effective education leaders encourage *all* staff members to become part of the professional community. Strong math professional communities share the following elements:

- shared and clearly defined goals for student learning
- collaboration and collective responsibility for meeting the goals
- professional inquiry by the staff concerning how to most effectively meet the goals
- opportunities for members of the community to influence school decisions (Newman, King, and Youngs 2000, 263)

Because one of the essential elements of professional communities is opportunities for members to influence school decisions, effective education leaders include teachers in decisions that affect mathematics instruction. Leaving those most impacted by instructional decisions out of the decision-making process inevitably leads to poor results. "If leaders do not foster mathematics teachers' participation in improvement processes, then improvement will not go beyond a superficial, show-and-tell level" (Balka, Hull, and Miles 2010, 12). Sadly, most schools have experienced too many show-and-tell improvements and are ready for more substantial efforts to increase student achievement.

To create a strong and engaged professional community, education leaders must establish a sense of trust, empower members of the community, encourage collaboration among members, and build and support teams working to achieve school improvement. (See Figure 2.1.)

Figure 2.1 Creating a Mathematics Professional Community

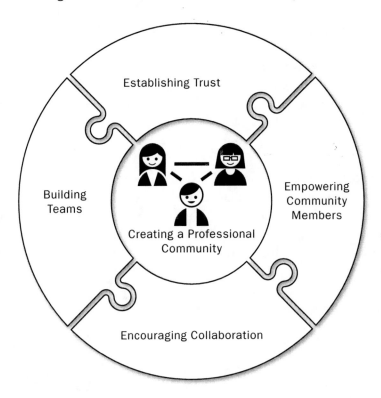

Establishing Trust

Imperative in the establishment of professional communities in schools is nurturing trust among community members—not only between administrative staff and teachers, but also between teachers. For much too long, math teachers worked on their own—never venturing into the classrooms of others, planning independently, and yet doing their best to teach their young learners in their own ways. Some teachers have even been territorial about their classrooms—reluctant to have others come in to observe, reluctant to share their successes or struggles with their peers. These teachers may engage in friendly chitchat with other teachers during breaks or after school, but are unwilling to engage in rich and constructive professional discussions. In that climate, professional communities focused on mathematics education initiatives fail to thrive.

This type of behavior often stems from a basic lack of trust and can be remedied. Within any school, the principal is "the key to building a trusting environment" (Short and Greer 2002, 63). For a district, the key may be the superintendent or other district personnel. How mathematics leaders in a supervisory role interact with those they supervise determines the level of trust between community members. Fullan advises leaders to "…name trust as a value and norm that you will embrace and develop in the organization; you model it in your day-to-day actions; and you monitor it in your own and others' behavior" (2014, 130).

The issue of trust goes beyond just integrity and fairness. It also involves the issue of competence (Fullan 2014). For trust to exist, members of the mathematics education community must not only believe that they will be treated fairly as they implement new instructional strategies like Guided Math, but also that other members are capable of carrying out duties that support the implementation. Teachers may *like* leaders, but still not *trust* them if they do not believe that they will carry out their responsibilities in a capable manner. A lack of trust within an educational team can torpedo change efforts.

Kirtman (2013, 71–73) describes a cycle for building trust with individuals and groups. Its five stages are implicit in many of the mathematics education leadership functions listed in Chapter 1.

1. **Communication.** Trusting relationships are created when leaders clearly communicate their expectations to members of the education community with whom they are working.

2. **Shared Understanding.** This is an area where many leaders struggle. Simply communicating expectations to the community is not sufficient. Its members must also truly understand those expectations. Since members interpret the expectations shared by leaders in light of their own experiences, their interpretations are likely to vary considerably. While it is tempting to assume shared understanding exists once expectations have been communicated, effective leaders take time to ensure that these are not just clearly communicated, but also accurately understood by everyone. Many times, leaders hesitate to check for this in fear that disagreement among the group will impede change. Yet,

if underlying disagreement exists and is not addressed early on, it may well disrupt progress later in the initiative.

3. **Predictability (Shared Expectations).** Most people find it easier to trust those who are predictable. In this stage of building trust, a clear sense of predictable behavior from leaders and team members emerges. Trust flourishes when predictions prove to be accurate; mistrust arises when the lack of shared understanding results in unpredictable behavior.

4. **Commitment.** Relying on the trust established in the first three stages of this cycle, members of the group assume the responsibility for carrying out the tasks required for change. During this stage, trust continues to build. The group gains confidence that all of its members can be depended upon to fulfill their responsibilities.

5. **Teamwork (Shared Efforts).** Effective teamwork is the final stage of the trust cycle. It consists of shared and coordinated efforts to attain the common goals that developed in a safe and trusting environment.

While the stages of this cycle are essential in building trust, there are other elements that should be considered as well in an educational setting. Too often, decisions regarding mathematics initiatives are made at the top and then passed down for implementation by classroom teachers, with little or no input from those most impacted. Short and Greer (2002) found teachers' involvement in and support of change efforts to be directly related to the degree to which they were genuinely trusted and empowered by the administration. Trust is engendered when teachers are truly valued as members of the education community. Leaders who trust others earn reciprocal trust from the members of their education community. Building trust within the mathematics education community creates a more fertile environment for implementing the Guided Math framework.

Empowering Community Members

Amabile and Kramer (2011, Kindle Location 90) maintain that "one of the most basic human drives is toward self-efficacy—a person's belief that he or she is individually capable of planning and executing the tasks required to achieve desired goals." Efficacy is itself an outcome of empowering teachers and engaging them in a professional community that supports the change process (Balka, Hull, and Miles 2010, 13). Perhaps "teacher efficacy" is the most available resource for increasing student learning. When disempowered, teachers come to believe that their students' success or failure depends not on their efforts, but is determined instead by "factors, conditions, or problems that are outside the control of the school or the teacher" (20). If math teachers are convinced that little that they do in the classroom impacts the mathematical achievement of their students, they have little inclination to try new instructional methods.

In this sense, the impact of self-efficacy on teachers is similar to Dweck's (2006) theories about the import of growth mindsets on students. Just as Dweck finds that students tend to be risk averse and unmotivated when they have a fixed mindset of intelligence—nothing they do will increase their intelligence—teachers who believe that factors affecting student achievement are beyond their control often tend to be defensive and equally unmotivated to change.

Empowered, confident teachers are similar to students with a growth mindset. They are likely to be more deeply engaged and willing to take risks to improve both their teaching and their students' learning. It is this kind of engagement that leads math teachers to improve their effectiveness through the use of new instructional techniques. Guided Math offers them an opportunity to enhance their mathematics instruction. But, to implement it, teachers have to be willing to move out of their comfort zones.

To paraphrase basketball coach Phil Jackson's advice for sports leaders, effective mathematics leaders empower and engage teachers by relating to their professional community members as *whole persons*, not just *cogs* in the education machine (Jackson and Delehanty 2013, Kindle Location 229). In this regard, Pink advises education leaders to "create an atmosphere in which people have a sufficient degree of freedom; can move toward mastery on something that matters; and know *why* they are doing it" (quoted in Azzam 2014, 15). To encourage mathematics educators to deeply engage with Guided Math implementation rather than just comply with a mandate, their autonomy must be increased *the right amount at the right moment* (14). Mathematics teachers more willingly move toward the kind of instructional shift inherent in Guided Math when they feel they have the autonomy to tweak it so that it works well in their classrooms.

Encouraging Collaboration

As leaders build trust and begin to empower mathematics educators, greater collaboration within the professional community typically emerges. "The school moves from an individualistic culture to a collaborative one; teachers stop thinking about 'their kids' only and 'their classroom' and become committed to the success of all kids in the school" (Fullan 2014, 87)—a reflection of trust between members of the community and the desire to work together toward shared goals. There develops a sense of both shared success and risk—"a feeling that 'we're all in this together'" (Conzemius and O'Neill 2001, 67).

For both principals and teachers who have been autonomous for so long, the process of shifting to a collaborative culture is difficult. "Collaboration requires us to surrender some of our control. It also requires us to be open to others' perspectives and to be willing to find out that perhaps we don't always know 'the right answer' or the 'best answer'" (Conzemius and O'Neill 2001, 77). Yet, it is well worth the effort. When math leaders are open to new ideas and nonjudgmental of those who adopt fresh teaching methods, the community of mathematics teachers becomes more willing to take risks and work together to implement change.

Schmoker (2004, 431) warns education leaders that "we can no longer afford to be innocent of the fact that 'collaboration' improves performance." Indeed, collaborating members of the community are "more powerful, intellectually or physically, than any one individual" (Costa and Kallick 2008, Kindle Locations 866–867). Collaboration is especially important for teachers who are in the process of implementing Guided Math in their classrooms. It allows teachers to share ideas and helps combat the negative effects of working in isolation.

Collaboration within a professional community does not occur simply because a leader decides it is a good idea. Even with a culture of trust and empowerment within the community, a sense of collegiality and collaboration must be nurtured. It is important to note that "collegial relationships are deeper than and different from personal friendships or simple courtesy during professional interactions" (Balka, Hull, and Miles 2010, 110). While school climate amongst its staff may be cordial, collaborative relationships involve more than a cordial staff.

According the Balka, Hull, and Miles (2010, 24), "effective collaboration must ensure that groups of teachers and administrators are both engaged and empowered in work that directly and positively affects student learning." This goes back to the notion of a professional community as one in which its members assume collective responsibility for shared purposes—which, for an educational institution, is student learning—which is exactly what is needed for the successful implementation of Guided Math. It is significant that Balka, Hull, and Miles include both groups—teachers *and* administrators—in the collaborative process. This understanding of collaboration is a far cry from leaders deciding that collaboration is a worthy goal and then excluding themselves from its practice.

An observer might also find that because of their ongoing participation in these rich conversations, members of collaborative professional communities tend to share a common vocabulary to describe their missions. The Guided Math framework consists of seven components. Without a community-wide understanding of the philosophy supporting the framework and the vocabulary related to the structure itself, collaboration is difficult. Since "language and thinking are closely entwined; like either side of a coin" (Costa and Kallick 2008, Kindle Locations 756–757), this is not surprising. While every profession has a "language of practice, one that captures the important concepts and understandings shared by members of the profession" (Danielson 2007, 5–6), the vocabulary used in collaborative communities as they work to implement Guided Math becomes more precise and clearly understood because teachers are engaged in focused conversations about their values, their profession, instructional practices, student achievement, and the shared goals of their educational community and how the framework supports those aspects of the mathematics education culture.

Another significant characteristic of collaborative professional communities is a consistent scheduled time for its members to meet. Conzemius and O'Neill (2001, 69) advise leaders that "there is simply no getting around the need to set aside concentrated amounts of time for school staffs to come together—away from the distractions of classrooms and cell phones—to develop shared vision and learn new skills." This is especially important when math teachers are shifting their instructional techniques.

Finding this time is not easy. There never seem to be enough hours in the day. In addition, structural barriers arising from complex scheduling often make it difficult for educators to find opportunities to get together to collaborate. If collaboration is a priority, however, time can be found. The business agenda of faculty meetings might be restructured to be more efficient and allow time for collaboration. Some schools decide to schedule their special classes (e.g., art, physical education, music, technology) to allow grade-level meetings during those times. With creativity and determination, leaders can find ways to make time for collaboration to support Guided Math implementation.

Building Teams

Business management guru, Peter Drucker wrote

> The leaders who work most effectively, it seems to me, never say "I." And that's not because they have trained themselves not to say "I." They don't think "I." They think "we"; they think "team." They understand their job to be to make the team function. They accept responsibility and don't sidestep it, but "we" gets the credit. This is what creates trust, what enables you to get the task done.
>
> (Drucker 1990, 14)

Just as teams are essential in business to accomplish common goals, they are also essential in schools. Schmoker (2004) urges leaders that instead of just focusing on reform, school improvement should focus on creating teams of teachers working collaboratively to achieve specific short-term, data-based goals—creating, in essence, a collaborative, inquiry-based culture in schools. The creation of such a culture leads Guided Math implementation to flourish. According to Fullan, large-scale reform does not work because "it feeds into the dependency of teachers and principals" (quoted in Sparks 2003, 57). Rather, teachers should be supported in assuming the role of scientists "who continuously develop their intellectual and investigative effectiveness" (57). Math teachers, working in teams to focus on student performance and then develop action plans for the implementation of Guided Math, can have enormous impact in bringing about change.

One trait of effective mathematics leaders is their ability to share the leadership responsibilities. Conzemius and O'Neill (2001, 11) describe a framework of shared responsibility for teams composed of these three elements:

- **Focus.** This element leads members to clarity of thought, direction, and purpose as to change initiatives and goals. An unwavering commitment to the goal of improving student achievement and ongoing attention to the effectiveness of mathematics teaching practices leads math teachers to try new instructional methods to promote student achievement. This kind of focus is essential in efforts to implement Guided Math.

- **Reflection.** This element encourages members to use what they have learned from their past experience to find better methods of working toward their goals. This practice leads "educators to go beyond best guesses or informed hunches about what is and is not working" (14). This kind of reflection enables math teachers to shape the Guided Math framework so that it addresses their students' needs and is compatible with their own teaching styles. Moreover, it promotes a willingness to change based on data-based evidence and supports professional inquiry by team members to address challenges in meeting common goals.

- **Collaboration.** This element brings team members together on an ongoing basis to focus on student learning goals, share ideas, and, in general, work through the "messiness of humanity" to build a strong foundation of learning. This process involves "developing interdependent relationships where all are focused on a common purpose and set of goals and where people must rely on each other to achieve these goals" (15–16). Throughout this collaborative process, mathematics teachers work together to make the Guided

Math implementation process successful. Teachers share what works for them, challenges they encountered, and the impact of the instructional changes on student achievement. Together they brainstorm methods for continued improvement of their mathematics instruction.

Because these three elements are so strongly interrelated—relying so heavily upon one another—the framework is effective only when all three exist and are equally robust. Not only are they essential for team building, they are vital in all aspects of building professional communities.

Once teams have been established to support teachers as they implement Guided Math in their classrooms, a leader's focus shifts. How can math education leaders support ongoing teamwork? These suggestions offer some guidance for mathematics education leaders.

- **Monitor the workings of teams of math educators that have been established to ensure that they are meeting as scheduled, are functioning smoothly, and are maintaining fidelity to the overarching shared values and goals of the school community.** Effective leaders refrain from micromanaging, but leave nothing to chance. Leaders may ask team leaders to provide regular reports. The process of monitoring should address questions such as these: Are the meetings occurring as planned? If not, why not? Do team meetings include adequate time for joint reflection, inquiry, and goal-setting regarding math instruction? Are team members working together productively in support of the Guided Math initiative? If not, what can be done to encourage collaboration—or even, at times, civility? Is progress being made by each team that is consistent with the values and goals established by the professional community as a whole? Will goals be met according to established timelines? If not, what can be done to support the effort, or should adjustments to the timeline be considered?

- **Stay informed about what is occurring in the meetings and educated about relevant curricular and instructional issues.** The monitoring process should provide information to leaders about the general content of each team's work, giving leaders opportunities to fulfill their functions as mathematics curriculum and instructional leaders. When teams are researching math education issues or ideas, leaders also have the responsibility to do some research themselves. How else can they effectively monitor improvement efforts?

✎ **Participate as often as possible in meetings, but be careful not to usurp the leadership of the team.** Obviously, leaders cannot attend all team meetings. In fact, leaders should *not* attend all team meetings. But, a leader's presence should be evident periodically during team meetings. Leaders should feel free to participate in but not to dominate a meeting. Being aware that others tend to defer to an authority figure, supportive leaders strive to minimize their impact on the meeting; instead they encourage the team itself to shape its content and structure. It is especially important that the internal leadership of the team be respected.

✎ **Maintain an open mind and actively listen when meeting with teams—even when you are not in agreement.** Leaders should participate in meetings with the goal of learning rather than imparting knowledge or exercising control. In the leader's presence, team members may need to be coaxed to share their honest observations and ideas, particularly if they fear that they may be at odds with those in leadership roles. This is particularly true during the implementation of a new instructional framework like Guided Math. When leaders listen actively, it is a sign of respect. It frees others to honestly participate in the discussion. That is not to say that leaders should never express their ideas within a team meeting—just that it must be done respectfully, aimed at addressing the ideas being discussed and not individuals.

✎ **Encourage teams to share and consider the ideas of all group members before decisions are made.** When monitoring team progress or attending team meetings, strong math education leaders work to ensure that all ideas are shared before decisions are made. To avoid dissension, it is sometimes tempting for team leaders to make decisions prior to a meeting to be rubber stamped by the team during the meeting. In the long run, this creates many problems— mistrust of leaders by team members, the stifling of valid points of discussion, and a lack of support for team decisions. By participating in meetings, listening actively, and developing the capacity to "hear what isn't being said," as Peter Drucker often says, leaders can identify team problems and head them off.

◈ **Remain flexible and willing to make changes if they are warranted.** Plans are only of value when they can be successfully carried out. Invariably, once goals have been established and action plans created, teams will discover that some aspects of the plans are unworkable or even undesirable. The Guided Math framework is a flexible instructional structure that allows teachers to adapt it to work effectively in diverse classroom settings. If team members are under the impression that the leader is inflexible and wedded to initial implementation plans in spite of any flaws in them, they will be reluctant to openly and honestly share their concerns. This creates a scenario that almost certainly leads to failure—both because the plans themselves are unworkable and because of a lack of motivation by team members who see inherent problems with the established plans. Effective math leaders consider concerns of the professional community openly and try to find resolutions. If changes are needed, they work closely with those directly involved to revise them and then support those revisions.

◈ **Be honest and open with team members—both within and outside of meetings.** This is a simple guideline: honesty is the best policy. That is not to say that *everything* must be shared. Good leaders use their judgment in what information should be shared, but never mislead others to make things go more smoothly. Behavior of that sort—providing misleading or false information—builds mistrust and will create problems in the future.

◈ **Continuously support a sense of community.** Lead members recognize that each member of the mathematics education community has something of value to offer and that together they are working toward common goals. The appearance of favoritism by leadership quickly disrupts any sense of community that has been established and should be avoided.

◈ **Support the autonomy of teams within reason.** Strong leaders establish, monitor, and support teams that work for school improvement, but they also allow them to function without being micromanaged. People are more motivated and engaged when they are given responsibilities and then trusted to carry them out. There are instances when leaders need to intervene, but without very strong reasons for intervention, the autonomy of the team may be compromised.

✎ **Recognize and celebrate team accomplishments.** Quite often, the attention of the education community is so focused on continuous improvement that it tends to overlook what it has already accomplished. Without a doubt, the ongoing striving for improvement is a good thing. But, it re-energizes people when they take the opportunity to see how far they have come toward reaching their initial goals and to celebrate what has already been accomplished.

Review & Reflect

1. What do you believe are the most compelling reasons for establishing a strong sense of professional community within your school or district? What distinguishes a professional mathematics education community from a general professional education community?

2. What have you done already to create a professional mathematics education community within your school/district? What has gone well? In what areas would you like to improve? What steps will you take to improve in those areas?

3. Are you satisfied with the degree of collaboration occurring in your school/district among math educators? What can you do to increase collaboration within the community?

Chapter 3

Embracing a Shared Vision and the Implementation of Guided Math

A shared vision is not an idea. It is not even an important idea such as freedom. It is, rather, a force in people's hearts, a force of impressive power. It may be inspired by an idea, but once it goes further—if it is compelling enough to acquire the support of more than one person—then it is no longer an abstraction. It is palpable. People begin to see it as if it exists. Few, if any, forces in human affairs are as powerful as shared vision.

Peter Senge (2006, Kindle Location 192)

While creating a vibrant professional educational community in support of Guided Math is a worthy accomplishment for a leader, it will not lead to school improvement unless the community also embraces a shared vision for the improvement of mathematical achievement of students—one that inspires and motivates its members to implement Guided Math. Just how does a mathematics leader bring educators together to not only identify the vision, but also inspire "a force in people's hearts, a force of impressive power," as Senge describes above?

What Is a Shared Vision?

"A vision is an inspirational picture of the desired future. It is a promise: a commitment to the students, staff, and community" (Conzemius and O'Neill 2001, 26). A shared vision motivates members of the community and impacts all aspects of a classroom, school, or district. Visions act as filters for the decisions that are made at all levels. They lead to focus and consistency. By engaging the entire professional community in "deep dialogue about their hopes and dreams and their underlying beliefs and values, what emerges is a description of *the community's* preferred future. This vision is based on a solid foundation of shared understanding and has the momentum necessary to sustain change" (27).

The best visions have the power to move people, both emotionally and professionally, because they reflect the most compelling aspects of the many individual visions of the community. According to Conzemius and O'Neill (2001, 26–27), strong visions have these features:

- They express a belief in a better future.
- They establish a clear time frame.
- They focus the community on a higher purpose—above the normal daily routines.
- They elevate the entire community and help them recognize their worth as they contribute work toward the vision.
- They derive from deeply held core values and beliefs.
- They are clearly defined.
- They invite the participation of all members of the community and serve as a consistent point of focus.

A shared vision serves as guidance for all aspects of planning and decision-making. There is a tendency for people to want to go their own way, but when "teachers, staff and administrators are working in schools where *focus* is a part of everything they do, they have a deep sense of their collective 'true north'—it helps them get unstuck when they don't know how to proceed and guides them back when they've lost their way" (Conzemius and O'Neill 2001, 34). While a shared vision does not specify the means that will lead to its realization, it is the vision that leads community members to focus on Guided Math as a means to achieving the vision.

The Process of Creating a Shared Vision

Leaders can use a variety of methods to gain a community consensus about a shared vision for mathematics instruction leading to the implementation of Guided Math. As discussed earlier, establishing a sense of community is an effective first start to the process. All members of the community should feel that their ideas are valued and are heard. Leaders must call upon their skills as motivators and change agents to accomplish this. To identify elements of a shared vision, a three-step brainstorming process can be used (Conzemius and O'Neill 2001, 30–31).

1. **Brainstorming.** Participants are encouraged to freely share ideas that occur to them, without evaluating them or discarding any. At this point, quantity is the objective, rather than quality. After a period of silent reflection, people record their ideas on sticky notes. Most frequently, prior to deciding to implement Guided Math, brainstorming will focus on the desire to improve students' mathematics achievement. Members of the professional community often suggest the need to identify and implement more effective instructional strategies to create a stimulating learning environment that maximizes students' mathematical learning—leading students to greater conceptual understanding, computational fluency, and proficiency in the mathematical practices.

2. **Creating Affinity Diagrams.** The sticky notes are placed on a large piece of paper or wall display—grouped by similarity. The placing of the sticky notes is done silently. Once this is done, members of the group can begin talking about the ideas that have been posted and can label categories by which the notes can be grouped. When brainstorming by the educational community focuses on the mathematical achievement of learners, it is likely that quite a few of the sticky notes will address teaching and learning. Mathematics leaders then encourage members of the brainstorming session to recognize this similarity and group them together. In addition, some sticky notes may mention the need to improve students' conceptual understanding and proficiency with the mathematical practices standards. Because the Guided Math framework creates a learning environment that cultivates greater rigor and student engagement, its implementation is often identified as a means of making the shared vision a reality.

3. **Multi-voting.** After the grouping and discussion, participants are given a limited number of sticky dots to be placed on the categories that they feel are most important and that should be a part of the shared vision. Essentially, the dots represent votes for particular ideas.

This process is one method of teasing out elements that the community deems to be important for a shared vision. In establishing a shared vision that leads to a Guided Math initiative, the professional community usually identifies essential elements of teaching and learning that correlate with improved mathematics proficiency. The practical instructional strategies of Guided Math make its implementation an obvious action step in the community's efforts to attain its shared vision.

A second method for reaching a community consensus about a shared vision can be accomplished with carousel brainstorming.

1. Members of the community are divided into smaller groups.

2. Each group is asked to discuss its thoughts about a vision for the future and then draft a sample vision based on the discussion. A recorder from each group records the sample vision on chart paper. These charts are then displayed on the walls around the room.

3. The small groups then engage in a carousel activity in which they visit each of the sample visions, discuss them, and then leave feedback using sticky notes.

4. If desired, the group can reconvene as a whole and share its thoughts about what they believe to be the most important elements of a shared vision.

With either of these methods of brainstorming, the actual drafting of the vision statement is delegated to a small team of community members who base their work on the ideas generated during the brainstorming sessions. The work of the drafting team is crucial. Obviously, not every idea proposed can be included in the final statement. This team has the job of sifting through the dreams and ideals proposed by many to arrive at a concise and coherent statement that can be embraced by the community as a whole. This draft is then brought back to the whole group to be finalized. It must be a version that the entire community can agree upon—not every aspect of it, perhaps, but enough to define it as a unifying vision. "A vision not consistent with values that people live by day by day will not only fail to inspire genuine enthusiasm, it will often foster outright cynicism" (Senge 2006, Kindle Locations 207–208). This vision should clearly spell out where the community is headed and what is desired for the future. Yet, the vision is not a blueprint and does not specify how the school or district will get there. That will be the next step of the process.

During this step, mathematics educational leaders share their views with the community, but for the process to result in a fully shared vision, it must be a forum in which the views of the community as a whole prevail. A shared vision cannot be imposed by leaders; if a focus on establishing a more stimulating and challenging mathematics learning environment for students is not a part of what the community envisions, the likelihood of success in implementing Guided Math is slim. If this occurs, math leaders must take a step back and regroup. Building a shared vision takes time, so leaders should be patient and continue their work in helping the community recognize the need for changes in mathematics instruction.

Keeping the Vision Meaningful as Mathematics Educators Work to Attain It

So now the professional community has a shared vision for mathematics instruction and student achievement. What are the next steps? If the process of creating a shared vision is done well, the community members feel good about it. They have engaged in powerful conversations, listened to one another, and collaborated to establish a clear vision of an attainable future. Momentum for change is building. Effective leaders work to continue these discussions and to be sure their leadership reflects the vision. As Senge (2006) writes, "visions spread because of a reinforcing process of increasing clarity, enthusiasm, communication and commitment. As people talk, the vision grows clearer. As it gets clearer, enthusiasm for its benefits builds" (211).

Conzemius and O'Neill (2001) suggest that leaders should reinforce the shared vision "by continually encouraging people to dream and hope beyond the day; by using planning and goal-setting sessions that include visioning; and by providing time to pursue the vision and goals" (31) so that it is internalized into "their daily behavioral repertoire" (32).

To monitor the degree to which community members have assimilated the vision of enhancing mathematics learning, effective leaders look for evidence that it is pervasive throughout the school or district, that collaborative meetings are driven by it, that it influences decisions throughout the institution, and that school improvement plans align with it. These conversations should provide fertile ground for exploring the implementation of the Guided Math framework as a means of providing effective teaching methods to nurture students' mathematical proficiency. If evidence of a pervasive focus on mathematical instruction is lacking, leaders must determine why and then take action to remedy it.

Certain factors can keep the vision from being fully assimilated by the community even after an inclusive process to develop it. If the growing enthusiasm and ongoing conversations about a mathematics focus expand without corresponding open reflection and inquiry, "the diversity of views dissipates focus and generates unmanageable conflicts. People see different ideal futures" (Senge 2006, 211). Thus, if people begin to consider the vision to be set in stone—totally unrelated to their individual emerging values and visions of mathematics instruction—the support for the vision "can grind to a halt with a wave of increasing polarization" (211). "Similarly, when almost every faculty member has a divergent view of what a prospective change initiative really means, the problem is not with the faculty. Rather, the work of effective change implementation requires considerably more clarity and consistency from the leader" (Reeves 2009, Kindle Locations 1083–1085).

To counteract this erosion of support, leaders should continue to solicit feedback about the vision from the school or district community—inviting comments and suggestions for refining it. Conzemius and O'Neill (2001) advise leaders to "reinforce a vision within your organization by continually encouraging people to dream and hope beyond the day; by using planning and goal-setting sessions that include visioning; and by providing time to pursue the vision and goals" (31). By listening respectfully and exploring these ideas through ongoing dialogue, shared visions for improving mathematics instruction through the implementation of Guided Math remain vibrant.

Another situation in which community members become disillusioned with shared visions is when "people get overwhelmed by the demands of current reality and lose their focus on the vision" (Senge 2006, 213). Reeves (2009) warns that "educators are drowning under the weight of initiative fatigue—attempting to use the same amount of time, money, and emotional energy to accomplish more and more objectives" (Kindle Locations 238–239). While dreams and visions are appealing, reality often gives them a swift jolt. Reeves offers a solution to leaders: "pull the weeds before you plant the flowers" (Kindle Location 218). This is certainly easier said than done. But, Reeves goes on to ask strategic leaders to consider these three ideas (Kindle Locations 253–269) for "pulling weeds."

1. **Use intergrade dialogue to find the essentials.** Vertical team meetings allow teachers to give advice to their colleagues in the next-lower grades—specific and succinct advice—about what is essential and what might be weeded out without greatly impacting student achievement.

2. **Sweat the small stuff.** Encourage teachers and other staff members to share time saving tips. Anything from suggestions for efficiently handling routine classroom tasks, for managing transitions, or for adjustments to the schedule can save seconds or minutes in a day. That might not seem like much, but they add up and can amount to large timesaving in the long run and allow teachers to be more receptive to the implementation of new and often challenging mathematics instructional strategies such as Guided Math.

3. **Set the standard for a weed-free garden.** Show respect for teachers' time by eliminating unnecessary meetings and announcements, by starting and ending meetings on time, and avoiding interruptions to the instructional day whenever possible. When leaders model weed pulling, teachers are more likely to give it a try within their classrooms and collaborative meetings.

Yet, even with Reeves' suggestions, finding time for community members to focus on a shared vision that calls for changes in instruction like the Guided Math framework without becoming overwhelmed is a delicate balancing act for leaders.

Finally, visions can languish if community members forget their connections to one another. "One of the deepest desires underlying shared vision is the desire to be connected, to a larger purpose and to one another. The spirit of connection is fragile. It is undermined whenever we lose our respect for one another and for each other's views. We then split into insiders and outsiders—those who are 'true believers' in the vision and those who are not. When this happens, the visioning conversations no longer build genuine enthusiasms toward the vision" (Senge 2006, 214).

Because a vision becomes a living force only when people truly believe they can shape their future, members of the community must be aware of the impact of their own actions in creating the current reality. Only when this happens can they envision change that is based on their own actions and those of their colleagues. They gain confidence that improvement in students' mathematical achievement through the implementation of Guided Math is indeed something that can be accomplished when the community is connected and works together. This is why collaboration and building a sense of collective efficacy is essential. Rather than individuals "going it alone," the members, in a collective effort, continue to shape the vision and work to attain it.

Working to Achieve a Shared Vision of Mathematics Instruction

The term strategic planning brings to mind for some people a disciplined and thoughtful process that links the values, mission, and goals of a school system with a set of coherent strategies and tasks designed to achieve those goals. For others, strategic planning induces a cringe brought about by memories of endless meetings, fact-free debates, three-ring binders, and dozens—perhaps hundreds—of discrete objectives, tasks, strategies, plans, and goals, all left undone after the plan was completed. As one frustrated administrator said to me, "When do we get to stop planning and start doing?"

(Reeves 2009, Kindle Locations 943–947)

The creation of a shared vision alone does not bring about change. It is only a commencement of an ongoing community effort by individuals who have "a similar picture of what they want to achieve" (Kaser et al. 2013, Kindle Location 61) and are convinced that "they can achieve it most effectively by their collective, not individual, actions" (61). It does not provide, however, specific goals or steps to be taken to achieve a vision of improved mathematical achievement. At this point, to focus and direct this joint undertaking, wise leaders provide people with opportunities for the disciplined and thoughtful process envisioned by Reeves (2009).

During the strategic planning process, members of the community examine relevant data in order to identify existing strengths and needs so that goals with coherent strategies and tasks to support them are devised. Careful attention to strategic planning avoids the frustrations described by Reeves (2009): "endless meetings, fact-free debates, three-ring binders, and dozens—perhaps hundreds—of discrete objectives, tasks, strategies, plans, and goals" (Kindle Location 945).

Within this part of the process, leaders gather data on mathematics instruction so that members of the educational community can consider its effectiveness. The choice of appropriate data significantly increases the likelihood that the community will choose to focus on the implementation of Guided Math. Data should include not only student assessment results, but should also document the kinds of instruction currently provided to students for members of the community to examine. In this way, members of the community can gauge the effectiveness of the mathematics teaching and learning within the school or district.

Based on a needs assessment developed from the examination of this data, specific goals can be established. Once the members of the community are receptive to learning about alternative instructional techniques, math leaders can present information about the Guided Math framework. At this point, its implementation may be agreed upon as a method of reaching the shared vision of improvement in mathematics achievement.

Without going through these steps, there is little chance that Guided Math implementation efforts will be collective, or even effective, in reaching the agreed upon vision. Efforts will not be collective because there has been no agreed upon road map drawn up for all to follow, nor are efforts likely to be effective because nothing has been done to determine what actions will best address the existing needs. Instead of a community acting in harmony, without these steps, what results are a multitude of almost random individual efforts. So, while it is tempting to step back and feel good about the establishment of a shared vision, in reality, this is the time when the real work begins.

Identifying Strengths and Needs

Examining classroom, school, and district data reflecting the degree of mathematical proficiency of its students is an excellent way for educators to identify current strengths and needs in light of their shared vision and also to chart their progress toward common goals in the future. To be of value, the data studied must be both specific and relevant. Educators analyze data to answer questions such as the following:

- Are there noticeable trends evident in the data?

- In what areas have the data stayed constant?

- What, if any, improvement in mathematical achievement is noticeable?

- Are there areas in which the data indicates decline?

- How does the community's data compare with data from other classrooms, schools, or districts with similar demographics?

- Based on the shared vision that has been developed, what areas should be targeted for improvement? Why should these areas be targeted?

- What instructional strategies are teachers using during mathematics lessons?

- To what degree are students engaging in hands-on tasks?

- How do the current methods of instruction impact the mathematical learning of students?

If trends are evident, community members should be encouraged to try to determine what might account for upswings or declines in achievement and how those influences impact future plans for instruction. This is an appropriate time for the community to consider the impact of current instructional practices. After all, data only gives us "*information*, nothing more and nothing less" (Conzemius and O'Neill 2001, 46). What is more important is what the professional community does with the data. "When applied with knowledge and integrity, data heighten our ability to make informed and reasoned decisions about our work; this kind of reflection is what distinguishes the professional practitioner from the technician" (46).

Brief classroom visits by mathematics educational leaders can provide a wealth of data concerning the types of teaching and learning that are most prevalent in the school or district. A form can be used to record observations. The form provided in Figure 3.1 may be adapted to meet the needs of individual schools. Using data compiled from this form, the community can analyze the common teaching techniques being used. Please see Appendix D for a full-size version of Figure 3.1.

Figure 3.1 Mathematics Instruction Observation Form

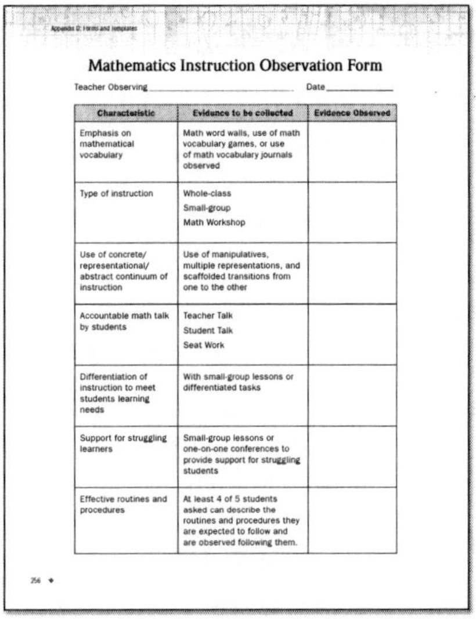
Appendix D: Forms and Templates

Mathematics Instruction Observation Form

Teacher Observing________________ Date________

Characteristic	Evidence to be collected	Evidence Observed
Emphasis on mathematical vocabulary	Math word walls, use of math vocabulary games, or use of math vocabulary journals observed	
Type of instruction	Whole-class Small-group Math Workshop	
Use of concrete/ representational/ abstract continuum of instruction	Use of manipulatives, multiple representations, and scaffolded transitions from one to the other	
Accountable math talk by students	Teacher Talk Student Talk Seat Work	
Differentiation of instruction to meet students learning needs	With small-group lessons or differentiated tasks	
Support for struggling learners	Small-group lessons or one-on-one conferences to provide support for struggling students	
Effective routines and procedures	At least 4 of 5 students asked can describe the routines and procedures they are expected to follow and are observed following them.	

256 ◆

Accordingly, the ongoing process of collaboratively analyzing data about students' mathematical learning and the predominate mathematics instructional practices accompanied by professional reflection is "one important aspect in shaping a culture for continuous learning and improvement" (Conzemius and O'Neil 2001, 59). It does not only occur immediately following the creation of a shared vision. Instead, it is ongoing—allowing for the identification of needs, the setting of goals, the measurement of progress in meeting goals, the revision of goals, and the refinement of the shared vision, if desired, by the educational community. It promotes the emergence of "informed professional judgment" in school improvement efforts as "teachers collectively focus on student performance and develop action plans to improve it" (Fullan quoted in Sparks 2003, 57). This kind of extensive examination gives members of the community the impetus to consider the value of implementing Guided Math as a way of increasing students' mathematical proficiency.

Figure 3.2 shows an example of a needs assessment form with data evidence collected during classroom observations that identifies the strengths and needs of mathematics instructional methods.

Figure 3.2 Sample Needs Assessment Form

Mathematics Instruction Needs Assessment	
Type of Data Examined: Mathematics Instructional Methods Observation Form	
Data Collection Period: September 10, 2015	
Describe specific evidence from data that indicates strengths and needs.	
Strengths	**Specific Evidence from Data**
Focus on mathematical vocabulary	In 95 percent of the classrooms visited, the use of Math Word Walls was evident.
Remedial assistance for struggling learners	In 10 percent of the classes visited, the teacher was engaged in small-group remediation.
Consistent expectations for student behavior during mathematics instruction	In 90 percent of the classrooms, students were able to describe the routines and procedures they were expected to follow.
Needs	**Specific Evidence from Data**
Increased use of Concrete/ Representational/Abstract instruction	Use of manipulatives during instruction was present in only 10 percent of the classrooms observed.
Increase in accountable student math talk	Teacher talk was the primary mathematical communication in 80 percent of the classrooms, student talk in 10 percent, and students engaged in seat work or other tasks accounted for the remaining 10 percent.
Increase in differentiation in mathematics instruction	Evidence of differentiation was observed in 15 percent of the classrooms through the use of small group instruction and only 5 percent of the classrooms had differentiated tasks.

Setting Goals

One is hard pressed to think of any organization that has sustained some measure of greatness in the absence of goals, values, and missions that become deeply shared throughout the organization.

(Senge 2006, Kindle Location 9)

By this point, a shared vision of improvement in students' mathematical achievement has emerged and an analysis of data has been done by teachers and staff members to identify instructional strengths and needs. The community has a pretty good idea of where it wants to go and what impediments stand in its way. Now, it is time for decisions to be made regarding the specific ways in which needs will be addressed in order to achieve the common vision. Of all the possible paths to improvement in mathematical teaching and learning, which of them most closely align with the vision, the existing strengths, and the identified needs? How can the school or district most effectively move forward to meet those needs? What specific goals will lead to attaining the vision? It is during this process that the implementation of Guided Math becomes a goal.

Process Goals and Results Goals

Building upon both the shared vision and the knowledge gained from examining data, the community must then construct a plan that establishes goals to address needs and lead the school or district toward attaining its vision of improved mathematical performance by students. Ideally, the improvement "plans have to be 'sticky'—concise, actionable, memorable" (Fullan 2014, Kindle Location 131). Yet, the plans should not be too complex. "When plans are elaborate, they rarely are clear enough to be understood and actionable. When plans focus on a few clear goals and corresponding actions, they are much more likely to stimulate action" (Fullan 2014, 130).

According to Conzemius and O'Neill (2001), there are two kinds of goals to be considered—process goals and results goals. "Process goals identify the methods, actions, and activities school staffs can use to build their capacity for improvement" (88). Results goals "identify what all that capacity building adds up to" (88). A solid strategic plan should include both kinds of goals. They keep the educational organization focused on the critical factors that will determine the degree of success of the school or district in fully achieving its vision.

During discussions about possible goals, "mathematics leaders need to work closely with teachers and carefully review research to determine initiatives and strategies that seem likely to have the greatest effect on student learning" (Balka, Hull, and Miles 2010, 99). This is an excellent time for staff members to consider instructional initiatives such as the implementation of the Guided Math framework as a process goal.

Implementation of Guided Math as a Process Goal

If the data indicates that there is a need to improve mathematics instruction, Guided Math can be adopted as a process goal to increase students' mathematical proficiency.

Guided Math is a multifaceted approach to teaching math that emphasizes students' conceptual understanding, competence in mathematical practices, and computational fluency. It offers teachers an instructional strategy that allows them to differentiate their mathematics instruction based on their students' learning needs. Moreover, all seven components of the framework encourage students to think as mathematicians and engage in the mathematical practices specified in the Common Core Math Standards (NGA and CCSSO 2010) and NCTM's process standards (2000). As such, it is an attractive option for educators as they focus on ways to improve student achievement in math.

In addition, because many teachers are already familiar with the Guided Reading approach, Guided Math's similar structure is one that can be readily incorporated into daily instruction. Teachers who are teaching reading with small-group lessons find that the same small-group format for teaching math makes sense. Students who are already familiar with the Reading Workshop routines and procedures easily adapt to Math Workshop.

Initial suggestions that the implementation of Guided Math may be an effective way of moving toward the common vision may come either from educational leaders or from other members of the school or district. In any case, interest is aroused when educational leaders give the entire community opportunities to learn about the framework and how it supports increases in mathematical achievement. The professional community has to become familiar with its structure and to see how it can be integrated into classroom instruction before any decisions are made to make its implementation a process goal.

What can educational leaders do if they are convinced that implementing the Guided Math framework is an effective strategy for improving mathematical achievement? In spite of their beliefs, leaders must be patient as other members of the community learn more about this instructional approach. A top-down decree that Guided Math is to become the method of mathematical instruction may work in some settings, but implementation is rarely as effective when imposed from the top as it is when teachers buy into its adoption and are convinced that it will help the educational organization reach its shared vision. Here are some suggestions for helping the mathematics educators understand the Guided Math framework and how its implementation will help the school or district attain its vision of improvement in students' mathematical achievement:

- Make Guided Math resource materials available for all to review or to support a team or teams to investigate the effectiveness of the approach, how it supports the shared vision, and how it could be implemented.

- Send a team of math teachers and other support staff to attend Guided Math training. Have them present what they learn to the community.

- Allow interested educators to pilot the Guided Math framework in their classrooms before the educational community as a whole considers it for school-wide or district-wide implementation. An effective way of convincing teachers and other staff members of the value of implementing Guided Math is having their colleagues present evidence of its benefits from their own experiences piloting it.

- Arrange for math educators to visit other schools or districts that use the Guided Math framework to observe it in practice and to discuss its impact with those who have found it to be effective.

When people have the opportunity to work together to research the best methods for attaining a shared goal, it generates a sense of inclusiveness among the community. But, of course, it is never possible to please everyone. Leaders who try to do that often wind up pleasing no one. "At the beginning, it is less important that the plan meet everyone's approval than that the plan starts a process of buy-in" (Fullan 2014, Kindle Location131).

Once a decision is made to implement Guided Math as a part of a strategic improvement plan, it is important to bear in mind that this goal is a *process* goal—a way of building instructional capacity with the aim of improving the mathematical achievement of students. As such, it should be accompanied by site-specific *results* goals. What improvements in proficiency are desired? How will the success of the implementation be measured or assessed? After all, the implementation of an instructional framework is *only a means to an end, not an end in and of itself.* The *end* is the hoped-for improvement in mathematical proficiency of students. In the long run, the most important goals are the results goals that specify exactly what improvement is desired and how it can be measured.

Results Goals for Guided Math Implementation

Results goals play an essential role in providing specific expectations for success. Throughout the time frame established, the measurement of progress toward reaching these goals also provides valuable feedback on how effective the process goal of implementing Guided Math is in making a difference. Because these goals should align directly with the results of the data analysis completed and the shared vision developed, they provide a direct measure of the effectiveness of the process goals (Guided Math implementation). Are the actions called for in the goal of implementing this instructional framework making a positive difference in the mathematical learning of students? If so, how much of a difference? If it is not making enough of a difference, this rich data informs the community in making necessary changes in the process goal determined by the community. This can occur only when the needs identified by the data evidence are linked directly to the process goals and are also reflected in the results goals.

SMART Goals for Guided Math

The most effective goals can be represented by the acronym SMART as described by Conzemius and O'Neill (2001, 89). A SMART goal has the following characteristics:

✎ **Specific and strategic**—The goal is specific in that it clearly identifies what it aims at improving. It is strategic in that it focuses on needs that emerged from the examination of relevant data.

✎ **Measurable**—The goal is written so that its results can be quantified in some way to determine the degree of success. All community members know at the beginning of the initiative what indicators will be examined for evidence of progress.

✎ **Attainable**—The goal is written so that it is achievable by community members. Think of it as a Goldilocks goal—not too conservative, not too ambitious, but just right.

✎ **Results-oriented**—The goal describes the desired outcome—not the process or change that will contribute to that outcome.

✎ **Time bound**—Time frames are set for accomplishing the goal. Community members realize that progress toward meeting the goal will be measured at given intervals and that by a given date it is expected that the goal will have been accomplished.

The adoption of the Guided Math framework is one possible method for improving student achievement in mathematics—clearly a process goal. Yet, its implementation does not describe a measurable outcome linked to an identified need. To accompany this process goal of implementation, results goals focus on the specific measurable improvement in students' mathematics success to be achieved as a result of the use of this instructional framework.

Figures 3.3 and 3.4 provide examples of Guided Math process/results goals and measures.

Figure 3.3 Sample Guided Math *Process* Goals and Measures

Sample Goal	Sample Measure
At least one classroom in each grade level will implement the Guided Math framework.	Checklists completed by mathematics coaches during classroom visits show evidence of implementation of at least 5 of the 7 components of the Guided Math framework by January and 7 of the 7 components by March in these classrooms.
All classroom teachers will create a classroom environment of numeracy by the end of September.	Teachers will complete a self-assessment form rating their level of implementation and documenting evidence of implementation.
All mathematics teachers will participate in a year-long professional learning community study of Guided Math which will meet monthly.	Each PLC will submit minutes following each meeting describing their study and actions for the month.
The math coach will conduct Guided Math demonstration lessons in each classroom during the months of September and October followed by debrief conferences with the teachers.	The math coach will provide a schedule of these lessons and debrief sessions to administrators on a weekly basis.

Figure 3.4 Sample Guided Math *Results* Goals and Measures

Sample Goal	Sample Measure
By the end of the year, 88 percent of fifth-grade students will score as proficient or advanced in mathematics on the state mandated test.	State-mandated tests
By the end of the year, 90 percent of third-grade students will score as practitioners or experts in problem solving on the district-developed problem-solving rubric.	District-developed problem solving rubric
By the end of the first quarter, 90 percent of sixth graders will demonstrate proficiency on the grade level performance task selected by the district.	Grade level performance tasks selected by the district
Eighty-five percent of fourth-grade students will show an improvement of 15 points on the midyear math benchmark test over what was scored on the fall math benchmark test.	District-wide benchmark tests

Finalizing the Plan for Improvement

With the process of developing SMART goals complete, there is one more step that effective math leaders undertake—ensuring that the entire community understands the vision and ensuing goals. Every part of the educational organization should be aware of their responsibilities according to the plan and how essential they are to its achievement. If people are unclear about how they are impacted by the plans, it is much better to discover it now rather than later. Some leaders choose to review these plans in depth at grade level meetings to get final feedback. Although this is not a time for substantial revision, this final consultation with teachers and staff demonstrates respect for them and for the importance of their contribution to the success of the plan. The plans then become internalized by the community as a whole.

Another reason for this final review is to emphasize the expectation that the entire community will actively support these measures. Too often in the educational community, plans for improvement have been established to meet requirements, but with little commitment to them by the community or the leadership. A plan was drafted—in place in case anyone checked—but the staff continued to do business as usual. There was little done to ensure compliance, much less buy-in, by the community. Thus, little was achieved by having a plan. Nor were staff members terribly interested or committed to the plan.

By involving the entire educational community throughout the process of developing a shared vision and plans for achieving that vision, the message is clear that this is a joint endeavor. With the final review of the plan in small grade level groups, leaders can clearly articulate that the responsibility for its success rests with individuals working together with a common and focused purpose.

A sample improvement plan for the implementation of Guided Math is shown in Figure 3.5. A blank template can be found in Appendix D.

Figure 3.5 Sample Mathematics Improvement Plan

Mathematics Improvement Plan

Shared Vision
Our students will become mathematically literate by developing deep conceptual understanding of mathematical content, computational fluency, and proficiency in the mathematical practices. Mathematics learning will be enhanced as teachers continuously reflect on their teaching and collaborate to refine their instructional strategies and to meet the learning needs of their students.

Action Plan
The school will pilot the use of Guided Math in one classroom in each grade level. Through the implementation of the effective Guided Math instructional strategies, teachers will provide rigorous instruction that leads students to think mathematically, become proficient in the mathematical practices, and develop computational fluency. Throughout the year, all teachers will learn about these instructional strategies during their grade level meetings as the piloting teachers share what they are learning and by participating in peer observations in the Guided Math classrooms.

Process Goals and Measures

Goals	Measures
One teacher from each grade level will pilot the implementation of Guided Math during the upcoming school year.	Checklists completed by mathematics coaches during classroom visits show evidence of implementation of at least 5 of the 7 components of the Guided Math framework by January and 7 of the 7 components by March in these classrooms.
Teachers who are piloting Guided Math will reflect on their implementation experiences and provide training on its components in collaborative monthly meetings with their grade levels.	Each teacher receives a copy of *Guided Math: A Framework for Mathematics Instruction* in August. The grade level minutes from the monthly Guided Math meetings submitted to the principal document the reflections on Guided Math implementation and the training provided by the Guided Math teachers to their peers.
Teachers will make at least three peer observations in Guided Math classrooms to increase their knowledge of the framework.	A calendar of these visits compiled by the math coach documents visits by each teacher in October, January, and March.

Results Goals and Measures

Goals	Measures
By the end of the school year, 85 percent of students in the Guided Math classrooms will report that Guided Math *somewhat positively* or *greatly positively* affected their understanding of mathematics.	Self-assessment survey created by the math leaders and administered to students in the Guided Math classes
At least 10 percent more students in the Guided Math classrooms at each grade level will demonstrate as practitioners or experts in applying mathematical knowledge and skills to real-life problem solving than students in other classrooms.	District-developed problem-solving rubric

Building Capacity for Change

Asking educators to embrace new instructional strategies without adequate training is unfair and ineffective. Teachers and other staff members deserve to know exactly what it is they are being asked to do, to be given comprehensive initial training, and then to receive ongoing job-embedded support as they begin the implementation process. The effectiveness of a brief book study or a one-day workshop is questionable. Schmoker warns that one-day workshops and isolated staff development measures are "a failed model for improving instructional practice: training, in the form of workshops or staff development" (Schmoker 2006, Kindle Locations 1611–1612). Some people will easily adopt new measures with little assistance, but most require considerably more support. At this point of a change initiative, the leadership function of building capacity comes heavily into play.

The implementation of new initiatives involves much learning and practice before expertise can be expected. As educators explore new ideas, it takes time for them to assimilate and perfect new skills. Almost certainly, things will go wrong before they go smoothly. It is not unusual for an implementation dip to occur as teachers adopt new methods of instruction. In fact, when things go too smoothly, it may be a sign that only superficial or trivial change is being made, rather than the more substantial changes called for in the improvement plan (Fullan and Miles 1992, 749; Huberman and Miles 1984, 86).

Leaders ease the difficulties inherent in the implementation process of Guided Math by creating a climate in which risk-taking is encouraged so educators are willing to venture beyond the familiar and engage in the "anxiety, difficulties, and uncertainty [that] are *intrinsic to all successful change*" (Fullan and Miles 1992, 749). In professional climates that are most supportive of change, teachers and other staff members rely on their leaders to recognize that difficulties are a natural part of the change process. An implementation dip is viewed as evidence of change, rather than failure. Encouragement and support are provided to teachers who may feel distressed as they engage in new practices.

Another responsibility for leaders in supporting change is supplying the extra resources that are invariably needed for successful change initiatives. When the professional community is asked to make meaningful changes as part of an improvement plan, those changes must be fully funded and adequate time allocated for the implementation. The responsibility for providing the funding, materials, or time needed falls squarely upon leadership. School districts may pool resources from several schools to offer district training for teachers. Lead teachers or coaches may attend training and share what they learn with other staff members. Collaborative brainstorming with staff members will sometimes generate ideas for shifting funds or materials to supply these resources. Pursuing funding through grants is another possible solution for short-term funding needs. Time needs may be met by closely examining schedules to see if there are ways to use time more efficiently. Some schools routinely hire substitute teachers during school hours to free time for teachers to engage in the needed training or collaborative planning. Others may schedule common planning time after school for grade level teams.

Providing Clear Expectations

A good strategic plan for increased mathematics achievement includes specific process goals such as the implementation of Guided Math and results goals with a well-structured timeframe for implementation. Having specific goals and a timeframe for implementation in place, however, is just the first step in the process. All members of the community must understand and be willing to carry out their responsibilities under the plan. Otherwise, the improvement plan with its goal of Guided Math implementation may be an initiative in word only.

Teachers and other staff members should be able to describe the plan and what they will do to implement it. Fullan (2014) calls it "talking the walk when people are doing something that is essential, deep, and related to success, and they are doing it using common language and transparent actions" (Kindle Location 87). Evidence of the implementation process should be pervasive throughout the school or school district—in classrooms, in coaching sessions, and in meetings. When the plan includes the implementation of the Guided Math framework, it should be common to hear members of the professional community discussing aspects of Guided Math, reflecting on their experiences with the implementation, assessing its effectiveness, and planning how to make the implementation even more effective.

The creation of a rich environment for change is largely dependent on leadership. Effective leaders model it; they are explicit in sharing their expectations with teachers. For them, the plan is not something that is compiled and then forgotten. The leader's ongoing engagement in the process communicates a commitment to make the initiative succeed and, thus, increases the likelihood that the entire community gets onboard to support it.

Sustaining a Guided Math Initiative

After building a firm foundation for change, a leader's responsibilities shift somewhat. The real work of implementing change now begins. How do leaders sustain the momentum? As mentioned earlier, with any improvement efforts, difficulties should be expected. Fullan and Miles (1992) offer leaders seven basic propositions for success to keep in mind as the implementation process continues.

1. **"Change is learning—loaded with uncertainty"** (749). Leaders must continue to understand that learning is a messy business and to create conditions that support ongoing learning. It helps to remind teachers of the struggles their students experience when learning something new. Just as teachers are patient with their students, educators must have patience with themselves as they work to implement changes. At times, leaders only need to extend encouragement and understanding. At other times, however, they may need to make

adjustments to the plan to address the difficulties. As adjustments are made, it is important to keep the end goals in mind—to be sure that the revisions continue to align with those goals.

2. **Change is a journey, not a blueprint.** "There can be no blueprints for change, because rational planning models for complex social change... do not work. Rather what is needed is a guided journey" (749). Rather than rigid adherence to a fixed plan, effective improvement efforts are continuously shaped and reshaped flexibly as new situations arise. As Fullan and Miles advise, "Do, then plan...and do and plan some more" (749).

3. **Problems are our friends.** "Problems arise naturally from the demands of the change process itself, from the people involved and from the structure and procedures of schools and districts" (750). Only problems that are ignored truly impede progress. Research shows that schools that successfully bring about change respond to problems by making both structural changes and, if the problem is relatively minor, applying "band-aid" solutions instead of ignoring the problems, easing off the change initiatives, or increasing pressure on the professional community. "In short, the assertive pursuit of problems in service of continuous improvement is the kind of accountability that can make a difference" (750).

Kaser et al. (2013) advise leaders that "in failing forward, we advance by the way we respond to a situation. Instead of reacting to the event and attempting a quick fix, we dig deeper to determine the root cause of the problem and to correct what organizational policies, programs, or practices are at the core. In that sense, problems are opportunities for us to broaden our attitudes, knowledge, and skills while moving our organizations forward" (Kindle Location 71).

4. **Change is resource-hungry.** Resources are essential for substantial change. How leaders allocate resources, both in terms of energy and money required, is crucial to the success of change efforts. When resources are available and used wisely, they support needed professional "training, consulting, coaching, coordination, and capacity-building" (Fullan and Miles 1992, 750). Effective leaders explore creative ways of providing needed resources, sometimes through purchases, through

re-allocation from one use to another, or through schedule changes. As teachers collaborate to implement Guided Math or pursue any shared vision, these resources are imperative. See Appendix B for suggested Guided Math resources.

5. **Change requires the power to manage it.** According to Fullan and Miles (1992, 751), there are four essential ingredients in managing change successfully. First, management is most effective when it is done by a cross-role group, possibly composed of teachers, coaches, and administrators. The composition of the group may vary according to the nature of the change initiatives and the educational institution itself.

   Second, that managing group must have legitimacy that is widely understood throughout the school or school district. The legitimacy should be conferred at the time that the group is selected and then, later, the group earns respect through its actions.

   Third, successful management is dependent upon the cooperation and the collaboration of all. Members must realize that change means there will be some disequilibrium, but that trust of one another is essential to the process. Leaders have to be willing to delegate some of the managing responsibilities to others without fear of losing control.

   Fourth, management of change goes most smoothly when there is support throughout the wider community.

6. **Change is systemic.** Change is systemic in the sense that it is aimed not only at the specific components of the system, such as curriculum, instruction, and student support, but also targets the entire culture of the school or district. Successful change, in other words, "involves both restructuring and 'reculturing'" (Fullan and Miles 1992, 751).

7. **All large-scale change is implemented locally.** "Change cannot be accomplished from afar" (Fullan and Miles 1992, 752). Without the active involvement of the professional community, meaningful and lasting change is impossible.

Overcoming Resistance to Change

A powerful strategic plan for school improvement, such as Guided Math, always calls for changes of one kind or another. Even mutually agreed upon changes, however, may cause discomfort and unease among educators. The leader as a motivator and change agent has a powerful role to play in supporting change within the educational community even when some resist it.

What are some of the most common reasons members of the professional community fail to implement the changes specified in the improvement plan?

✎ **People lack an understanding of the change and what is expected of them to bring about the change.** This is primarily a communication problem and can be fairly easily addressed. Although this may be a problem for an entire group of educators—perhaps a grade level cadre of teachers—most often it occurs with individuals.

To solve this problem, a leader can meet either with the individual teacher or the group who seems to lack an understanding of what is expected of them to clarify the expectations and answer any questions they may have. Leaders should then follow up by monitoring their performance to ensure that they now understand and are implementing the changes.

This problem is sometimes misdiagnosed. Individuals who choose not to implement changes may justify the lack of compliance by feigning ignorance of expectations. Follow-up monitoring sends a clear message that these members of the community are not only expected to, but are required to make these changes.

When there appears to be an overwhelming lack of understanding among teachers and other staff members, the leaders who drafted the plan which calls for Guided Math implementation should meet with the entire community to review all components of the plan, link it to the shared vision, explain in detail the called-for changes, and set out the time frame for implementation.

✎ **People lack the knowledge or skills needed to make the changes.** Leaders are responsible for providing the necessary training for educators who are expected to make changes. If many individuals are experiencing this problem, it is an indication that additional support in the way of training or coaching is needed for the whole community. If it is a problem with only a few people, this support should be targeted more precisely to include only those individuals who need it.

With either situation, however, it is important to determine the kind of support that is necessary. Do teachers need to go "back to the basics" with professional training to reintroduce the knowledge and skills required for the implementation of Guided Math or do they only need support from coaches who might model lessons, observe classroom practices, and give feedback? Or, do they just need some positive feedback on what they are doing to give their confidence a boost?

Following the additional training or support, ongoing monitoring is needed to be sure that it was sufficient to allow these teachers or other staff members to make the changes required.

✎ **People are not convinced the changes will make a difference or disagree with the changes.** When this problem occurs, it is time to listen to concerns, but also for leaders to reassert the expectation that *everyone*, as a part of an inclusive educational community, will play an active role in implementing Guided Math because it is best for the students. For some who resist initially, actually implementing all or part of the framework and finding it is effective will convince them of the efficacy of the plan. Others may never be convinced, but even these individuals must come to understand that participating in the implementation plan is their responsibility as members of the greater group. Although this compliance is much less desirable than motivation from within, it is a step in the right direction.

✎ **People choose not to make the effort to change.** For a very few individuals, it may seem to be too much effort to change the way they have always done things. This can be the most challenging problem that leaders encounter. Clarification of expectations will not solve it. Additional training and support will not solve it. In this situation, the steadfastness of the leader is critical. When educators are opting out of participation because they just do not want to change or make the effort to change, it must be made clear to them that they have no other option than to comply. Even then, frequent monitoring should occur to verify compliance. Continued lack of compliance should be well documented, along with documentation of the supports that have been provided. If a member of the community continues to resist, the leader may choose to discuss with the individual whether his or her professional position is a good fit for the educational community and for the individual.

Figure 3.6 summarizes the necessary steps in achieving a shared vision for the implementation of the Guided Math framework.

Figure 3.6 Steps to Achieving a Shared Vision of Mathematics Instruction

Develop a Mathematics Shared Vision	Lead the educational community in identifying what they want their mathematics instruction to provide students. What is the commitment of mathematics educators to students, staff, and community?
Complete a Needs Assessment	Analyze data reflecting both students' mathematical achievement and the current mathematical instruction students receive to determine strengths and needs as evidenced by the data.
Set Process and Results Goals	As a community, establish how the vision can be achieved (process goals) and define targets for improvement in student achievement (results goals). Once schools or districts choose to implement Guided Math as an instructional framework that will lead them toward their shared vision, its implementation becomes a process goal.
Build Capacity for Change	Provide targeted and consistent professional development, essential resources, and opportunities for collaboration to support the attainment of both process and results goals.
Sustain the Vision	Monitor and evaluate the progress toward meeting both process and results goals. Revise the plan as needed. Continue to engage members in discussions focused on the shared vision.

Review & Reflect

1. Ask five members of your professional community to describe their vision of mathematics education. How can the implementation of Guided Math support these visions?

2. As a mathematics educational leader, what do you think is your most important function in creating a shared vision for mathematics education? Why is the creation of a shared vision important for Guided Math implementation?

3. What are some of the school improvement plans in which you have participated? How can you draw upon these experiences to support the use of the Guided Math framework as a process goal in a math improvement plan?

Chapter 4

Implementing the Guided Math Framework

This chapter examines models for the implementation of the Guided Math framework (Sammons 2010, 2013). When a needs analysis leads the professional community to focus on improving students' mathematics achievement, the adoption of the Guided Math framework may be considered as a process goal for an improvement plan. Some school districts, schools, or even individual teachers may choose to implement the framework without having gone through the process of creating an extensive improvement plan at all. The following implementation models may be used regardless of whether the processes described in the first three chapters have been carried out first.

In some districts and schools, the decision to implement Guided Math may be a result of mathematics leaders seeing the need for improvement in mathematics achievement and engaging in a search to find effective strategies for improving mathematics instruction. In other instances, the decision to implement the Guided Math framework may be spurred by individual teachers or schools that began using the framework and shared their successes with district mathematics leaders. Regardless of the initial motivation for implementation, there are several models for Guided Math implementation that leaders may choose to employ or to adapt and employ.

To Mandate or Not?

There are a number of things to be considered when schools or school districts are deciding whether to mandate the implementation of the Guided Math framework in all classrooms. Reeves (2009) cites research finding that "implementation that was moderate or occasional was no better than implementation that was completely absent" (Kindle Location 533). To ensure deep implementation, mandates seem to be critical. Comprehensive professional development including ongoing job-embedded coaching coupled with explicit expectations that teachers use the framework for mathematics instruction are most likely to lead to the universal adoption of the Guided Math framework in classrooms.

Yet, many schools and districts choose to encourage and support implementation without mandating it for a variety of reasons.

✎ Teachers are usually more committed to an implementation initiative when they are empowered and feel they have a role in the decision-making process (Short and Greer 2002, 159). Even when teachers have been included in a decision to mandate Guided Math implementation, if given a choice, many would rather begin the implementation by learning about it and then adopting it at their own pace. With that method, educators tend to develop a greater sense of ownership in its implementation.

✎ Perhaps several different approaches to improving mathematics achievement are being considered. Teachers are given the option of choosing one of them to try. Later the school may examine the effectiveness of the various approaches and decide to mandate its implementation.

✎ Teachers who initially choose to implement Guided Math will later be asked to act as models for others.

✎ Teachers are accorded a deep respect for their professional knowledge and so diversity in teaching methods is encouraged. Thus, while results goals may be included in an improvement plan, teachers are given the responsibility to decide how they can best achieve them.

The drawbacks to optional implementation of Guided Math are the difficulties in providing adequate training for teachers who decide to use it and the confusion resulting from the creation of a patchwork quilt of instructional methods being implemented throughout a school or district.

Piloted Guided Math Classrooms

Some schools and school districts choose to begin implementation with pilot classrooms to model the use of Guided Math. Teachers may choose to be a part of the pilot program or may be asked to participate by school leaders. A school or district planning to mandate Guided Math implementation in a year or two might initiate pilot classrooms as a first step. Alternatively, this method might be a way of establishing a system of voluntary implementation. Beginning Guided Math implementation with pilot classrooms serves several purposes.

- The school or district has a test-run with implementation which allows the fine-tuning of the professional development and coaching support needed.

- The effectiveness of Guided Math as an instructional framework can be assessed before district-wide or school-wide implementation.

- When Guided Math is shown to enhance student achievement, the motivation of other teachers to implement it in their classrooms increases.

- Other teachers see Guided Math fully implemented in classrooms *in their own schools*—not just as described by a consultant or by the book. This helps convince teachers that the implementation really can be done successfully in their classrooms. Additionally, the pilot teachers are a valuable source of information for their colleagues, giving practical suggestions for making Guided Math work.

- Pilot classrooms function as labs as other teachers begin the implementation process. Teachers can observe first hand the classroom environments of numeracy established, the effective use of Math Warm-Ups, when to use whole-class instruction, how small-group lessons differ from whole-class lessons, and how to manage Math Workshop. The piloting teachers and their classrooms become an integral part of professional development.

Because the pilot classrooms will be used to assess the effectiveness of the framework and will serve as prototypes of Guided Math implementation, it is imperative that adequate professional development is provided. West and Cameron (2013) suggest the term "model classrooms" be avoided. The label "model" implies that these teachers are "modeling" best practices for others rather than focusing on the fact that they are acting as a part of a collaborative inquiry into school improvement by the entire professional community.

Voluntary Classroom Implementation

Voluntary implementation of Guided Math differs significantly from the establishment of piloted Guided Math classrooms. With optional implementation, schools or districts are not promoting the implementation, but are *allowing* it. Professional development opportunities may or may not be provided for teachers. When training is provided, it is usually done by paying for interested teachers to attend Guided Math workshops sponsored by regional education services agencies or other organizations, either profit or nonprofit. If the school or district has math coaches, they may support these teachers as they set up the framework in their classrooms. If not, teachers either work together to support each other or else go it alone.

In many instances, teachers who want to try Guided Math will participate in a Professional Learning Community (PLC) composed of their colleagues. The idea for using Guided Math may have evolved from the work of a PLC or a PLC may be established specifically for the purpose of learning more about Guided Math. No matter where the idea came from, the value of the group study is substantial. In PLCs, teachers work together to not only engage in book studies, but also to examine data, plan lessons, observe each other's lessons, look at student work, reflect on their own experiences and their observations, and in general encourage each other as they implement Guided Math in their classrooms.

As with piloted classrooms, leaders may encourage teachers who are interested in implementing Guided Math to do so in order to introduce the framework to other educators. If this is their intention, the teachers who are using Guided Math may be asked to report on their experiences in grade level meetings, curriculum meetings, or other faculty meetings. If their experiences are positive and their students' mathematical achievement improves, others are likely to become interested in implementing Guided Math with their own students.

Leaders should encourage the Guided Math teachers to open the doors of their classrooms to other interested teachers who wish to see what Guided

Math looks like in a real classroom. Only with leadership support is this kind of authentic professional learning possible. Leaders must be willing to provide release time to allow teachers to make peer observations and to confer with one another. Although this may be an example of incremental change, it can be better than no change at all in that it stimulates interest in and enthusiasm for mathematics instruction throughout the professional community.

District-Wide Mandates

Whenever school districts mandate the implementation of the Guided Math framework, it is imperative that teachers, administrators, and other education leaders be provided adequate professional development for successful implementation. The small-group lessons and workshop format are a considerable change in instruction for many teachers—particularly teachers who have never used the Guided Reading structure for teaching literacy. It is important that administrators and other leaders understand both the demands of the framework and how it should look when implemented. Effective monitoring of its implementation is impossible unless these leaders can accurately assess the level of implementation by teachers and other staff members. To do that, adequate professional development for all members of the educational community is essential.

Starting with Professional Development

Using Consultants

Usually district Guided Math mandates are supported with considerably more resources than mandates by schools or individual teachers who implement voluntarily. Frequently, funding is available to bring in a consultant who provides an initial overview of the framework for teachers, coaches, and sometimes administrators. Teachers learn about each of the components and how to use them in the classroom to support conceptual understanding, computational fluency, problem-solving skills, and proficiency with mathematical practices. The training gives grade level teachers time to work together as they envision how the components can be implemented effectively in their own classrooms. Districts usually provide teachers with professional resources to support the implementation. (See Appendix C for a list of Guided Math resource materials.)

An overview consisting of one or two days is minimal training for teachers. Implementation is more successful when a consultant also goes into classrooms to demonstrate small-group lessons or other components of the framework as teachers observe and meet with the consultant later to debrief. These training opportunities allow teachers to actually see the components come alive in the classroom. The ensuing debrief sessions promote reflections and analysis as teachers discuss their observations, share questions, and hear the consultant's reflections on the lessons.

For districts that do not have math coaches to support mathematics instruction, some consultants now offer job-embedded coaching as part of their professional development services. Consultants work directly with teachers, planning lessons, observing teachers' lessons, and then offering immediate specific descriptive feedback.

As the implementation process continues, districts may opt to have consultants return to focus on a particular component of the Guided Math framework. Teachers who have gained proficiency in some areas are ready to move on to learn more about other components of Guided Math. For instance, after beginning with the implementation of small-group lessons and Math Workshop, teachers may decide they need more training to learn how to effectively conduct one-on-one Guided Math conferences with their students.

Using Mathematics or Instructional Coaches

When a district chooses to rely on their coaches to train teachers for Guided Math implementation, the district usually brings in a consultant to train the coaches. If that is not feasible, mathematics leaders may lead a book study of *Guided Math: A Framework of Mathematics Instruction* (Sammons 2010) with the district coaches. Coaches then provide the overview training and subsequent demonstration lessons for teachers based on what they learn from the book study.

Even when a consultant provides the overview training, if funding is unavailable for follow-up demonstration lessons by a consultant, in districts that are fortunate enough to have mathematics or instructional coaches, the coaches might provide demonstration lessons in classrooms with debrief sessions for teachers. The coaches then work with individual teachers to plan lessons, observe instruction, and offer feedback. The support provided by district or school coaches can be crucial for successful implementation. Teachers who experience problems with the instructional framework have someone to whom they can turn for suggestions, encouragement, and resources.

Implementation Structures

When districts decide to mandate Guided Math implementation, they not only have to plan how to provide professional development, but they also have to decide on how to roll out the implementation. There are many ways this can be accomplished. Some districts establish a schedule for implementation that is adhered to by all schools in the system. Other districts opt to ask each school in the district to devise its own schedule for implementation. An example of each of these kinds of implementation initiatives is included below.

Sample District-Wide Implementation Plan

When the Chinook School Division in Saskatchewan, Canada decided to implement the Guided Math framework as part of the Math Momentum initiative, their curriculum leaders had already explored Guided Math with their math coaches. They asked me to work with them to help facilitate the implementation of Guided Math throughout the division. I provided training to their elementary and middle school teachers in early spring. In addition to the daylong overview presentation, I visited schools, both elementary and middle, for two days working directly with students, teaching small-group lessons as teachers observed. Each of the classroom lessons was followed with debrief sessions where teachers had an opportunity to share their observations and reflections and ask me questions. The lessons and debriefs were videotaped so they could be used in the future for ongoing professional development.

Following the initial training in March, teachers were encouraged to begin thinking about how the framework could be implemented in their classrooms. Many of them actually gave it a try immediately after the training. During the spring of that year, the math coaches provided some additional professional development on managing Math Workshop, the component of the Guided Math framework in which students work independently and an area of great concern for teachers.

The expectation of the division was that their teachers, with the support of their math coaches, would begin a process of implementing Guided Math during the upcoming school year. In August of the implementation year, during pre-service professional development, I again worked with the Chinook teachers—spending half a day with teachers from grades kindergarten to 4, and half with teachers from grades 5–8. The agenda for this training included:

- A review of the Guided Math framework components,
- Routines and procedures for Math Workshop,
- Suggestions for math workstation tasks,
- Planning of differentiated small-group lessons,
- Addressing questions that had been submitted prior to the session by teachers, and
- Introducing a plan for preparing students for Guided Math during the first 15 days of school.

For the upcoming school year, the division also contracted with me to meet via online conferencing with the coaches during their monthly meetings to answer questions they had and to assist them as they continued to plan the Guided Math implementation.

Rather than roll out the implementation of the entire framework at once, the Chinook mathematics leaders decided to break the process down into four blocks. (See Figure 4.1 for the District-Wide Guided Math Implementation Plan [Coaching Overview].) During each block of time, the topics to be emphasized, the coaches' roles, and the teachers' roles varied. This implementation plan provided specific guidance for teachers and for coaches. Expectations were explicitly shared with everyone involved in the process. Coaches were coordinated in their support for teachers. They demonstrated new instructional strategies for groups of teachers, and then followed up with classroom observations so they could provide feedback to teachers as they tried the strategies that had been demonstrated earlier.

Figure 4.1 District-Wide Guided Math Implementation Plan (Coaching Overview)

	Topic	Coach's Role	Teacher's Role	Observations
Block 1 **September/ October**	Guided Math First 15 Days; Numeracy Rich Environment; Math Warm-Ups; Assessments	Conversations and observations; Demonstrate a grade level appropriate math workstation	Implement first 15 days; Create Numeracy Rich Environment; Use Math Warm-Ups; Make an assessment plan	Assessment check-up; Numeracy Rich Environment (anchor charts, word wall); Classroom set-up (small-group table, desk arrangement, manipulatives)
Block 2 **November/ December**	Management of Math Workshop; Small-group lessons; Grouping; Workstations; Student Accountability (journal, student folders, observation notes)	Demonstrations; Transitions; Student accountability; Scaffolding for different abilities; Debriefs; Observations; Reminders to review First 15 Days after holiday	Prepare for coach visit; Group students; Prepare workstations; Observe coach's small-group lesson with debrief; Teacher small-group lesson observed by coach with debrief	Assessment check-up; Differentiated lesson plans; Numeracy Rich Environments (anchor charts, word walls); Classroom set-up (small-group table, desk arrangement, manipulatives)
Block 3 **March/ April**	Whole-class Instruction with a focus on the use of Read Aloud to highlight math in literature	Provide needs assessment to teachers; Demonstration of whole-class lesson (10–15 minutes) with debrief session; Observation of teachers as they teach a whole-class lesson using a strategy of their choice	Observe Coach's whole-class lesson with debrief; Choose a whole-class strategy for a lesson to be observed by Coach; Teach whole-class lesson using a strategy of their choice to be observed by Coach with debrief	Assessment check-up; Differentiated lesson plans; Student accountability (journals, student folders, observation notes); Whole-class lesson
Block 4 **May/June**	One-on-one Guided Math Conferences; Scheduling; Questions; Teaching Points; Record Keeping; Follow-up	Review Guided Math Conferences; Demonstrations of conferences in classrooms	Prepare for Coach's visit; Confer with selected students; Meet with Coach to reflect on conferring experiences	Assessment check-up; Differentiated lesson plans; Conferences (reflections/ record keeping)

(Adapted from Chinook School Division, Saskatchewan, Canada)

The yearlong implementation plan was supplemented in November and March with four hour-long professional development sessions designed and carried out by the coaches. During these sessions, teachers were able to share their implementation experiences with each other. After the workshop, coaches provided follow-up demonstrations in the classrooms and continued observations with feedback for teachers.

The division found that providing only one year of support was not sufficient. Coaching support of Guided Math implementation continued the following year. Year Two of the implementation plan consisted of three blocks. Block 1 was similar to Block 1 of Year One—a review of what teachers need to do to begin use of the Guided Math framework with a new class. Block 2 provided intentional coaching for small-group instruction. Coaches taught demonstration lessons and then observed teachers as they conducted small-group lessons. Finally, Block 3 offered teachers differentiated coaching, targeting needs identified by teacher self-assessments. During this phase, teachers reflected on their strengths and weaknesses regarding the use of the Guided Math framework in their classrooms to determine their greatest need for the final block of coaching support.

The Chinook School Division created a comprehensive implementation plan that was consistent throughout the division. With this step-by-step approach, teachers knew precisely what was expected of them. Well-trained mathematics coaches first demonstrated what was being expected to support them. Just as teachers were being asked to differentiate instruction for their classes, the coaches modeled the differentiation of coaching during Block 3 of the second year of support. Coaches continued to support teachers and monitor the implementation of Guided Math as teachers gained experience using the framework. The Guided Math training sessions were recorded so that they could be used with new teachers. In addition, coaches were available to provide support for those who were just beginning the implementation process. According to Ed Varjassy, Curriculum Coordinator for the division, "the professional learning model of workshops with follow-up classroom coaching has been very successful in changing teacher practice" (Laney Sammons, pers. comm.).

Sample District-Wide Implementation Plan with Individual School Implementations

When Danville Public Schools in Danville, Virginia decided to implement the Guided Math framework in their elementary schools, they took a different approach from the Chinook School Division. As with Chinook, they had mathematics coaches available to help with the implementation. The availability of coaches was more limited because they were classroom teachers who worked as coaches on a supplemental basis. The district was also sensitive to the fact that Guided Reading had recently been implemented and teachers were still feeling stress from that implementation.

As a first step in the implementation process for the district, I was asked to spend a day working with the mathematics coaches giving them an overview of the Guided Math framework. Following this training, the coaches worked closely with the district leadership to plan how to introduce the concept of Guided Math to their teachers. District leaders introduced the Guided Math framework to school administrators in preparation for the district-wide implementation. In individual school meetings, administrators and coaches shared information about Guided Math and plans for its implementation. Teachers were reassured that the Guided Math framework was similar in many ways to Guided Reading, but that teachers were encouraged to exercise a great deal of professional judgment in establishing it in their classrooms—in other words, it was not expected to look exactly the same in each classroom. There would be flexibility.

In the fall, I returned to the district to provide two half-day overview sessions for all elementary school teachers. On subsequent days, I visited each elementary school in the district and demonstrated small-group lessons with groups of students as teachers observed. Each lesson lasted an hour during which time I taught three separate small-group lessons. After each demonstration lesson, I met with the teachers who had observed the lesson to answer their questions, to encourage them to share their observations, and to share my reflections on the lessons.

Up until this time, the implementation approaches of the Chinook School Division and the Virginia school district were similar. At this point, their approaches diverged according to Catiia Greene, Title I Director. Instead of creating an implementation plan for all schools to follow, Danville Public Schools requested that *each school* complete a school-wide needs assessment and then create a "specific and detailed timeline/plan for school-wide implementation of Guided Math instruction" (Catiia Greene and Laney Sammons, pers. comm.) to be submitted to the district. A sample needs assessment document (See Figure 4.2) was provided to the schools to be used if desired or schools were able to make their own assessment form for teachers. Instead of one district-wide implementation plan, each elementary school was responsible for developing a plan specific to its needs. Please see Appendix D for a full-size version of Figure 4.2.

Figure 4.2 Guided Math Needs Assessment

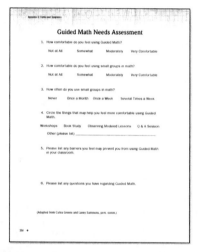

(Adapted from Catiia Greene and Laney Sammons, pers. comm.)

The school-specific implementation plans were clearly intended to address the needs of teachers in each school—thus giving teachers and school leaders more input and attempting to make the process as effective as possible.

The district provided a sample school-wide plan (See Figure 4.3) to give school leaders an idea of the kind of plan that was expected. Plans were expected to establish detailed timelines to ensure that the implementation of Guided Math could be monitored. Principals and coaches were responsible for monitoring the implementation of the Guided Math framework by their teachers and for identifying any further support teachers needed.

Figure 4.3 Sample School-Wide Guided Math Implementation Plan

When?	Who?	What?
November 18	Teachers	• Will have reviewed the Guided Math handouts. • Email Guided Math Needs Assessment responses to the Math Coach.
November 18	Administrators Math Coaches	• Review the Guided Math First 15 Days: Setting the Stage. • In faculty meeting, ask teachers to review strategies for small-group lessons. Share expectation that they will be prepared to provide feedback regarding implementation of First 15 Days at faculty meeting on November 25. Teachers will keep a journal of reflections.
Week of November 18	Teachers	• In grade level meetings, analyze assessment data to establish groups and create a schedule for Guided Math. • Begin implementation of First 15 Days.
	Administrators	• In grade level meetings, review with teachers observation and specific lesson plan "look-fors."
November 25	Teachers	• During faculty meeting, teachers will share feedback from their reflection journals concerning First 15 Days.
Week of December 2	Teachers	• Each teacher will implement Guided Math with small-group lessons at least one day a week.
December 9	Administrators Coaches	• During faculty meeting, review observation and lesson plan "look-fors." (How were groups determined? Size of group appropriate? Evidence of data analysis to inform instruction? Guided Math components included in lesson plans?) • During faculty meeting, share clear expectations that Guided Math will be implemented daily with supportive math workstations beginning December 11. Observations to begin December 18.
December 9	Teachers	• During faculty meeting, discuss "grows and glows" from the initial Guided Math implementation.
December 11	Teachers	• Full implementation of the Guided Math framework.
December 18	Administrators	• Begin observations. Observational feedback will include "grows and glows."

(Adapted from Catiia Greene and Laney Sammons, pers. comm.)

District-Wide Implementation Plan without Mathematics Coaches

These are examples of how mathematics leaders in two districts established effective plans for the mandated implementation of Guided Math. Both Chinook School Division and Danville Public Schools decided to implement the Guided Math framework throughout the district, but structured their implementation plans in very different ways. In both these examples, the districts had mathematics coaches to support teachers during the implementation process. Districts without math coaches should focus on alternative methods of support. In many instances, administrators act in the capacity of coaches. After participating in Guided Math training, they collaborate closely with teachers, observe Guided Math lessons, provide feedback in a nonevaluative way, and offer teachers opportunities for peer observations. By working closely with math teachers, they can identify needs (i.e., resources, time adjustments, and professional learning) so that teachers can more successfully implement Guided Math in their classrooms. The following chapters on how math coaches can support teachers during the adoption process can guide administrators as they act as math coaches.

Some districts without coaches establish and nurture strong Professional Learning Communities (PLCs) so that teachers support one another during the implementation process. The ongoing focus on the Guided Math framework by PLCs is an effective method of encouraging the adoption of these instructional strategies. Later chapters focus on how PLCs are formed and how they function.

Regardless of the support system provided for teachers within the district, it is recommended that initial professional development be offered to give educators an overview of the seven components of the Guided Math framework and suggestions for its implementation. This might be accomplished by bringing in a consultant or through in-house professional development conducted by mathematics leaders within the district. This type of professional development leads to a common vocabulary among teachers and a similar vision of how the Guided Math framework can become a part of their mathematics instruction. It is unwise to mandate implementation without first building a solid foundation for it.

Following that overview training, teachers will also need a time frame for implementation—either created by the district or by individual schools.

Teachers' collaboration is essential during the process of implementation. Districts should ask school level administrators to encourage teachers to learn from one another by offering release time for collaborative planning and for peer observations followed by debrief sessions to encourage reflective deliberation on what is working well and what needs to be improved.

School-Wide Mandates

Perhaps even more common than district-wide mandated implementations of the Guided Math framework are school-wide implementations. The decision to focus on Guided Math in individual schools usually results from the development of school improvement plans. Having engaged in processes similar to those described in previous chapters, school leaders and their staff members decide to focus on the improvement of the mathematical achievement of their students. With the recent calls for increased rigor and depth in mathematics instruction, this is hardly surprising. It is no wonder that educators are increasingly seeking new strategies for improving their mathematical instruction.

Typically, a single school has fewer resources available for professional development than districts do. Some resourceful schools pool their resources to bring in a consultant who provides training for their teaching staffs. In addition to being a cost-saving measure, joint efforts offer an additional benefit—building collegial communities between the two (or more) professional teams so that ideas and experiences can be shared. These efforts may also lead to later visits between the two campuses so that teachers can observe the Guided Math implementation in schools other than their own.

If funding is lacking for professional development by a Guided Math professional consultant, schools may have mathematics coaches who can provide the initial overview, along with coaching to further support the implementation. If not, administrators may serve in that capacity—conducting training, making classroom visits, providing feedback, meeting with teachers to determine needs, and serving as cheerleaders when things go well. Follow-up coaching greatly increases the likelihood of successful implementation.

Monitoring the Effectiveness of Implementation and Change

As implementation gets underway, an important function of a leader is progress monitoring. The most effective monitoring involves a two-prong approach—monitoring the success of the implementation and also monitoring its impact on achievement. Thus, monitoring efforts should focus both on the *process* goals and the *results* goals of the improvement plan. Careful monitoring of the process goals guarantees that agreed upon changes are being implemented with fidelity. Monitoring the effects of the changes on student achievement lets leaders know whether or not the changes being implemented are having the desired results.

The monitoring process begins with a focus on the articulated goals of the improvement plan. What changes are called for in the improvement plan? What is the time frame for implementation? What results are desired? How are they to be measured? The answers to these questions will guide leaders as they critique the success of the initiative.

Monitoring the Implementation

To ensure that the implementation of changes occurs, leaders have to know what is happening in classrooms throughout the school or district. Brief classroom visits by leaders are a valuable method of getting an accurate picture of how well an implementation process is proceeding. Leaders gain a true feel for the level of teacher support for the initiative by spending time in classrooms and observing firsthand how it is being implemented. They are able to observe both the positive impacts of the changes being made and any difficulties that teachers are experiencing.

Because classroom observations by principals are often used to conduct teacher evaluations, these visits may cause some anxiety if teachers do not understand the purpose for these visits. To ease the anxiety, leaders should clearly communicate their reasons for making classroom visits. Not only should leaders "clearly recognize and be able to articulate differences between evaluative classroom observations and supportive classroom visits in order to avoid crossing the line of authority" (Balka, Hull, and Miles 2010, 49), but *everyone* in the professional community needs to be aware of the underlying purpose of the brief progress monitoring visits and how they differ significantly from teacher observations conducted for the purpose of evaluation. (See Figure 4.4.)

Figure 4.4 Monitoring Visits Versus Teacher Observations

Observation Protocol	Classroom Monitoring Visits	Classroom Teacher Observations
Measures	Implementation progress	Teacher performance
Amount of Time	About 10 minutes or less	Often 45 minutes or more
Mandated by	School Improvement Plan	State or district
Purpose	Assessment of the Guided Math implementation	Evaluation of teacher performance
Information Gathered	Cumulative data to identify trends and patterns to support implementation	Individual data based on teacher performance

(Adapted from Balka, Hull, and Miles 2010, 49)

What is most significant about the differences between the two is the fact that classroom visits serve as a formative assessment tool to rate the success of the school or district as a whole in implementing change. Information gathered from these visits guides the entire community in their efforts to make the changes as effective as possible. These visits allow leaders to support teachers in the implementation process. On the other hand, the classroom observations are evaluations designed to give leaders information to rate an individual teacher's proficiency.

Keeping classroom visits brief not only allows leaders to make more visits, but also helps distinguish them from evaluative teacher observations (Balka, Hull, and Miles 2010, 50). To allay any lingering anxiety, leaders can include teachers in the process of identifying the specific behaviors or evidence of successful Guided Math implementation that will be used to monitor progress. When these teacher-generated expectations are incorporated into a classroom visit checklist, it ensures that everyone knows precisely what leaders will be looking for when they visit.

Figure 4.5 is a Guided Math Implementation Classroom Visit Checklist that can be used as a formative assessment tool. This checklist can be used for a single classroom visit or to tally observations when a number of classrooms are visited. When used to compile tallies, the results give an overall picture of the level of implementation of Guided Math within the classrooms visited. See Appendix D for a full-size version of Figure 4.5.

Figure 4.5 Guided Math Implementation Classroom Visit Checklist

A sample completed checklist is provided in Figure 4.6.

Figure 4.6 Sample Guided Math Implementation Classroom Visit Checklist

Guided Math Components		Evident	Not Evident	Notes
Environment	Table or floor space for small-group lessons	✔		
	Math word wall	✔		*Words displayed with nonlinguistic representations*
	Math anchor charts		✔	
	Student work displayed	✔		*Several problem-solving posters explaining student thinking*
Instruction: Small-Group	Hands-on, active engagement by students	✔		
	Accountable math talk	✔		*Students were prompted by teacher to use mathematical terminology.*
	Focused teaching point		✔	
	Differentiation based on needs	✔		
	Lesson uninterrupted by students working independently	✔		
	Informal assessment with method of recording		✔	*No method of recording anecdotal notes was obvious.*
Instruction: Math Workshop	Clear routines and procedures	✔		*Students clearly knew the expectations for their behavior.*
	Students productively engaged in math tasks or games	✔		
	System of accountability for students	✔		*Students recorded their work in math journals.*

In many ways, classroom visits are beneficial for more than simply monitoring progress. Because all members of the community have been included in a comprehensive and ongoing process for improvement, they know where they, as a community, want to go and how they plan to get there. Based on these visits, leaders can give teachers valuable and precise feedback garnered from the jointly formulated checklist. A mutually supportive partnership—almost a symbiosis—develops between leaders and classroom teachers who are working in concert to bring about school improvement through the use of the Guided Math framework.

As leaders move into the role of providing timely and targeted feedback based on the classroom visit checklists, leaders are engaged in a coaching function. Balka, Hull, and Miles (2010) believe that "feedback appropriately collected and used serves as a tipping point for change. Supportive, specific feedback accelerates the teaching/learning process and increases student achievement" (93).

Another very powerful way to assess the success of the Guided Math implementation process is calling upon teachers to self-assess the level of implementation in their classrooms. As with classroom visits by leaders, a checklist of behaviors and evidence of implementation can be compiled by the professional community as a whole. Encouraging self-assessment by educators is in some ways one of the most powerful methods of monitoring progress. Teachers and staff members become even more aware of the expectations because they are asked to examine their own practices in light of those expectations.

As an alternative to a checklist, teachers might be asked to rate the degree of implementation that is evident and how it has impacted both instruction and student learning. This self-assessment document should also contain questions to be answered based on teachers' reflections. Leaders learn much about teachers' perceptions and needs as well as the progress of Guided Math implementation by reviewing these documents.

Figure 4.7 is a template self-assessment questionnaire for the implementation of the Guided Math framework. See Appendix D for a full-size version of Figure 4.7.

Figure 4.7 Guided Math Implementation Self-Assessment Questionnaire

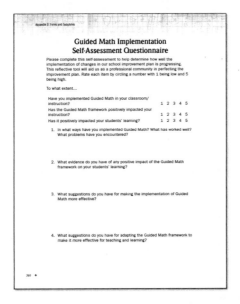

A sample completed questionnaire is provided in Figure 4.8.

Figure 4.8 Sample Guided Math Implementation Self-Assessment Questionnaire

Guided Math Implementation Self-Assessment Questionnaire

Please complete this self-assessment to help determine how well the implementation of changes in our school improvement plan is progressing. This reflective tool will aid us as a professional community in perfecting the improvement plan. Rate each item by circling a number, with 1 being low and 5 being high.

To what extent...

Have you implemented Guided Math in your classroom/instruction?   1 2 ③ 4 5

Has the Guided Math framework positively impacted your instruction?   1 2 3 ④ 5

Has it positively impacted your students' learning?   1 2 3 ④ 5

1. In what ways have you implemented Guided Math? What has worked well? What problems have you encountered?

   I am doing small-group instruction 3 days a week. The lessons are wonderful—my students are talking math, and I know so much more about what they are thinking. I am still trying to perfect the routines and procedures for my students. Some of them get off task too easily.

2. What evidence do you have of any positive impact of the Guided Math framework on your students' learning?

   Students are now able to justify their mathematical thinking! Whoo Hoo! I love it when they get excited about math.

3. What suggestions do you have for making the implementation of Guided Math more effective?

   I would like to have someone come to my classroom to observe Math Workshop to give me feedback and suggestions to make it go more smoothly. It would also be great if my grade level was given some release time to develop math workstation tasks.

4. What suggestions do you have for adapting the Guided Math framework to make it more effective for teaching and learning?

   Initially, I was trying to teach a mini lesson before my small-group lessons, but I found that it was not very effective. Instead time seems better spent in small-group lessons. Also, I find it hard to limit my Math Huddle discussions. The class is learning so much from them. I am thinking that maybe I should devote a little more time for those discussions than 5 to 7 minutes.

Monitoring the Change

At the same time the success of the implementation of change initiative is being assessed, it is important to monitor the effects of these changes on student achievement—which, after all, is the primary motivation for the implementation of Guided Math. More than likely, the cumulative effects of the changes will not be apparent immediately. Nevertheless, the results goals included in the improvement plan should guide the expectations for success. Well-conceived plans for improvement using Guided Math will specify how the results should be measured. Leaders should look to these goals as they monitor the preliminary results. Just as the analysis of data is a crucial part of developing an improvement plan, the monitoring process also relies on it—although during this process the data examined will be much more specific and targeted.

Patience is key during the early stages of the monitoring process. Understandably, people hope to see quick positive results as justification of the time and effort invested in the Guided Math initiative. It is easy for educators to become discouraged if positive changes are not obvious as the monitoring process begins. When "stepping stone" targets are included as a part of the goals statements, it is much more likely that the community will be able to celebrate some achievement in the journey toward their long-term goals. Reeves (2009, Kindle Location 115) recommends the use of ongoing formative assessment to identify short-term gains in student achievement—making them more apparent—rather than waiting for summative assessment results. Formative assessments are valuable not only for spotlighting student gains early on, but also for informing upcoming instruction to make it more effective.

Short-term goals for Guided Math implementation can be determined by the education community. For example, looking back at Figure 3.3, one process goal is "At least one classroom in each grade level will implement the Guided Math framework." A mid-year goal of checklists completed by mathematics coaches during classroom visits showing evidence of implementation of at least 5 of the 7 components of the Guided Math framework by January is established. But, after two months, teachers could celebrate if checklists indicate that 3 of the components are implemented.

Looking at data as a way of assessing interim success is rewarding when improvement is evident. But, what happens when the hoped-for improvement is not apparent? At the beginning of the implementation process, leaders should be patient, but also be open to any concerns or difficulties teachers are reporting. Later, if data still fails to show improvement, it becomes crucial to find out why it is not evident. Are the methods of measure well aligned with the initiative and with the kinds of improvement desired? Are the specified changes being carried out consistently? If the changes are not being implemented, why not? Are there impediments to the process of change that should be addressed to make implementation more successful? Or, is it possible that the change being implemented is just not going to bring about the desired improvements in achievement?

These are difficult questions to answer. But, to bring about the desired improvement, the Guided Math implementation process must be examined to find the answers. The answers will determine how to proceed. Thinking back to the advice of Fullan and Miles, leaders must "Do, then plan…and do and plan some more" (1992, 749). This is the time for "plan some more."

Plans for improvement may fail when schools or districts rigidly adhere to it in spite of the fact that it is not working or when the professional community simply gives up the effort to improve because of the lack of initial success. Instead of giving up when a plan is not bringing about the desired results after sufficient time has passed, it is time to regroup and revise the original plan based on what has been learned through the implementation process. It takes a skilled leader to know when this regrouping should be done. If it happens too soon, the original plans may not have been given enough time to show positive results. If done too late, valuable time has been wasted. Members of the community may become discouraged and then lack enthusiasm for embarking on a new or revised plan.

When needed, effective leaders do not hesitate to refocus the professional community on the shared vision, ask them to reflect on the plans that were implemented, decide why those plans did not bring about the improvements that were anticipated, and then revise the plan to make it more workable.

Sustaining Guided Math Implementation through PLCs

Professional Learning Communities (PLCs) are defined by Hord and Sommers (2008) as "communities of professionals caring for and working to improve student learning together, by engaging in continuous collective learning of their own" (Kindle Location 46). Although PLCs may be structured differently from school to school, the model "flows from the assumption that the core mission of formal education is not simply to ensure that students are taught but to ensure that they learn. This simple shift—from a focus on teaching to a focus on learning—has profound implications for schools" (DuFour 2005, 32). Directly related to that shift in focus is the recognition by the educators that to help all students achieve at high levels, they must work collaboratively. While "the PLC structure in a school is one of continuous adult learning, strong collaboration, democratic participation, and consensus about the school environment and culture and how to attain that" (Hord and Sommers 2008, Kindle Locations 257–258), its predominant focus is on the extent of student learning.

The implementation of the Guided Math framework may be supported through teacher participation in PLCs. These learning communities may be established as a part of mandated Guided Math implementations or of voluntary implementations. In some situations, the impetus for Guided Math implementation emerges from the work done in previously established PLCs. In others, PLCs are established in order to support the implementation process. Part III of this book will provide more information about PLCs, suggestions for how education leaders can support them, and a yearlong Guided Math implementation plan for PLCs.

Choosing and Supporting an Implementation Model

This chapter has provided examples of ways in which the Guided Math framework can be implemented—ranging from implementation in which a single teacher chooses to implement it in a classroom to district-wide mandates. Educational leaders are responsible for deciding, with the input of community members, what works best in their educational community and then providing the support needed to make it work.

Once an implementation model has been selected, the work of mathematics leaders is only just beginning. Their leadership is essential in monitoring the implementation to assess its effectiveness and to determine additional needs. As the initial interest in trying something new diminishes or obstacles arise, the role of leaders continues. Effective leaders recognize their ongoing responsibilities in ensuring the success of the implementation process.

Review & Reflect

1. Think of an implementation process that was used in your school or district. Reflect on its effectiveness. What aspects of it worked well? How could you improve it?

2. Design a sample Guided Math implementation plan. What do you think will be your greatest challenges? How will you address them?

3. As teachers begin to use the Guided Math instructional strategies, how can math leaders best monitor the implementation and sustain the adoption momentum?

Chapter 5

The Role of Coaching in Guided Math

Not all schools and districts have academic coaches, but that should not discourage schools from working to implement Guided Math. Educational leaders—whoever they may be—can play a powerful role in supporting implementation. This section may provide ideas for any leader, but it is specifically aimed at giving guidance to those who are in a coaching position.

What exactly is coaching in the world of mathematics? Mathematics coaches are individuals who are knowledgeable about mathematics content and pedagogy and who work directly with teachers with the goal of improving students' learning of mathematics. "Mathematics coaches hold a unique position as leaders. Their primary responsibility is to work with classroom teachers to increase student learning by implementing decisions made by leaders in line authority positions" (Hull, Balka, and Miles 2009, Kindle Location 68–69). Although coaches may not be the decision makers, their roles can be quite demanding and very diverse. Overall, though, their primary purpose is "to help teachers increase their effectiveness" (Marzano et al. 2013, 1) and thereby positively impact student achievement. To do this, "mathematics coaches influence instruction by building trusting relationships, challenging ineffective instructional practices, supporting teachers as they learn new practices, providing meaningful and focused feedback, and implementing manageable, effective improvement processes" (Hull, Balka, and Miles 2009, Kindle Locations 69–70).

According to Marzano et al. (2013, 8), coaches have several goals as they work with educators:

✎ To point teachers toward best practices

✎ To show teachers what good teaching looks like

✎ To help teachers maintain their best performance

✎ To help teachers achieve "flow"

✎ To help teachers take risks

The responsibility for change implementation described aligns well with the goals Marzano et al. 2013 set forth. In assisting with the implementation process, coaches are pointing teachers toward best practices—some which may be new to teachers. Lessons demonstrated by coaches show teachers what good teaching looks like. As teachers practice these techniques in their own classrooms observed by coaches and provided with feedback, they are being helped to maintain their best performance. As coaches encourage and reflect with teachers about teaching practices, they help them achieve "flow"—that mental state when one is fully immersed in a feeling of energized focus and enjoyment in what one is doing. And, the very presence of coaches supporting change helps teachers take the risks necessary to move their teaching performance to a whole new level.

The Efficacy of Mathematics Coaching

With the drumbeat of demands for school improvement and the increasing focus on teacher proficiency, professional development practices are in the limelight. Current practice "runs the gamut from one-shot workshops to more intensive job-embedded professional development, which has teachers learn in the day-to-day environment in which they work rather than getting pulled out to attend an outside training" (Zarrow 2014, para. 2).

Oft-quoted research by Joyce and Showers (2002) showed dramatically different outcomes from frequently used methods of professional development. (See Figure 5.1.) The table below documents the percentage of participants who attained the specified outcomes after training.

Figure 5.1 Effectiveness of Teacher Training

Methods of Training	Thorough Mastery of Knowledge (%)	Strong Skill Acquisition (%)	Classroom Application (%)
Theory (Workshops or Book Studies)	10%	5%	0%
Theory and Demonstration	30%	20%	0%
Theory, Demonstration, and Practice	60%	60%	5%
Theory, Demonstration, Practice, and Coaching	95%	95%	95%

(Adapted from Joyce and Showers 2002, 78)

What is striking about the research findings of Joyce and Showers is the minimal amount of transfer to classroom application for any of the methods of training, unless coaching was also provided. This was even true for a combination of theory, demonstration, and practice—where the percentage of participants mastering the knowledge and acquiring the skills was at sixty percent, yet only five percent of these teachers actually used what they had learned in their classrooms. Joyce and Showers concluded that "continuing technical assistance, whether provided by an outside expert or by peer experts resulted in much greater classroom implementation than was achieved by teachers who shared initial training but did not have the long-term support of coaching" (85).

It seems apparent that, as with learning any new skill, merely gaining knowledge about it is much easier than implementing it. Gulamhussein (2013) advises educational leaders that "crafting effective professional development means confronting this reality and building a significant amount of support for teachers during the critical implementation phase in one's actual classroom" (12). In fact, teachers may require as much as 50 hours of instruction, practice and coaching to master and implement a new teaching strategy. Teachers who are supported during the implementation phase with coaching are much more likely to be successful in changing their teaching practices, while teachers who participate only in a workshop frequently lose interest quickly without ever implementing it in their classrooms.

"Coaching can build will, skill, knowledge, and capacity because it can go where no other professional development has gone before: into the intellect, behaviors, practices, beliefs, values, and feelings of an educator" (Aguilar 2013, Kindle Locations 501–503). Because of this, the benefits of ongoing, job-embedded coaching extend beyond the increase in application of the new skill by teachers. Joyce and Showers (2002) found that the impact of coaching on teachers included the following:

- Coached educators practiced newly learned strategies more often and as a result became more competent at implementing Guided Math than educators who were not coached but had received the same amount of *knowledge* training.

- Coached educators used newly acquired skills more appropriately in terms of their teaching objectives than those who were not coached.

- Coached educators retained their newly learned knowledge and skills, which increased their use over time as compared to non-coached educators.

- Coached educators were more likely to discuss the new models of teaching with their students, so that students understood the purpose of the strategy and how it impacts them.

- Coached educators had a clearer understanding of the purposes and uses of the newly implemented instructional strategies as shown in interviews, lesson plans, and classroom performance (85–88).

A comprehensive study on instructional coaching by the Annenberg Institute for School Reform (2004) offers powerful validation for coaching. It found the following:

- Effective coaching encourages collaborative, reflective practice.

- Effective embedded professional learning promotes positive cultural change.

- A focus on content encourages the use of data analysis to inform practice.

- Coaching promotes the implementation of learning and reciprocal accountability.

- Coaching supports collective, interconnected leadership across a school system (2–3).

According to the study, coaching provides more varied opportunities for professional learning that results in improvements in the instructional capacity of teachers.

Educational leaders of schools or districts in the process of implementing the Guided Math framework should take heed of these findings. When significant resources are devoted to an improvement plan calling for the implementation of Guided Math, it is counterproductive to offer teachers knowledge-only professional development. Through the use of coaches, leaders build the professional capacity of the entire community. Effective coaches recognize that "organizational growth depends on collaborative teams, not independent work…. They encourage teams of teachers to take ownership of all their students, share their best practice, and promote inquiry about their profession" (Hansen 2009, 4).

When coaches are not available, leaders can support teachers' participation in Professional Learning Communities. Through the structure of a PLC, teachers can be involved in collaborative planning, peer observations, and peer coaching experiences. "Teachers learn best by studying, doing, and reflecting; by collaborating with other teachers, by looking closely at students and their work; and by sharing what they see" (Darling-Hammond 1999, 2). That is exactly the kind of learning experience PLCs provide.

The Role of a Mathematics Coach

"Successful math coaches have clearly defined roles, responsibilities, and goals" (Hansen 2009, 13). For some math coaches, the coaching responsibilities are determined for them by administrators. The expectations for their work are clearly defined. Effective leaders design initiatives for their coaches while keeping the shared community vision and end goals in mind. A math coaching initiative should include the training that is needed for the teachers and other staff members, define the roles of all participants, and identify the funding sources for needed resources (West and Cameron 2013, 23). If leaders collaborate closely with their math coaches in developing a coaching plan, there is a greater likelihood that it will be thoroughly understood by both leadership and coach, resulting in an increased probability that the goals of the coaching initiative will be achieved.

While some math coaches have well-defined roles, many math coaches find they are given little direction for their work. "Confusion about their roles and the lack of a developmental process are key challenges faced by mathematics coaches. These challenges are exacerbated if school leaders have launched a coaching initiative with little preparation or planning for success through supportive internal structures" (Hull, Balka, and Miles 2009, Kindle Location 55).

When this is the case, coaches are "left to their own devices to figure out their job—where to work, who to work with, what to do, and how to actually increase student learning" (Kindle Locations 60–61). When possible, math coaches should work closely with principals or curriculum leaders to identify needs and then devise plans for meeting those needs. While the lack of a clearly defined role may be disconcerting for some coaches, others enjoy the challenge of designing their own coaching structures.

"The job of a school-based coach is a complex mix of teacher, resource provider, change agent, facilitator, mentor, and curriculum specialist—in general" (Jones and Vreeman 2008, 74). Confer (2006) adds that math coaches are responsible for creating "a mathematically rich school environment" (14). And while doing all of the above, Jones and Vreeman (2008, 139) remind coaches to remain focused on those they ultimately serve—the students.

Obviously, the work of coaching is complex and multifaceted. Increasing the complexity of the role of math coaches is the fact that the expectations for them vary considerably from place to place. Commonly, mathematics coaches have the following interconnected responsibilities:

✎ work with teachers to improve mathematics achievement by increasing their content knowledge and helping them develop more effective teaching practices

✎ collaborate with teachers in planning, teaching, observing and providing feedback

✎ assist teachers in understanding the mathematics standards

✎ examine student work with teachers

✎ manage and control curriculum and instructional resources

- arrange and provide professional development
- monitor implementation of mathematics initiatives and programs
- build the mathematics program by using its strengths and reducing its weaknesses
- maintain and share best-practice research
- build and support collaborative teams (PLCs) and networks
- assist teachers in gathering, analyzing, and interpreting data from assessments and benchmark tests to determine the effectiveness of instruction and to inform future instruction

(Hull, Balka, and Miles 2009, Kindle Locations 174-176; Hansen 2009, 2).

It is likely that most math coaches could add to this list. However, coaches who aspire to regularly check off *all* of those tasks daily, or even weekly, will find themselves severely challenged. On a regular basis, effective coaches have to take into account the unique circumstances and needs of their schools as they pencil in their schedules on their calendars each week and then prioritize so as to keep from being overwhelmed or spread too thin.

Mathematics coaches around the country also vary greatly in personality, age, experience, and training. The best of them, however, share certain knowledge, skills, and even personal traits.

Figure 5.2 Essential Knowledge, Skills, and Personal Traits for Mathematics Coaching

Professional Knowledge	Professional Skills	Personal Traits
• Content • Pedagogical • Organizational	• Listening • Communication • Data analysis • Instruction • Questioning to encourage teacher reflection and inquiry • Resource gathering • Leadership • Ability to empower others	• Intellectual curiosity • Compassion • Respectful of others • Sense of humor • High expectations of self and others • Trustworthiness • Dependability • Timeliness • Supportive of others • Willingness to accept diversity • Patience

Because the roles of mathematics coaches are so numerous, so are the essential abilities they must possess. There is much overlap between the categories of professional knowledge, professional skills, and personal traits. Undoubtedly, the distinctions between the three categories are fuzzy. Nonetheless, it is helpful to recognize that these differences exist—just as it is worthwhile to examine performance standards to differentiate required student *knowledge* from required student *skills*.

Assessing Current Mathematical Instruction

Coaches can support the implementation of Guided Math by providing valuable professional learning opportunities for teachers. According to Hull, Balka, and Miles (2009), coaches "start the change action by serving as a catalyst, by introducing teachers to new information about classroom practices supported by research, and by engaging teachers in meaningful professional conversations" (Kindle Locations 233–234). This foundational work by coaches in collaboration with teachers facilitates the implementation process.

The process begins with an initial assessment of the current mathematics instruction in the school or district. Looking at data offers coaches information about how well students are doing and also gives them a better idea of how teachers are doing. "Because student learning mirrors teacher beliefs about teaching and learning, coaches can analyze the data they collect and gain insights into teacher beliefs and values" (West and Cameron 2013, 91). If a needs assessment has already been completed in the development of an improvement plan, it can serve as the basis of this assessment.

If a needs assessment has not been conducted, mathematics coaches will need to examine student data pertaining to mathematical achievement. To build a strong foundation for Guided Math implementation, coaches should include both teachers and administrators in this process. Unless a need for change is evident to the educational community, it is unlikely that meaningful change will occur.

Data Analysis

One of the basic responsibilities of coaches is working with the professional community in examining data in a meaningful way. Hull, Balka, and Miles (2009) stress that "it is virtually impossible to determine student achievement growth without some form of assessment" (Kindle Location 663). Interpreting assessment data allows educators to arrive at a better understanding of not only their students' strengths and weaknesses, but also of their own mathematics instruction. As Mike Schmoker writes, "Data are to goals what signposts are to travelers; data are not end points, but are essential to reaching them—the signposts on the road to school improvement" (1999, 36). Unless coaches and all members of the school or district know where they are beginning their journey, it is not likely that they will ever reach their desired destination.

The types of data collected for analysis will vary depending upon the kinds of assessments conducted in a school or district and upon the specific purpose for looking at data. When trying to determine whether to implement Guided Math, most educational leaders look for evidence of overall mathematical achievement by students. This type of data may come from standardized testing, benchmark testing, chapter tests, or other summative assessments. It is helpful to be able to compare achievement to similar demographic populations, so when possible, data that can be compared to other schools or districts should be examined.

If the purpose is informing and improving instruction—particularly for purposes of differentiating small-group lessons—the focus is on formative assessments. Data may be obtained from informal assessments (anecdotal notes from small-group instruction), student work samples collected from the same assigned task, quizzes, or tickets-out-the-door (exit tickets). Unless the purpose of looking at data is to assess computational fluency, it is important that the data collected reflect not only computational fluency, but also student proficiency in the mathematical practices. The analysis of the data collected should lead the educational community to identify student strengths and needs, which then provides fodder to a rich discussion of how their instruction can be adjusted to meet student needs. Leaders can encourage teachers to consider how the components of the Guided Math framework can be tapped to align instruction to students' learning needs.

One of the responsibilities of educational leaders is evaluating the success of instructional initiatives—both the degree of implementation and the effect of implementation on student achievement. To evaluate the implementation process itself, educational leaders must collect data that reflects how the Guided Math framework is being incorporated in instruction. For example, if an administrator or coach conducts a series of classroom visits to check on the level of Guided Math implementation and compiles the results from the observation form (See Figure 3.1), staff members may meet to analyze the data. Having the opportunity to assess the extent of Guided Math implementation going on in the school, teachers may decide to intensify their own implementation efforts or leaders may discover obstacles to implementation that need to be resolved.

To determine the effects of Guided Math implementation on students' mathematical achievement, data from both formative and summative assessment may be used for analysis—depending upon when the analysis is being conducted. Examining formative data provides ongoing checks on the effectiveness and affords educators the opportunity to tweak the implementation process throughout the school year. A year-end analysis of summative data gives the educators an overall sense of how the use of this instructional structure has impacted student learning. It may still be used to tweak the use of Guided Math in the future, but will not have the same potential for spurring immediate changes in implementation practices.

When looking at data with teachers, it is important to have a protocol to use to ensure that the analysis focuses on the relevant aspects of the data. This is generally easier to do with small groups, although it can be accomplished with large groups. If the data analysis process is to be done by a large group, perhaps on a school-wide data day, it is best to break the group into subgroups—each with a leader. Each subgroup analyzes the data, then reports its findings to the group as a whole. The group as a whole then reflects on and discusses what was learned and what actions they should take. In this way, the entire professional community shares the same experience.

While protocols for data analysis are available, it is usually best to use one that is simple and straightforward, so that the protocol itself does not distract from the analysis. Protocols establish guidelines that the group understands and agrees to in advance. They provide structure for meaningful conversation. The protocol is a "guiding template that is used consistently to keep the group focused on the task at hand" (Moran 2007, 109).

Initially, the protocol format may seem difficult to follow because people seldom engage in this kind of structured talk. Moran describes protocols as being "vehicles for *building the skills and culture necessary for collaborative work*" (2007, 109). Because a structure is imposed on the conversation, everyone participates in a measured way. Trust is built as teachers perform this important work.

The protocol in Figure 5.3 is for a data analysis session of 45 minutes. The times specified in the protocol may be adjusted as needed in advance of the meeting, but once those times have been set they should be adhered to. The analysis process is most effective when the data to be examined is concise and highly relevant to the process of school improvement. It is also important that the sheer quantity of data being studied is not overwhelming to teachers.

Figure 5.3 Data Analysis Protocol

I. Establish the purpose for looking at the set of data. Appoint a recorder to list the responses from Parts IV and V on chart paper to be displayed, so they can be referred to in Part V. (2 minutes)

II. Present the data to be examined. Explain the context of the data. (3 minutes)

III. Examine the data in light of the stated purpose.

    1. Teachers examine the data and make notes without conversation. (5 minutes)

    2. Working in pairs, teachers discuss the data. (5 minutes)

IV. As a group, answer these questions about the data. The recorder lists the responses on chart paper. (20 minutes)

    1. What do we *know* from looking at this data?

       List facts, quantifiable statements, and statements that cannot be disputed.

    2. What do we *think* as a result of looking at this data?

       What do we think it tells us about what students know and can do?

       What do we think it tells us about areas with which students struggle?

       What does it tell us about our mathematics instruction?

       What other ideas do we have about what the data shows?

    3. What *don't we know* as a result of looking at this data?

       List information that we do not know from looking at this data.

       Do we need more information?

       What else do we need to know?

V. Reflecting on the responses to the questions in Part IV, how does this data *help us improve* instruction and learning? Decide on next steps in teaching and learning improvement and how they will be monitored. (15 minutes)

(Adapted from Moran 2007, 111)

While analyzing data is important, the benefit of this collaborative exercise stems from what occurs as a result of what is learned. The *next steps* to be determined by the group in Part V of the Data Analysis Protocol are what directly impact student learning. These steps may call for further analysis and research into instructional strategies or for specific action steps regarding instruction. Whatever steps are called for, coaches should ensure that the group clearly specifies what they will be and how they will be monitored. In this way, the coach is able to follow up to be sure they are carried out.

To lead teachers in identifying next steps, it is helpful to first ask teachers to reflect silently on what they have learned from the data and how they can use that information to increase student achievement. Once the group has had time to reflect, encourage them to share their ideas with the group. Have the group agree upon one or two steps they will take based on what the data indicated and how these steps will be monitored. Although many ideas for next steps may be suggested, limiting the steps to one or two will make follow-up much more likely. The group may decide to plan another data analysis session to assess the effectiveness of their next steps.

Classroom Instructional Practices Analysis

To supplement the data-based needs assessment that reflects students' mathematical achievement, many coaches choose to make brief classroom visits to get a feel for the instructional practices being used by teachers. Although the landscape of mathematics instruction is in flux with the introduction of more rigorous standards, traditional mathematics instruction has been characterized by the following traits (which are still evident in classrooms):

1. Teacher-centered classrooms where teachers are the providers of information

2. Passive learning by students

3. Rigid instructional structure: check homework, introduction of new topic and how-to lesson by teacher, student guided practice, assignment of homework

4. Textbook curriculum

5. Assessments primarily procedural—lacking rigor

6. Emphasis on rote learning and recall

(Adapted from Hull, Balka, and Miles 2009, Kindle Locations 242-276)

Some teachers find comfort in perpetuating these traits. Since most teachers experienced this kind of mathematics instruction in school, they tend to teach the way they were taught. Yet, the calls for greater rigor and increased student achievement dictate that teachers adopt more effective teaching practices. Instead of teacher-centered classrooms with passive learning by students, there are demands for greater student engagement and challenge. In these classrooms, students assume greater responsibility for their learning. Teachers focus on teaching the standards—not just covering the textbook. Teachers use a variety of assessment tools to more accurately assess student understanding. And, with the demands for greater depth of learning, students go beyond simple rote learning to develop true conceptual understanding of the mathematics.

Math coaches can use an observation form (See Figure 5.4) during classroom visits to gauge how well teachers are making the transition away from traditional instructional methods. To obtain a true picture of the overall instructional climate of a school, numerous classrooms must be visited and then the results compiled. These findings should be shared with both administrators and teachers, so that the entire professional community is aware of the current instructional environment of its classrooms.

The information gathered from classroom visits can be shared in a data analysis session. Instead of examining student work or assessment results, the focus is on data regarding their own teaching practices. This is particularly valuable as schools or districts begin to implement Guided Math. The process leads teachers to identify how using Guided Math impacts the quality of mathematics teaching and learning. Conversations arising from this type of reflection increase teachers' understanding of how they can use the framework to provide more rigorous mathematics instruction for their students. Please see Appendix D for a full-size version of Figure 5.4.

Figure 5.4 Mathematics Instruction Observation Form

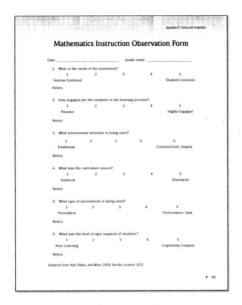

(Adapted from Hull, Balka, and Miles 2009, Kindle Location 352)

Methods of Coach Support for Guided Math Implementation

Optimally, when a school or district decides to support the implementation of Guided Math, a Guided Math consultant provides the initial training. When this training is not available to educators, coaches often provide it. Although usually lacking extensive experience with the Guided Math framework, most mathematics coaches have considerable knowledge of both content and pedagogy. They may have experience using Guided Reading for literacy instruction upon which they can draw. With their own teaching expertise and the Guided Math resources (See Appendix C) designed to support implementation, coaches can offer teachers basic Guided Math training. The professional resources *Guided Math: A Framework for Mathematics Instruction* (Sammons 2010) and *Strategies for Implementing Guided Math* (Sammons 2013) offer coaches and teachers a comprehensive description of Guided Math and each of its seven components.

Full-Day Guided Math Overview

If professional learning days are available, a full day of training that includes information about each of the seven components is recommended. This training is best presented in late spring, during a summer institute, or on a pre-service day before the school year begins so that teachers have the information they need for implementation at the beginning of the school year.

During the training, teachers should be given ample opportunities to share their ideas, ask questions, and plan together. See Figure 5.5 for a sample agenda for a daylong Guided Math training presentation.

Figure 5.5 Sample Guided Math Training Agenda (Full Day)

Presentation Chapters	Chapter Content
Introduction	· Welcome · Expectations
The Guided Math Framework	· What is Guided Math? · Why implement it? · What are the seven components of Guided Math?
Creating an Environment of Numeracy	· Why is this important? · How can you create this in a classroom? · What are mathematics anchor charts?
Math Warm-Ups	· What are Math Warm-Ups? · Why are they important? · What are some examples of Math Warm-Ups? · Teachers work in groups to create Math Stretches.
Whole-Class Instruction	· What are its drawbacks? · When should it be used? · Teachers play a whole group vocabulary game.

Presentation Chapters	Chapter Content
Small-Group Instruction	• What is it? • How are small-group lessons different from whole-class lessons? • What are its benefits for student learning? • How are the lessons planned? • How can lessons be differentiated? • Teachers brainstorm: What are characteristics of a good small-group lesson?
Math Workshop	• What is it? • Why is it important? • How is it implemented? • What routines and procedures are necessary? • What are some workshop models? • What are some appropriate math workstation tasks? • How can students be held accountable?
Math Conferences	• What are Math Conferences? • Why are they important?
Assessment	• What are balanced assessments? • Why is assessment so important for Guided Math instruction? • How is assessment used for small-group instruction?
Putting It All Together	• What does the daily schedule look like? • Questions? • Teachers set implementation goals.

At the conclusion of the daylong training, teachers should be asked to set personal goals for implementation. If desired, coaches can ask the participants to work together as a cohort and to set implementation goals for the group as a whole. The advantages to this approach to goal setting is having teachers working at the same pace so they can readily share their experiences—both successes and struggles—with one another. Also, if they work together as a cohort, the monitoring process for coaches is less cumbersome. Coaches are aware of where in the implementation process teachers are at any given time and can provide relevant support and resources for them.

If teachers are asked to set personal implementation goals, they may assume responsibility for monitoring their own progress or be asked to submit these goals to their coaches. If the coach is aware of individual teacher goals, they can monitor the implementation progress and differentiate the support they provide to meet individual teachers' needs.

Incremental Guided Math Component Training

When the schedule does not permit a full day of training for teachers, coaches may opt to provide the training incrementally—component by component. In fact, some coaches may prefer to present it in this way. A full day's overview of the Guided Math framework encompasses an enormous amount of information for teachers to absorb at one time. Although a full day does give teachers an understanding of the framework as a *whole*, only a portion of what is presented is truly processed and retained by teachers.

With an incremental learning approach, coaches present an abbreviated overview of the Guided Math framework at the beginning of the year and then focus on specific components over the next several months or over the entire school year. This approach requires less teacher time for each training session, so the training may be conducted during a planning period or even after school. Following the introduction of each component, teachers focus on implementing that component in their classrooms. Since all teachers are on the same implementation schedule, it simplifies the coaches' supporting role. In addition, teachers can work collaboratively to plan and then reflect on the success of their implementation efforts.

The advantage of this professional learning approach is that each component is spotlighted at a specific time, encouraging teachers to delve more deeply into its implementation without distraction. Likewise, the coach can focus exclusively on particular components by providing demonstration lessons, classroom observations with feedback, and providing component-specific resources for teachers.

Demonstration Lessons

Demonstration lessons are integral to the professional learning process. Although the coach presents the lesson in one classroom, several teachers can observe. Administrators are often able to provide release time for lesson observations and debriefing sessions following the demonstration. Coaches make the framework come alive for teachers when they go into classrooms to teach Guided Math lessons. These lessons might include working with students to create an anchor chart, conducting a Math Huddle based on students' work in a Math Stretch, teaching a whole-class lesson, or working with a small group of students. These should always be billed as *demonstration* lessons rather than *model* lessons. The term *model* implies that they are perfect, and that the person teaching the lesson is an expert. It sets the coach, or whoever is presenting, above the observing teachers. Coaches are more effective when they are regarded as partners with teachers—all of whom are working to increase student achievement by examining and improving their own teaching practices. With the use of the term *demonstration,* coaches signal that they are showing how a lesson might look, but are not claiming to be *experts*. They signal that they are there to learn, too. Debrief sessions are an important part of demonstration lessons. These should always be done face-to-face and scheduled as soon after the lesson as possible. Although scheduling is sometimes challenging, these follow-up conversations may occur immediately after the demonstration if release time is possible, during planning time, or after school.

During these debrief sessions, coaches reflect on their lessons and ask for specific feedback from the teachers who were observing. When coaches put themselves in scenarios similar to what teachers experience when working with coaches, teachers tend to be more open and more willing to take risks trying out new instructional strategies.

If the incremental approach to Guided Math professional learning is being presented to teachers, coaches might plan several demonstration lessons for each of the components to ensure that all teachers have a chance to see an example of the component. (See Figure 5.6.)

Figure 5.6 Guided Math Demonstration Lessons

Guided Math Component	Possible Demonstration Lesson
Environment of Numeracy	Creation of an anchor chart with students about "Why Mathematicians Ask Questions"
Math Warm-Ups	Math Stretch "How Did My Family Use Math Last Night?" with a Math Huddle discussion
Whole-Class Instruction	Math Vocabulary Game
Small-Group Instruction	Small-group lesson topic to be determined by the classroom teacher
Math Workshop	Creation of an anchor chart with students on what Math Workshop "Looks Like, Sounds Like"
Math Conferences	Math Conferences conducted with three students regarding their math work
Assessment	Use of Tickets Out the Door with students to determine grouping and differentiation of a small-group lesson being planned

It is recommended that these lessons be scheduled so that groups of teachers are able to observe. The observing teachers may be from the same grade level or from multiple grade levels. Some coaches prefer to provide teachers with observation forms asking that they look for specific things during the lesson. Others prefer to leave the observation more open-ended. Sometimes when teachers are directed to look for certain things, they become so focused that they miss other important aspects of the lesson.

There are two advantages of having a group, rather than just one teacher, observe a demonstration lesson. First, it is a more efficient way of providing the demonstration lesson experience for teachers. More teachers view each demonstration lesson. The other advantage is the richer debrief conversation. Because the teachers each notice different aspects of the lesson, when their observations and questions are shared, it broadens the perspectives of everyone in the debrief session.

Debrief sessions are most meaningful when teachers reflect and summarize what they have learned as the session concludes. Several methods may be used to structure their reflections and summaries.

✏ **3–2–1:** Teachers jot down three things they learned, two things they liked, and one thing they will go back to their classrooms and use.

✏ **$2.00 Summaries:** With each word worth ten cents, teachers write a summary of their reflections that is worth two dollars.

✏ **Important Things:** Teachers list three important things they noticed and then add "The most important thing I learned is _____."

✏ **Tickets Out the Door:** A question is posed to which teachers respond. An example might be "Now what?" or "What do you want to learn more about?"

✏ **Reflect and Share:** This is one of the simplest and many times the most effective of these strategies. Teachers reflect for a few minutes and then share something of value they learned from the observation—either with a partner or with the whole group.

Pilot Classroom Observations

Observations of pilot classrooms are especially useful when there are teachers who are piloting Guided Math implementation—although coaches should avoid scheduling a group observation of a teacher who is just beginning the implementation process. Later in the chapter, a different kind of peer observation, one in which a single teacher visits to observe a lesson in another classroom as part of the teacher coaching process, will be described. For pilot classroom observations, coaches arrange for several teachers to visit to observe a lesson. These visits should be aligned with the current focus of the professional learning. For example, as teachers learn about Math Warm-Ups, they observe a lesson related to that component.

These visits may be scheduled during teacher planning periods to minimize the need for substitute teachers. If needed, some schools assign teaching assistants or paraprofessionals to cover teachers' classes during these observations. Another option is providing a substitute who will move from class to class to facilitate these observations. While it may seem logical to have coaches cover classes so teachers can observe their peers, it is not recommended. Coaches should join the teachers observing the lesson. By being a part of the observation group, coaches ensure timeliness and participation of the teachers engaged in this professional learning opportunity.

Coaches who are involved in this type of professional learning observe the lesson with a more practiced eye. Since these observations are followed by debrief sessions, just as demonstration lessons are, coaches can then facilitate and guide the debrief conversation to ensure that important features of the lesson—some of which may have been overlooked by the observers—are discussed. In addition, by being a part of the observing team, coaches are aware of the experiences teachers have had and can refer to them specifically in future training and during individual coaching with teachers.

Guided Math Focus Walks

Teachers can get a feel for the flexibility of the Guided Math framework when they see it implemented in several classrooms. In a Guided Math focus walk, a group of teachers visit several classrooms, but not to observe an entire lesson. Instead, they visit a number of classrooms briefly to look for evidence of implementation.

To prepare for Guided Math focus walks, teachers first brainstorm what they would expect to see in a classroom in which Guided Math is fully implemented. Or, if the focus walk highlights a single component of the framework, the teachers would come up with a list of things they would expect to see related to that component. For example, if the focus is an environment of numeracy, some of the things teachers might see are:

✎ a math word wall
✎ math-related literature
✎ student math work displayed
✎ a number line
✎ instruments of measure (e.g., rulers, measuring cups, scales)
✎ anchor charts about math
✎ manipulatives

Coaches or teacher leaders then compile the teacher-created list and plan the focus walk. With the brainstormed list in hand, teachers whose classrooms will be visited know exactly what the focus group will be looking for. Four or five teachers are selected to visit four or five different classrooms during a math lesson.

As the focus walk begins, the group meets to receive a copy of the brainstormed list. The group visits each classroom together, accompanied by the coach. As they visit each classroom, they are instructed to focus their attention on the listed classroom attributes. Only five to seven minutes is spent in each classroom. After each classroom is visited, the group briefly reviews what they observed and then moves on to the next classroom. When all of the scheduled visits have been made, the group meets for a debrief session. Teachers share what they noticed, any questions they might have, and together reflect on their experience. The entire focus walk takes approximately an hour. See Figure 5.7 for a sample schedule.

Figure 5.7 Sample Guided Math Focus Walk Schedule

Guided Math Focus Walk: Creating an Environment of Numeracy

The visiting members will be observing classrooms for the following evidence of a classroom environment of numeracy and how they are being used:

- a math word wall
- math-related literature
- student math work displayed
- a number line
- instruments of measure
- anchor charts about math
- manipulatives

Date of Visit	Members of Focus Walk	Classes and Times to Visit
October 1	Hampton	Hernandez 8:30
8:30–9:30	Smith	Sanders 8:40
	O'Neal	Walsh 8:50
Meet the coach by C Hall	Carty	Hsu 9:00
		Debrief 9:10–9:30
Date of Visit	**Members of Focus Walk**	**Classes and Times to Visit**
October 22	Hernandez	Hampton 1:00
1:00–2:00	Sanders	Smith 1:10
	Walsh	O'Neal 1:20
Meet Coach by D Hall at the Media Center	Hsu	Carty 1:30
		Debrief 1:40–2:00

If desired, a protocol might be used to provide structure to the focus walk discussion. The Wows and Wonders protocol works well for this type of professional learning experience. If used during the walk, the Wows and Wonders forms are copied for teacher use. Please see Appendix D for a full-size version of Figure 5.8.

Figure 5.8 Wows and Wonders Form

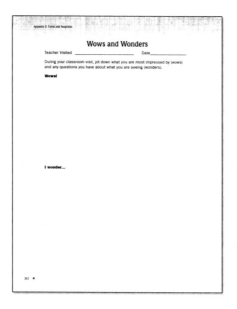

Teachers are given a copy of the form for each classroom to be visited. During the visit, they jot down their *wows* (what they were impressed by) and their *wonders* (questions they had about what they saw). These notes then form a basis for the debrief discussion. Coaches may also choose to collect the comments to give to the teachers whose classrooms were visited. Most teachers enjoy reading the wows and learn from the wonders. Obviously, any comments that may be hurtful would not be shared.

A few weeks later, another focus walk should be scheduled, but this time the teachers who were visited now visit the classrooms of teachers who were the visitors during the first focus walk. In this way, all teachers have the opportunity to both visit and be visited.

Focus walks are powerful learning experiences for teachers. When teachers engage in this type of professional learning, these are some benefits to the learning experience.

- ✎ Teachers come away from the focus walks with a variety of ideas for using Guided Math in their classrooms. The framework is flexible and will be implemented in different ways by different teachers.

- ✎ Teachers who are on the brink of trying Guided Math in their classrooms are nudged to go ahead with it when their classrooms are scheduled to be visited.

- ✎ Teachers become more familiar with the vertical alignment of the mathematics curriculum. Because teachers may visit multiple grade levels during focus walks, they see firsthand the glimpses of the instruction their current students have received in earlier grades and also what their current students will encounter in the years to come.

- ✎ Teachers develop a greater sense of collegiality. They become more comfortable having their peers visit their classrooms during instruction and in openly sharing their instructional ideas and concerns.

Surveying Teachers to Discover their Guided Math Learning Needs

The professional learning described so far in this chapter addresses needs determined by data analysis and by the goal of implementing Guided Math. The structure of the framework itself provides considerable direction for teacher training. To use Guided Math, teachers must understand its components and how to use them in the classroom. This understanding is just a start, as are demonstration lessons, pilot classroom observations, and focus walks. Math coaches will make a huge error, however, if they assume that *covering* the basics is sufficient. Just as classroom instruction should be tailored to meet the needs of students, effective professional learning must be designed to meet the needs of teachers.

Sometimes, these needs become obvious through conversations with teachers. Often, though, they remain obscured. It may be that the opportunity for a teacher to share a need with his or her coach never arose.

Or, it may be that a teacher is reluctant to ask for help for fear of appearing to be incompetent.

To discover unidentified professional learning needs, coaches may decide to survey teachers. Surveys may be simple paper and pencil varieties or may be conducted online. Teacher surveys are most revealing when they include both very specific suggestions for additional training as well as open-ended questions. The specificity spurs teachers to consider areas they may not have already considered and therefore spark their thinking. On the other hand, the open-ended format allows teachers to include areas that may not have occurred to the coach. Surveys may also be used to identify the preferred times of day and formats for additional training sessions.

If only a few of the teachers surveyed made specific requests, these can best be handled by arranging further support directly with those teachers. If there are training needs that many teachers requested, group sessions should be arranged. To meet a variety of training needs, coaches or educational leaders may create a menu of training options based on the survey results from which teachers pick and choose. This offers a differentiated approach to providing professional learning opportunities for teachers.

Coaching Challenges in Guided Math

As described earlier in the chapter, the roles of a coach are many and often not very clearly defined. "Coaches often find that they face a myriad of obstacles that seem to prevent them from coaching in any meaningful way" (West and Cameron 2013, xv). With so many demands, coaches may struggle to decide how to best allocate their time to support the implementation of Guided Math.

On-site coaches may find themselves to be the "go to" person for administrators when something needs to be done. They may be assigned an array of tasks that have little or nothing to do with coaching. Some of the responsibilities that are extraneous to math coaching include covering classes when teachers are out, bus duty, lunch duty, acting as testing coordinator, providing remediation for struggling students, monitoring dress code violations, and ordering and distributing textbook materials. Yet "none of these (mis)uses of a coach's time will help to *cultivate an adult learning culture that will upgrade teaching capacity system-wide to the degree that student learning will substantially improve,* which is the primary function of coaching in educational settings" (West and Cameron 2013, xvi). Working under these conditions, it is easy for coaches to lose sight of their main purpose and become ensnared in carrying out such tasks. Even when coaches maintain visions of supporting teachers as they adopt the instructional strategies of the Guided Math framework and refine their use of it, finding the time to work productively toward those visions is challenging under those conditions.

In the same way, district math coaches may be asked to coordinate testing, provide a wide range of professional development, and participate in district initiatives. In some ways this is a more challenging situation for coaches. On-site coaches are more likely to develop a close working relationship with administrators who are more aware of their coaches' day-to-day responsibilities in working directly with teachers as they learn more about the components of Guided Math. Once again, to be effective, coaches have to carve out a role that allows them to support their teachers in honing their implementation of Guided Math.

Administrators who recognize that it is their coaches' work with teachers that promotes overall mathematics academic excellence try to insulate coaches from responsibilities that are unrelated to that mission. Those coaches are indeed very fortunate. When an administrator fails to understand the importance of the coach's role and uses the coach as a "catch all" person, it is unlikely that the full potential of coaching will be realized.

Many coaches, both on-site and district, find it exceedingly difficult to discuss this problem with their administrative supervisors. To do so seems to send a message that they are unwilling to carry out their professional responsibilities. Some coaches are also concerned that if they do not assume the same kind of duties that teachers are assigned, it damages their relationships with classroom teachers—if classroom teachers have bus duty, why shouldn't a coach?

These are valid concerns that can only be addressed by honest and open discussions between coaches and their administrative supervisors—discussions that should clarify exactly what the administrators' expectations are and which of the many school responsibilities mesh well with those expectations. It sometimes helps for the administrator and coach to itemize coaching-specific tasks and then to jointly create a coaching schedule based on those responsibilities. Just as coaches go through a process of learning the ins-and-outs of the profession, administrators go through a similar learning process. Very often, they have never considered the importance of protecting their coaches' time so that it can be devoted to cultivating a strong professional learning environment.

Even when administrators wisely choose to insulate math coaches from these responsibilities, both administrators and coaches must remain sensitive to the perceptions of the rest of the educational community. It is best when the entire community understands the job description of a math coach and see firsthand how hardworking the coach is. Some coaches send out their weekly schedules to both keep the community informed about their work and to make it easier for teachers and other staff members to arrange times to meet with them.

Supporting the implementation of Guided Math by teachers makes great demands on coaches. All in all, effective coaches are most likely to be able to assist an educational community's move toward the implementation of Guided Math. If coaches are pulled in too many different directions, their ability to successfully support teachers in any way is diminished.

Strategic Coaching in Guided Math

In truth, every teacher *deserves* a math coach. In an ideal world, every teacher would have one. But, alas, who lives in an ideal world? Even when schools and school districts provide coaches, it is impossible for them to coach all teachers equally. Consequently, their mathematics coaching must be strategic. Jones and Vreeman (2008) warn coaches and other educational leaders that "trying to cover all classrooms will result in 'a spit, a lick, and a promise' type of practice. We all know from experience how ineffective this mode of operating can be" (90). Instead, coaches are much more effective when they work with fewer teachers, building capacity for Guided Math instruction with them before moving on to coach additional teachers.

On which teachers should coaches and leaders focus their Guided Math coaching efforts first? It is tempting to designate those teachers who are struggling. And, in many cases, coaches are asked by administrators to provide support for new teachers or less proficient teachers. Using coaches in this way, however, severely limits their coaching effectiveness. Low-functioning teachers have the potential of "drawing down the coaches' positive energy and monopolizing the coaches' time. They may be slow to progress because they either don't have the capacity or chose not to change" (Hansen 2009, 50). An ongoing lack of progress can doom Guided Math initiatives.

Another drawback to math coaches focusing on these teachers is that it creates the impression that all teachers who are being coached are struggling teachers. Coaching initiatives may be confused with commonly used *remedial* professional development plans created for teachers whose performance reviews are unsatisfactory. One of the best ways to counter this misconception is by "spending time building talent with the strongest teachers" (Jones and Vreeman 2008, 89). This is particularly true when coaches are assisting teachers as they are implementing new instructional practices such as Guided Math.

Smith (2006) advises coaches to "practice the 'water principle.' Specialists [coaches] should go with the flow and start with the area of least resistance" (122). When coaches begin work to support Guided Math implementation with teachers who are motivated and accomplished, "their journey will most likely be swift, successful, and public" (Hansen 2009, 49). With a small cadre of "teachers who are willing and able, the ones that have the most potential to make a change" (Hansen 2009, 50) coaches can work with intimate groups of teachers to establish the kind of risk-free learning environment that nurtures innovation.

The same strategic coaching approach can be applied when coaches are working with PLCs focused on Guided Math. In schools where PLCs are numerous, coaches and administrators must decide which of them should have the most coaching support. In some schools, that decision may be easy. Coaches play a crucial role in supporting implementation (e.g., resource gathering, demonstration lessons, observations with feedback, scheduling peer classroom visits).

Review & Reflect

1. Think back on a worthwhile professional development experience you have had. What aspects of the training made the experience valuable to you? Did you apply what you had learned in your role as an educator? Why or why not?

2. Consider a professional development opportunity that was of little value to you. Why do you think it lacked value? How could it have been improved?

3. With what aspects of the implementation of Guided Math would you expect teachers to struggle the most? What kinds of support can math coaches provide to alleviate those struggles?

Chapter 6

Guided Math Professional Development Provided by Coaches

One-on-One Coaching to Promote Guided Math Implementation

Both experienced and rookie teachers are fortunate when they have coaches to assist them in restructuring their mathematics instruction. The research of Joyce and Showers (2002) clearly documents the limited value of workshops, demonstrations, and practice activities in changing traditional teaching methods unless bolstered by ongoing coaching. Teachers may not feel especially fortunate, however, when they first encounter mathematics or academic coaches. In fact, less-confident or over-confident teachers may even feel threatened.

Building Trust with Teachers

It is hardly surprising that Balka, Hull, and Miles (2010) maintain that "trust is one of the most important attributes for mathematics leaders to establish" (105). Developing a trusting relationship with teachers is key for coaches who are supporting the implementation of the Guided Math framework. "Trust building is a slow process that requires disclosure, authenticity of work and action, follow through in meeting others' needs, respect for diversity, enabling teachers to take action in risk-taking environments without fear of reprisal, and basic ethical actions that demonstrate a concern for the well-being of others" (Short and Greer 2002, 159)—hardly an easy task. Undoubtedly, "during change initiatives, teachers need someone who is by their side, not looking over their shoulder" (Balka, Hull, and Miles 2010, 106).

Tips for Establishing Trusting Relationships

How do coaches go about convincing teachers that they are on their side, not looking over their shoulders? Covey and Merrill (2006) suggest the following tips for establishing trusting relationships.

1. **Talk straight.** Being honest and telling the truth is always the best policy for coaches. Of course, that does not mean being *brutally* honest. But, people need to know where coaches stand and not feel as if they are being manipulated.

2. **Demonstrate respect for others.** When coaches genuinely care about the teachers with whom they work, it shows. Effective coaches take time to show others that they care. They are respectful of the dignity of the teachers they support. It is more important in building trust to take time to show kindness to others, than to be perceived as extremely efficient.

3. **Create transparency.** Coaches must be open and genuine with all members of their professional community. Having hidden agendas hinders trust-building efforts.

4. **Right wrongs when they occur.** Coaches are human; they make mistakes. They sometimes hurt the feelings of others without intending to. Acknowledging mistakes and apologizing for them helps coaches establish trusting relationships. Effective coaches refuse to let their pride hinder them from doing the right thing.

5. **Show loyalty.** When working with others, it is important to acknowledge their contributions and give them credit when credit is due. At times, all coaches experience frustration with those they are coaching. To earn trust, however, coaches refrain from sharing negative comments about others or voicing their frustrations. People are more trusting of coaches who maintain a positive and supportive attitude about their professional community.

6. **Deliver results.** Teachers trust coaches who accomplish what they promise and can get things done. These coaches only promise what they can reasonably expect to deliver. And, in the event that they do

not deliver what was promised, they accept the responsibility for it rather than making excuses.

7. **Get better or improve constantly and deliberately.** Teachers are more trusting of coaches who personally model the concept of continuous improvement. Coaches who request and are open to feedback from others establish trusting relationships within the learning community.

8. **Confront reality.** While it is difficult to address some issues with teachers who are being coached, in the long run, confronting those realities helps strengthen trusting relationships—even when agreement is not reached. When teachers are confident that coaches have no hidden agendas—that they are addressing the tough issues—trust is more likely to flourish.

9. **Clarify expectations.** Clarifying expectations is closely akin to creating transparency. Just as teachers are expected to help students be aware of their learning goals, coaches build trust when their expectations for the teachers with whom they work are clearly defined and understood by all.

10. **Practice accountability.** Trusted coaches hold themselves and others accountable. When coaches give relevant feedback based on clearly defined expectations, teachers feel accountable for meeting common goals. They hold themselves accountable by meeting expectations or assuming responsibilities within the learning community.

11. **Listen first.** Good coaches make it a practice to listen before they speak. They actively listen to hear what is being expressed without assuming they already know what is going to be said. Teachers can trust their coaches to better understand their needs when this kind of listening is common practice.

12. **Keep commitments.** People trust those who do what they say they are going to. It is quite simple. Because education professions are so demanding and stressful, coaches need to be particularly aware of the importance of following through on their commitments.

13. **Extend trust to others.** One of the easiest ways to earn trust is to extend it to others. Certainly, extending trust has its limits. Covey and Merrill suggest that those who wish to build trust "extend trust abundantly to those who have earned your trust. Extend trust conditionally to those who are earning your trust. Learn how to appropriately extend trust to others based on the situation, risk, and credibility (character and competence) of the people involved. But have a propensity to trust" (Kindle Location 4458). Coaches find that extending trust brings out the best in others (Kindle Locations 2860–4460).

The Importance of Trust between Coaches and Teachers

Why is a trusting relationship between teachers and coaches especially important when teachers begin using Guided Math in their classrooms? Although teachers understand that they are accountable for the quality and quantity of learning that goes on in their classrooms, it is unsettling when the methods of assessing teacher proficiency vary from school to school and change from year to year. It is even more unsettling when major decisions involving teaching are being made by others—outside the classroom, outside the school, and in many cases outside the educational community. With reason, many teachers are hesitant to implement new instructional strategies. Even though they acknowledge the need for change and would like to improve their teaching methods, the process of change itself is frightening—especially for highly motivated and dedicated teachers.

In order to relieve some of this anxiety, coaches must help teachers feel confident that they are knowledgeable and informed—that, in the professional opinion of the coaches, the Guided Math framework *will* make a positive difference in the mathematical learning of students. Teachers must also trust that coaches recognize that it is likely there will be a dip as Guided Math is being implemented. They have to trust that their coaches realize not every lesson using the new teaching strategies will be successful. They must be able to trust that their coaches will be there to support them when things do not go as desired—offering encouragement, feedback, suggestions, and resources.

In order for teachers to turn to coaches for help, they have to feel comfortable sharing the fact that they *need* help. That is not always easily done. Requests for help made to coaches should remain confidential between teachers and coaches. Confidential conversations are "integral in laying the foundation for establishing trust" (Rapacki and Francis 2014, 560). Effective coaches help teachers to recognize that being able to identify how they would like to improve their instruction and then taking steps to make that improvement are characteristics of master teachers.

Teachers must also be able to trust their coaches to be conduits between teachers and administrators. Coaches earn this trust by educating administrators, if needed, about the Guided Math framework, its value and what they should expect to see in classrooms during the implementation process. Teachers feel vulnerable when trying new teaching methods and many rely heavily on their coaches for support in multiple ways. Reciprocal trusting relationships between coaches and teachers are essential.

Encouraging Teachers

Coaches also build trust by providing encouragement to teachers who are practicing new teaching strategies. Most teachers want honest feedback that will help them improve their teaching, but they also need to receive positive feedback on what it is they are doing well. Like all people, teachers need and appreciate recognition of their efforts to master new skills. Stopping by a classroom to give a teacher a thumbs up or leaving a note mentioning something specific a teacher has done well builds goodwill and brightens the teacher's day. Taking the time to affirm the efforts teachers are making to implement Guided Math is an essential responsibility for coaches who hope to truly make a difference in the professional learning of teachers. Coaches who anticipate teachers' needs and concerns and then are prepared to alleviate them, lay a foundation of trust that will be especially valuable during difficult times. An academic coach is most effective when he or she finds a way to balance being teachers' most enthusiastic cheerleader and being a trusted confidant who offers honest feedback to teachers about how to improve their teaching.

Steps for Coaching Individual Teachers

The needs of individual teachers are diverse; one coaching plan or strategy will not satisfy them all. Generally though, coaches scaffold their support in much the same way teachers scaffold their instruction, gradually releasing responsibility (Pearson and Gallagher 1983; Fisher and Frey

2008). With scaffolding provided by coaches, gradually teachers assume greater responsibility for using the Guided Math framework in their own classrooms. (See Figure 6.1.)

Figure 6.1 Gradual Release of Responsibility for Mathematics Coaching

Coaching Phase	Coach	Teacher
Coach Teaches/ Teacher Observes	Plans lesson with Teacher Demonstrates Lessons Debrief/Reflection with Teacher	Plans lesson with Coach Observes the Lesson Debrief/Reflection with Coach
Coach and Teacher Teach Together	Plan Lesson with Teacher Co-Teach the Lesson with Teacher Debrief/Reflection with Teacher	Plan Lesson with Coach Co-Teach the Lesson with Coach Debrief/Reflection with Coach
Teacher Teaches/ Coach Observes	Plans Lesson with Teacher Observes Lesson that Teacher Teaches Debrief and Provide Feedback to Teacher	Plans Lesson with Coach Teaches Lesson Debrief and Reflection with Coach

(Adapted from Pearson and Gallagher 1983; Fisher and Frey 2008)

Following the initial Guided Math professional development, some teachers will be ready and eager to go. Without any hesitation, they will map out ways to adapt the framework to make it fit their teaching styles and to meet their students' needs. They will begin using Guided Math immediately, adjusting their approaches as they go—if and when required. With these teachers, coaches may offer to supplement teachers' efforts with demonstration lessons on an as-needed basis. But, the coach's role will be minimal—mainly providing resources and feedback. These teachers are ready to assume responsibility for Guided Math instruction from the outset.

Other teachers may want to implement the framework, but will not be quite sure how to proceed. These teachers may need to see demonstration lessons and participate in co-teaching lessons with the coach before becoming comfortable enough to assume responsibility for implementing it independently in their own classrooms. As they begin this process, they may require a lot of handholding and encouragement.

Finally, there will always be a few teachers who would simply rather not implement Guided Math in their classrooms at all. They may be unconvinced that the instruction change will improve student achievement, lack confidence in their ability to implement it successfully, or would rather not put in the extra effort it takes to change their current teaching practices.

If Guided Math implementation is mandated, coaches have a responsibility to support these educators in whatever ways they can. It is important to remember, though, that coaches are not administrators. The coach's role is to support teachers in carrying out their professional responsibilities successfully. If a teacher refuses to change his or her instructional practices when change is mandated, administrators—not coaches—are ultimately responsible for handling the situation.

Pre-Teach Guided Math Lesson Planning with Teachers

Meeting with teachers to plan lessons is an essential component of the coaching process—whether the lessons being planned are demonstration lessons, co-taught lessons, or lessons to be taught by the teacher and observed by the coach. The planning process helps inform the coach about what the teacher hopes to accomplish with the lesson and what the students' needs are.

Hull, Balka, and Miles remind coaches that they "need most of all to be effective listeners" (2009, Kindle Location 737) during the lesson planning conferences. In some ways, the conference is a pre-assessment of what teachers already know about both content and instructional strategies. "Positive changes begin from this point, building on the teachers' knowledge base that coaches discover. The goal, after all, is not for mathematics coaches to prove how much they know but to assist teachers in learning and using effective instructional strategies" (Hull, Balka, and Miles 2009, Kindle Locations 739–740).

Without joint planning, the value of demonstration lessons, co-taught lessons, and observations of lessons by coaches is diminished. Planning discussions reinforce both content knowledge and pedagogy. The coach and teacher examine the standards to be addressed in the lesson and consider how the Guided Math framework can be utilized most efficiently to provide students tailored instruction to meet their learning needs.

One aspect of Guided Math lesson planning that is often overlooked is the consideration of prerequisite knowledge and skills that students must have to be successful with the upcoming lesson. When teachers are aware of the essential foundational understanding that students must have, they can draw upon assessment information to group students appropriately. Students who have gaps in needed knowledge and skills are grouped together so these gaps can be addressed before students are engaged in the current lesson. Likewise, students who may already have mastered the standards addressed in the lesson can be grouped together and given additional challenges. Coaches who include this aspect of planning in their conferences with teachers lead teachers to more accurate differentiation of instruction.

Also, during the planning session, coaches should encourage teachers to review their assessment data—both formal and informal—as they form instructional groups for lessons. Planning discussions should focus on answering the following questions as differentiation options are considered:

✎ What do students need to know and be able to do?

✎ How do we know whether students have gaps in what they know and can do?

✎ How do we know if students may be able to go beyond the lesson and need additional challenge?

This kind of conversation sets the stage for differentiation and underscores how important it is for teachers to know precisely where their students are at this point in time on their personal and grade level learning trajectories.

Describing her experience as a math coach planning lessons with teachers, Rapacki writes "I tried to make my planning process transparent to the teachers, showing them modified lesson plans, useful articles and books, and resources I had obtained at conferences. I hoped that making this process transparent would provide a template for the teachers to use in their future independent planning" (Rapacki and Francis 2014, 561). So, in planning lessons together, coaches and teachers learn from each other. In addition, the planning process has the potential of generating strong bonds between teachers and coaches that define their ongoing working relationships.

Demonstrating Guided Math Lessons

The demonstration of new practices, such as Guided Math lessons, by coaches "has been shown to be particularly successful in helping teachers understand and apply a concept and remain open to adopting it" (Gulamhussein 2013, 17). Teachers usually welcome coaches into their classrooms when coaches offer to conduct demonstration lessons. According to Moran (2007), coaches use demonstration lessons for the following three reasons:

- ✎ "To demonstrate particular teaching methods, strategies, or content to teachers who are less familiar or confident with them

- ✎ To provide a common experience of teaching that can serve as the basis for discussing and developing practice

- ✎ To foster teachers' self-reflection and creative problem solving" (75)

All three are relevant when coaches are supporting the implementation of Guided Math. As implementation begins, most teachers are unfamiliar with the framework and not confident in their ability to use it effectively. They want to see what it looks like with students before putting it into practice in their classrooms. Based on what they observe in the demonstration lessons, teachers are better able to decide how to adapt the framework for use in their own classrooms to make it fit their individual teaching styles and their students' needs.

In demonstrating lessons, coaches draw upon what they learned about students' learning needs during the pre-teaching planning session with the teacher. Demonstration lessons let teachers see firsthand how the Guided Math framework allows them to differentiate instruction based on their students' needs, to promote conceptual understanding, and to strengthen students' proficiency in the mathematics practices. Teacher and coach both experience the same lesson, but in different ways—the coach as teacher and the classroom teacher as observer. Their debrief conversations are made richer as they share their different perspectives on the lesson.

To support Guided Math implementation, coaches may choose to demonstrate lessons creating mathematical anchor charts with students, conducting Math Stretches and Huddles, teaching the whole class, or teaching small groups of students. Additionally, although some may not consider them to be lessons, coaches can demonstrate how to explore and assess students' mathematical thinking with Math Conferences and how to use a "well-planned approach to balanced assessment…[to obtain] the different kinds of data they need to be well-informed decision makers" (Huebner 2009, 86).

When teaching demonstration lessons, it is important that coaches "respect teachers' different ways of organizing classrooms and the special relationship they have built with their children" (Confer 2006, 9). Coaches who establish strong working relationships with teachers never lose sight of the fact that they are guests in another teacher's classroom. They adhere to the classroom rules and procedures unless the teacher has clearly given permission to deviate from them.

It is advisable for coaches and teachers to establish ground rules for demonstration lessons. The coach assumes responsibility for teaching the lesson, while the teacher remains in the classroom to observe. To avoid misunderstandings, coaches should explicitly share these expectations with teachers. While it may seem obvious that teachers should remain in the classroom to observe demonstration lessons, occasionally teachers decide that this is an opportune time to take a break while their class is with the coach. The teacher should understand that the lesson is being demonstrated for them, not just to teach the students. Teachers should not be grading papers or multitasking in any way. When expectations are clear, this kind of problem is avoided.

Some coaches prefer to have teachers participate actively in the lesson even as they observe; others would rather the teacher simply observe. This decision may depend on the lesson. There are valid reasons for coaches to ask teachers to limit their role to observation. When assisting with a lesson, teachers may miss important aspects of it that coaches hope will be noticed and discussed later in the debrief conversations.

Teachers who are engaged in the demonstration may also unintentionally misdirect the lesson. For example, a coach may be teaching a lesson aimed at prompting the teacher to discover how important it is to allow students to struggle productively when working with math. The coach knows that a student who engages in productive struggle to understand a concept or solve a problem "has a higher likelihood of retaining the information than if he or she were simply given steps to follow" (Hiltabidel 2012, para. 8).

Yet, in a misguided attempt to help, the teacher may step in and suggest strategies or even provide the answer to make it easier for students. Of course, should that occur, the incident itself can be discussed during the debrief session, but it has less impact because the teacher is unable to observe the positive consequences of productive struggle. It also puts the teacher in the awkward position of feeling as though he or she behaved improperly.

When planning and conducting demonstration lessons, coaches have dual responsibilities—teaching students and offering the observing teachers new insights into instruction. During pre-teach lesson planning, teachers may ask coaches to demonstrate certain instructional strategies or share problems they are having. Even when teachers make no special requests, coaches may have noticed a need or an administrator may ask a coach to target a particular instructional area. So, in addition to using information about student needs, coaches develop their lesson plans based on the teachers' needs. On some occasions, coaches may specify what they would like teachers to look for during the lesson. At other times, they may choose to leave it open-ended. To provide teachers a common method for recording their observations, some coaches choose to provide a recording sheet that may be completed either as the teacher observes or immediately after the lesson.

If the teacher is not completing the observation form during the lesson, coaches may choose to ask the teacher to sit with students or to walk around the room observing what students are doing. This is up to the coach. At times, teacher movement or presence sitting with students may be a distraction to both teacher and students. As teachers focus on what a student or students are doing, they may miss aspects of the lesson being demonstrated. Students may tend to focus more on their own teacher. Teachers may also be tempted to step in and disrupt the flow of the lesson. On the other hand, their observations of students during the lesson can generate additional insights into the demonstrated lesson.

The sample observation form shown in Figure 6.2 is general, but may be adapted to encourage teachers to attend to specific areas of teaching and learning. (See Appendix D for a full-size version.) The content of the form itself can lead teachers to focus on particular aspects of a demonstration lesson. Additional questions that might be included in an observation form are:

✎ How did the Guided Math structure support mathematical learning?

✎ How did the teacher support students' sense of being part of a mathematical learning community?

✎ How were students challenged to think mathematically and communicate that thinking?

✎ Were students allowed to struggle in a productive way to construct mathematical meaning or solve problems? Describe what occurred.

✎ How was the lesson differentiated to meet student needs?

✎ What kind of teacher/student and student/student interactions did you observe? Describe them.

✎ How were students encouraged to assume responsibility for their learning?

✎ What new ideas did you encounter during the observation?

✎ Is there anything that could have been done differently in the lesson that may have made it more effective?

Figure 6.2 Guided Math Demonstration Lesson Observation Form For Teachers

Co-Teaching Guided Math Lessons

Another method coaches use to encourage the use of Guided Math is co-teaching lessons with classroom teachers. Following a demonstration lesson in a teacher's classroom, the logical next step is a co-teaching experience, especially for teachers who lack the confidence to begin implementation. As Jones and Vreeman discovered in their experience as coaches, "many people were uncomfortable moving from watching a model lesson to being observed as *they* taught a lesson. One of the ways many of our coaches helped breakdown some of that anxiety was by inviting the classroom teacher into a co-teach model" (2008, 87).

With the co-teach approach, teachers and coaches share equally the responsibility of preparing and teaching the lesson. This coaching technique may be a bit intimidating for teachers if they are not yet accustomed to working with coaches. Yet, "when mathematics coaches have become a well-accepted presence in classrooms, teachers will feel more comfortable about the prospect of coteaching" (Hull, Bulka, and Miles 2009, Kindle Location 783).

Coaches and teachers may decide to co-teach a lesson for a number of reasons in addition to supporting Guided Math implementation. These include the following:

- To capitalize on the knowledge of content and pedagogy of both coach and teacher in planning and teaching a lesson
- To determine the effectiveness of currently used instructional strategies
- To support attempts to use new instructional techniques that teachers would be reluctant to try on their own
- To take advantage of diverse instructional styles and talents of both coaches and teachers
- To promote collaboration among the professional community to enhance student achievement by breaking down barriers between coaches and teachers
- To take advantage of having another set of eyes to observe and find solutions to problems
- To engage in a shared teaching experience that can be used as the basis for discussion in a post-observation conference

(Adapted from Moran 2007, 90)

Chris Confer, a mathematics coach, writes that although "math coaching has long been seen as a one-way street, a relationship where an 'expert' provides information, demonstration lessons, and specific feedback to teachers after observing their teaching...I find the most powerful way that I impact the teaching of others is through coteaching" (Williams and Confer 2006, 76). He likens the co-teaching experience to action research where teacher and coach, as a team, investigate to learn more about effective mathematics instruction. He further describes his experience stating

> *I learn from the teachers and they learn from me. This process is respectful of the experiences and expertise that teachers bring to professional development situations. It is honest about the fact that even very experienced math coaches cannot know everything, and that researching together is the most powerful arrangement for professional development.*

> (Williams and Confer 2006, 77)

As with demonstration lessons, the coach and teacher collaborate prior to the lesson to identify students' needs, decide on areas of instructional focus, and plan the lesson. "In true coteaching, teachers and coaches first plan collaboratively the roles that each will play. Neither will be the lead teacher or the assistant teacher. A level of equality is maintained" (Hull, Balka, and Miles 2009, Kindle Locations 786–787).

During the lesson, however, coaches and teachers assume either primary or supporting roles. Initially, co-teachers should decide how to allocate teaching responsibilities during the planning process tasks to avoid confusion during the lesson. But, when coach and teacher become comfortable working together, the roles can be traded back and forth spontaneously during the lesson. According to Hull, Balka, and Miles (2009), the primary teacher can be either the coach or the classroom teacher. The primary teacher

- ✎ determines the learning goals of the students,
- ✎ monitors the flow of the lesson to ensure it meets student needs,
- ✎ guides and directs the learning tasks,
- ✎ tracks the timing of the lesson, and then

✎ leads the summarization of the lesson learning (Kindle Locations 798–801).

The supporting teacher, on the other hand,

✎ follows the lead of the primary teacher regarding the pace and flow of the lesson,

✎ focuses on and supports the learning of individual students or small groups working independently,

✎ teaches one or more parts of the lesson,

✎ oversees activity in the classroom, and

✎ provides scaffolding for students who are struggling (Kindle Locations 802–803).

Coaches should always be aware that "even when sharing responsibility, the ultimate responsibility for classroom instruction rests with the teacher, not the coach. Coaches are, in practical terms, guests; it is classroom teachers who must deal with students when coaches are not present" (Hull, Balka, and Miles 2009, Kindle Locations 805–807).

Even after observing a demonstrated small-group lesson, teachers often require additional coaching support to manage students working independently in Math Workshop as they teach small-group lessons. The co-teaching model is ideal for providing the kind of support they need. This may be a logical next step for teachers who are not quite ready to teach a small-group lesson with the coach observing.

Probably the most effective division of labor in this situation is having both the teacher and coach each teach at least one of the small-group lessons. When either is not engaged with the small-group lessons, they assist in monitoring the independent work of the students. Whether the math coach teaches the first lesson while the teacher manages the workshop or the teacher assumes responsibility for the first small-group lesson while the coach oversees students working independently will depend on the confidence of the teacher. Teachers who are unsure of their ability to manage the workshop may prefer to have the coach take that role first.

With this teaching scenario, both coach and teacher actively participate in each of these Guided Math components—Math Workshop and small-group instruction. During the debrief conversation following the co-teach session, they are able to reflect on both the lesson and the workshop from their own unique perspectives as classroom teacher and coach.

Since the teacher is actively involved in a co-teaching lesson, keeping observational notes is not usually possible. However, teachers should take time soon after the lesson to jot down their reflections on the co-teaching experience to share at the post-observation conference.

Observing Guided Math Lessons

As teachers progress through the coaching process, they assume more responsibility for Guided Math implementation. When math coaches establish a reputation of being experienced and trustworthy, teachers value their feedback. "One of the most effective coaching approaches to professional development is observing the work of teachers and providing feedback. It is there that the coach can actually intercede, provide reinforcement, alter various behaviors, or augment the teaching approaches of those observed" (Bean 2009, Kindle Locations 2577–2578).

The observations of lessons by coaches described in this section differ from the classroom observations mentioned in Chapter 4 that are designed to take the instructional pulse of the learning community and identify overall coaching needs. In contrast, these observations are of specific Guided Math lessons and are an important part of the coaching process. They occur after a pre-teach planning conference with the teacher being observed and are designed to provide valuable feedback for teachers. What is perhaps the most important feature of these observations is their *non-evaluative* nature.

Even though they are non-evaluative, coaches must be sensitive to teacher concerns. "Any leadership position, especially one not clearly defined or understood, can evoke concern and resistance from those being observed, regardless of whether the leader is known by the teachers or not. Given the evaluative nature of regular observations, teachers are often fearful of appearing incompetent to colleagues and teacher leaders. These concerns should not be overlooked" (Rapacki and Francis 2014, 559). It must be clear to teachers that the coach serves as a resource and not as an evaluator.

Just as in pre-teach conferences prior to demonstration lessons or co-taught lessons, coaches and teachers meet to determine student needs and lesson focuses. Teachers describe what they hope students will learn from the lesson and the instructional strategies they plan to use. Teachers may also discuss what they would like the coaches to attend to particularly during the lesson. It may be that they are trying a new strategy or are having difficulty with a particular area of instruction and would like feedback. Teachers gain greater insight into their own teaching practices when an experienced educator observes to give feedback on strategies specified by the teacher. The perspectives of an "outside eye" lead to deeper reflection and often "aha" moments.

Coaches coming into a classroom to observe a lesson should try to avoid disrupting the lesson with their presence. Most teachers will have prepared their students to expect a visitor. When entering a classroom, it is best for the coach to be as unobtrusive as possible. In some instances, teachers may pause briefly to introduce the coach to the class. Since the visit is for observation, coaches do not usually play an active role in instruction, but may do so if invited by the teacher. See Figure 6.3 for a Guided Math Lesson Observation form that can be used by coaches. A full-size version of Figure 6.3 can be found in Appendix D. This form can be adapted as desired to reflect the focus of the observation. After observations, teachers and coaches meet to reflect on the lesson.

Even when teachers have shared specific areas of instruction on which they would like feedback, the observing coach should be aware of all aspects of teaching and learning—including the classroom environment, classroom management, instructional strategies, lesson content, student engagement, and teacher/student interaction. Obviously, during a debrief conference, coaches use their professional judgment to offer feedback that is specific and actionable, but not overwhelming. Additional feedback that was not requested by the teacher can be addressed, if the coach feels this feedback can potentially lead the teacher to make substantial improvements in teaching and if it is delivered in a tactful, supportive manner.

Figure 6.3 Guided Math Lesson Observation Form For Coaches

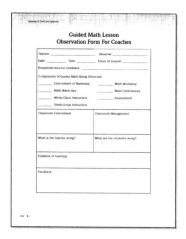

Peer Observation of Guided Math

Teachers can learn much from each other in a variety of contexts. Most commonly, teachers share their experiences and ideas during collaborative work or grade level meetings. What is shared in those meetings, however, is somewhat limited. Teachers may assume that some of the things that they do routinely in their classrooms are what other teachers do and, as a result, they do not share these techniques in collaborative meetings. Some teachers are not even conscious of very effective teaching practices they use on a regular basis in their classrooms. Furthermore, when strategies are shared in meetings, there are often disconnects between teachers' descriptions of their practices and the way others envision them.

To encourage teachers to learn in greater depth from each other, coaches facilitate opportunities for teachers to observe their colleagues who are using the Guided Math framework. Many teachers relish the opportunity to visit the classrooms of their peers. Van Tassel writes of her enthusiasm, "I wanted to visit their classrooms, I wanted them to visit mine, and I wanted us to build on our collective knowledge as we worked toward a common goal of implementing engaging, effective lessons" (2014, 77).

While it may seem convenient for a coach to cover the class of the teacher who will be observing a peer, it is better, whenever possible, to make other arrangements. Peer observations are most effective if the coach also observes the lesson and then participates in a post-observation conference involving both the teacher observing and the teacher who was observed. If substitute teachers cannot be provided, observations might be arranged during a class's special instruction (e.g., art, music, P.E., computer lab), a paraprofessional might be asked to teach the class, or students might be divided among several other classrooms during the observation time.

One way to make the most of these learning experiences is by helping teachers determine a focus prior to the observation. What does the teacher hope to learn from the experience? If time permits, a pre-observation conference between the two teachers and the coach can clarify expectations. Teachers who are being visited appreciate knowing in advance what their guest teacher hopes to gain from the observation. Clarifying the purpose also helps the visiting teacher remain focused and gives the coach insight into the needs of the teacher. The Guided Math Peer Observation form (Figure 6.4) can be used to help structure the pre- and post-observation conferences and make the purpose of the observation explicit to everyone involved. See Appendix D for full-size version.

Both teachers can be given a copy of the form prior to the pre-observation conference, so they will be prepared for the discussion. The coach records teachers' comments during that conference and makes a copy for both teachers so that everyone has the same information. During the post-observation conference, the coach can again act as scribe to document the conversation or teachers can complete their own forms.

Figure 6.4 Guided Math Peer Observation Form

Post-Observation Conferences

After a demonstration lesson, a co-teach lesson, a coach-observed lesson, or a peer observation, teacher(s) and coach confer in a post-observation meeting to debrief and reflect. These conferences are just as important as pre-observation planning meetings. Immediate reflection and review of the lesson reinforces and extends teacher learning by examining "what happened in the classroom as well as why it happened, thereby increasing teacher maturity and professionalism" (Boreen et al. 2009, Kindle Location 926). It gives teachers an opportunity to verbalize their thoughts, hear the reflections of others who may have noticed different aspects of the lesson, and consider how they will use what they learned from the experience.

Moran (2007) offers the following suggestions for coaches when planning and participating in reflection conferences. These conferences should:

- ✎ **Take place as soon as possible after the lesson.** In the busy lives of teachers, observation details are quickly forgotten without prompt reflection and conversation about what was noticed and learned.

- ✎ **Be scheduled for a time and place where the teacher and the coach will not be interrupted.** In addition to finding a time and place for an uninterrupted conference, all parties to the conference need to make a commitment to turn off cell phones and other electronic devices.

- ✎ **Structured to provide an opportunity for the teacher and the coach to walk through the main parts of the lesson.** Observation forms are valuable in helping create a structure that leads the teacher and coach to recall the parts of the lesson. Often, the review of the lesson leads teachers to reflect once more on what was observed or to put into context the feedback provided by coaches.

- ✎ **Focus on the specific aspects the observer wanted to see or on which the observed requested to receive feedback.** In these conferences, either the coach or teacher may be the observer. In either case, it is important that coaches respect teachers' judgment in determining areas of interest and need. When coaches recognize other areas of need, they can be addressed later in a different setting.

✎ **Encourage and support teachers in reflecting on their own role in the observation process.** The coach should ensure that reflections and feedback highlight instructional strengths as well as areas that can be improved. Although teachers should be encouraged to take the lead in these conversations, carefully crafted questions from the coach prompt teachers to think more deeply and to consider how they can incorporate what they observed or the feedback they received into their teaching.

✎ **Focus on the "next steps" for teacher action.** As teachers reflect, they should be encouraged to relate how it will impact their instruction. The teachers' next steps should be specific and detailed to ensure that teaching practices are impacted by their experience.

(Moran 2007, 80)

Coaches act as encouragers and active listeners in these sessions. Moran warns that "the coach should use the debriefing session to encourage self-reflection and creative problem solving by the teacher, *not* to tell the teacher what to do or not to do!" (2007, 80). But, because it is crucial that the learning is relevant to the classroom, coaches can prompt *teachers* to make connections between the observation and their teaching practices explicit.

These conversations should include a constructive critique of the lesson (whether taught by teacher or coach)—not of the person or persons teaching the lesson. Coaches can ensure that positive statements about what occurred are "supported with evidence of students' learning, and negative statements, with possible alternatives" (Rapacki and Francis 2014, 561).

The Value of Reflection

> *Reflection is essential to a fully lived professional life. Among teachers, the finest are those who consider their progress in the classroom, who ponder effective teaching strategies and devise creative classroom activities, who practice reflection to set personal and professional goals, who think on their feet as they teach.*

> (Boreen et al. 2009, Kindle Locations 748–749)

According to Hull, Balka, and Miles (2009), reflection is a strategic tool used to improve both teaching and learning. It "helps to solidify training and practice related to skills that teachers want to use in their classrooms" (Kindle Location 1029). To most effectively plan and teach lessons that promote students' mathematical understanding, teachers need to cultivate the practice of reflecting "on the outcomes of prior lessons (paying close attention to the concepts that students grasped as well as where they struggled) and use this information when planning for the future" (Rapacki and Francis 2014, 559).

Furthermore, Stronge finds that "effective teachers realize that reflective practices are more than simply preservice or inservice exercises. Indeed, reflective practices are crucial to lifelong learning and a professional necessity" (2007, 31). Structured debrief conferences with coaches facilitate that kind of professional reflection. By making the debrief process a fundamental part of the coaching process, coaches create opportunities for teachers to practice the reflective process. Their reflection reinforces training they have received and their experiences related to the Guided Math framework as well as other skills used in their classrooms.

In addition to leading teachers to identify and then apply new teaching methods, the reflection process also serves as affirmation of their efficacy. Especially as teachers attempt to implement new instructional strategies and teach more demanding, content-rich curriculum, they benefit from reassurance that their efforts make a difference. "While efficacy does change for teachers as they encounter new experiences, …they are more likely to have additional positive experiences as they reflect on these new experiences" (Stronge 2007, 31). Thus, as a vehicle for teacher self-reflection, post-observation conferences increase teachers' feeling of efficacy at times when they may be experiencing feelings of disequilibrium. And, "when teachers are confident, they communicate the belief of their own efficacy to students" (31) which has a positive effect on learning.

"Reflection seems uncomplicated, but truly purposeful reflection by teachers on their own actions and their students' responses can be a complex undertaking" (Hull, Balka, and Miles 2009, Kindle Locations 1025–1026). Coaches play a crucial role in assisting teachers as they reflect on their teaching. Post-observation conversations spur teachers' thinking about instructional strategies and encourage them to carefully assess evidence of student engagement and learning.

Coaches may decide to approach the post-observations conversations a variety of ways depending on the particular circumstances surrounding the session. Rita Bean (2009) suggests three methods coaches can use when meeting with teachers: the coach as mirror, the coach as collaborator, or the coach as expert.

With more confident and experienced teachers, coaches may decide on the first method—coach as mirror. With this approach, the teacher self-reflects and assumes a leadership role in the conference. The coach acts as a validator of what the teacher articulates. In many ways, the coach serves as a sounding board—allowing teachers to share observation reflections and plans for using what they have learned. Coaches serve as mirrors, reflecting back to teachers specific examples that support their reflections.

> **Teacher:** As I taught the small-group lessons, I noticed that students in my second group had some misconceptions about fractions. When they shared with partners, I heard several of them say that the greater number is always on the bottom, the denominator. I was wondering what I should do to help them understand fractions better. I think I will work with those students as a group tomorrow to review what they know and correct their misconceptions.
>
> **Coach:** Having students share what they know about fractions with partners to begin the lesson was an effective informal assessment tool. You discovered some crucial misconceptions about fractions and now you can address them.

In the second approach—coach as collaborator—coaches and teachers reflect as a team on the lesson, working together to determine what was most effective and what could be improved. This method of conducting post-observation conferences promotes the collaborative relationship between coaches and teachers. It works well with teachers who are not quite as confident—supporting them as they begin to assume a more active role in the process of reflection.

Teacher: *The students were eager to talk about the Math Stretch today in our Math Huddle. I am pleased that they are so interested and comfortable sharing their ideas. But, I noticed that they are not using many of the mathematical terms they have learned when they are explaining their thinking.*

Coach: *I noticed that, too. Let's see—I saw that you have a Math Word Wall in your classroom. I wonder if there is a way that you can encourage students to make better use of it.*

Teacher: *At the beginning of the year, we played several games using the word wall. The students really began to pay attention to it and were using those words when they talked or wrote about math, but lately I haven't had students do much to interact with it. I think you are on to something! If we revisit some of those games, I think students will be more likely to use it as a resource.*

When meeting with novice teachers or teachers who are attempting Guided Math for the first time, coaches may assume the role of expert. Coaches provide information that helps teachers understand whether they are implementing various components of the framework effectively.

Teacher: *When I was in Ms. Garcia's class today to observe Math Workshop, everyone seemed to know just what to do. They all worked hard and really appeared to be engaged in thinking about math. This just doesn't happen in my classroom. I don't think my kids can do it.*

Coach: *What kinds of problems are you experiencing during Math Workshop?*

Teacher: *My students constantly interrupt my small-group lessons with questions. They keep getting up and moving around the room bothering others, so I have to stop my lesson to attend to them.*

Coach: *I am impressed with all you have accomplished so far in your first year of teaching. The math workstations you have developed for your students are quite effective at reinforcing their mathematical understanding and giving them opportunities to practice computational fluency. That's a great start. Now, to address routines and procedures that will make Math Workshop run more smoothly, have you thought about returning to the First 15 Days plan? Sometimes, you just have to call a halt, so you can help students learn to work independently and you can teach small-group lessons. Let me stop by tomorrow, and we'll see if we can come up with a plan to get Math Workshop to work with your students.*

"Effective analysis and reflection require honesty, which holds true even if teachers are engaged only in self-reflective practice. When other teachers or mathematics coaches are involved, analysis and reflection also require trust" (Hull, Balka, and Miles 2009, Kindle Locations 1047–1048). Most teachers are deeply committed to their profession. They care about their students and work tirelessly to create lessons to inspire them to learn. It can be difficult to acknowledge shortcomings in lessons they have taught. Unless teachers are confident that those with whom they are conferring will be supportive, they are unlikely to acknowledge aspects of their lessons that could be improved or ask others for suggestions to increase their effectiveness.

In much the same way, when observing lessons demonstrated by coaches or taught by peers, teachers may be unwilling to share feedback that is not overwhelmingly positive for fear of offending others. After demonstration lessons, coaches have the opportunity to model honest self-reflection. When coaches are able to describe and discuss parts of their lessons that did not go as they intended or failed to bring about the desired student learning and then turn to others in the post-observation session to assist in problem solving, they establish a climate of collaboration in which teachers are more willing to take risks and follow suit.

Effective post-observation conferences always conclude with teachers reflecting on what they learned from the experience and on how they plan to use it in their teaching. Coaches should make note of the plans proposed by teachers so they can locate and provide resources teachers may need and also follow up to see how those plans are going. With the many demands teachers face daily, some of the plans they intend to implement will invariably be neglected as more pressing obligations arise. When coaches stop by to ask how it is going, it both reminds them of their plans and sends a message that there is an expectation of follow-through on the part of teachers.

After Demonstration Lessons by Coaches

During post-observation conferences following demonstration lessons, coaches have a chance to model active reflection from the perspective of the *teacher of the lesson*. By *thinking aloud* during the post-observation meeting, the coach engages teachers in an examination of the teaching practices used in the lesson from the coach's point of view. When highlighting something in the lesson that went well, the coach may mention specific evidence of student learning to support it. In discussing aspects of the lesson that were not successful, the coach should again look to student learning. These are some questions that can guide the post-observation conversation.

- What instructional strategies were used? Why do you think they were selected for this lesson? How effective were they?

- Was the lesson differentiated? If so, in what ways? How did it meet the needs of most learners?

- What evidence of student learning was observed during the lesson? How was it aligned with the standards being taught?

- What did you notice that made you think the lesson went well? Did not go well?

- What changes might be made to improve the effectiveness of the lesson?

- What are the next steps in learning for these students?

Reflection by the coach sets the stage for later post-observation conferences when the teachers are teaching or co-teaching lessons. The coach is not the only participant in the conversation, however. Teachers should be actively involved in the discourse. The coach should solicit feedback from teachers as well as suggestions for improvement of the lesson and what they noticed about student learning. As a part of this collaborative group, teachers should also be encouraged to ask questions and to share their observations, rather than being passive participants.

In addition to modeling reflective practices, coaches can use post-observation sessions to highlight important aspects of the lesson that they want teachers to notice. What teachers see when they watch a demonstration lesson is strongly influenced by their own background knowledge about teaching and any distractions that occurred during the lesson. Experienced coaches never take it for granted that teachers observing a lesson noticed what the coach intended them to see. Gently guiding post-observations, they ensure that teachers are aware of the important facets of the lesson.

After Co-Teach Lessons

In debrief conversations subsequent to co-teach lessons, coaches not only listen to and encourage teachers' reflections, but also share their own. It is advisable, however, for coaches to listen first as teachers describe their impressions and reflections, so that teachers begin to assume greater responsibility for guiding these conversations.

Because they know their own students so well, teachers usually have powerful insights regarding their students' performance during the lesson and are eager to share these observations with their coaches (co-teachers). But, regardless of how well teachers know their class, the co-teaching format provides teachers a different view of their students. For one, they are able to observe their students a little more intensely because the coach is teaching part of the lesson. Moreover, the students themselves may behave in a very different way when someone other than their math teacher is teaching the lesson.

One of the most important goals of post-observation conferences is "to promote teacher reflection to the highest degree possible, focusing on teacher and student behaviors (Who was doing what?), comparing actual and desired behaviors, or considering reasons why these occurred or did not occur" (Bean 2009, Kindle Locations 2747–2749). By the time teachers and coaches are co-teaching lessons, most teachers will have already experienced post-observation conversations focused on lessons demonstrated by coaches. They should have a good idea of what reflection entails. Even so, the process of reflecting on a lesson is a skill that takes practice to perfect. Teachers may require prompts and encouragement from coaches before they move beyond superficial observations.

Coaches can prompt teachers to reflect in more depth by asking questions that focus on pertinent aspects of the observation. These are some questions that mathematics coaches may use to encourage reflection on co-taught lessons:

- What impact did the Guided Math instructional framework have on our lesson? Did we use it as effectively as possible? If not, what do you think we could do to make it work better for this kind of lesson?

✎ What do you think were the strengths of our lesson? What makes you think so? How can these strengths be applied in other instructional contexts?

✎ Was there anything in the lesson we taught that surprised you? If so, what was it and why did it surprise you?

✎ If there was one thing you could change about the way the lesson went, what would it be? How would you change it? Why?

✎ How would you rate the degree of student engagement? What evidence supports that rating?

✎ Did you notice any misconceptions students had about the content of the lesson? What led you to recognize these misconceptions? Did we effectively address these misconceptions?

✎ Did the lesson achieve the desired learning goals? What evidence of learning leads you to that conclusion?

✎ Was the differentiation of the lesson we provided effective in meeting students' learning needs? What makes you think so? If not, how could we adapt the lesson to make it better?

✎ What do you want to take away and remember from this experience?

These questions stimulate thinking about the co-taught lesson and its consequences in regard to student learning. These are only suggestions, however. In these conversations, coaches can pick and choose from these questions or compose additional questions based on what they noticed about the lesson and what they believe will lead to the greatest improvements in mathematics instruction.

As with all post-observation conferences, teachers should be encouraged to share specific plans for how they will use what they learned in future lessons.

After Teacher-Taught Lessons Observed by Coaches

Hull, Balka, and Miles (2009) remind mathematics coaches that "teachers may feel vulnerable during the reflective phase" (Kindle Locations 1076–1080). This is certainly true when they reflect with the coach on a teacher-taught, coach-observed lesson while in the process of implementing a new instructional framework. During these conferences, the teacher assumes the leading role in reflecting on the lesson. Teachers share what they believe to be the strengths of their lesson, what they noticed about student learning, and what they wish they had done another way. Coaches listen during the initial reflections.

When coaches join these post-observation sessions more actively, their questions should be designed to clarify the thoughts teachers are expressing. The way these questions are asked and the way teachers perceive their role in the conversation are closely correlated. Downey et al. liken a reflective question to a gift. "It's planting a seed for future growth. Its purpose is to enhance a person's thinking on the journey and quest to learn about how he or she makes particular decisions and choices. It is not about answering to a supervisor" (2004, Kindle Locations 830–831).

Teachers should not feel that coaches are quizzing them. Instead, the coaches' questions should clearly reflect their desire to better understand the teachers' thinking and prompt teachers to examine their own thoughts. Questions like these may help coaches better understand the thoughts of teachers.

- How successful do you think you were in achieving the goals you set when we met in the pre-observation conference?

- You said you were not pleased with _____. Can you tell me why?

- What do you think you did during the lesson that helped your students the most as they worked to understand _____?

- How is the implementation of Guided Math affecting teaching and learning in your classroom?

As the reflection process continues, coaches can share what they noticed about the lesson and then offer specific and actionable feedback based on areas identified by teachers during the pre-observation conference. During the lessons, coaches may have noticed a number of instructional needs, but at this point, it is best to keep the feedback relevant to what the teacher requested. Delving into other areas at this time may seem to be overly critical and damage the relationship between teachers and coaches. This is not to say that those needs are never addressed. Coaches should maintain anecdotal notes that document areas of need, so that they can work on these at a later date.

"One of a coach's most important functions is to provide teachers with feedback on their performance. It stands to reason that if a teacher doesn't know what he or she is doing right or wrong, it will be difficult for that teacher to improve his or her knowledge and skill" (Marzano et al. 2013, 10). Many effective teachers call upon others for information about their teaching and depend on their honest critiques of their lessons. But, even when they have requested feedback during the pre-observation conference, "some teachers may react defensively and be unable to accept or benefit from feedback, unless it is provided in a carefully balanced manner" (Bean, 2009, Kindle Locations 2792–2793). Another hazard of providing feedback is "that coaches tend to drift into supervisory roles, which is counter to what…coaching is all about" (Moran 2007, 87). All in all, giving accurate and meaningful, yet tactful feedback requires considerable skill. Bean (2009) offers the following suggestions for feedback.

✎ **Be specific with the feedback.** Never assume that teachers will know what is meant by a vague observation. Just as writing "good job" on a student essay fails to provide sufficient information to let the student know what was done well and how the piece could be improved, telling a teacher the lesson was good or interesting is of little value. Comments such as *"Your questioning technique challenged students to think more deeply about the mathematics in the problem,"* or, *"You were patient and gave students time to struggle to come up with a solution instead of telling them how to solve the problem"* let teachers know that you recognized their teaching strategies and that they worked. And then, comments similar to the following will help teachers grow, *"You asked me to give you feedback on your questioning techniques. While you asked a number of high-level questions, I noticed that you gave students very little wait time before calling on another student or giving them the answer, usually just one second or so. I think you will find students are much more responsive when you give them at least three to five seconds of wait time."*

✎ **Use an approach that includes teachers in finding solutions to problems that were observed.** When giving feedback, describe what was observed and involve the teacher in finding a solution. They know their own teaching preferences and styles as well as their students much better than the coach. When they bring their expertise to the table, they are much more likely to respond positively to the feedback. Coaches might provide the following feedback: *"I noticed that quite a few of your learners struggled with using mathematical vocabulary* *terms. Let's talk about that. Have you thought about how you might address it? I'd like to hear what you are thinking of trying."* This prompts the teacher to consider ways to address the issue and is a perfect opening for the teacher to ask the coach for support, if needed.

- ✎ **Deliver feedback that is balanced.** Teachers need to hear not only what they need to improve, but also what they did well during a lesson. Feedback is more palatable when it begins with something positive. For example, *"Your students know and follow the routines and procedures you have established for Math Workshop very well. I noticed a bit of confusion, however, during transitions. Is there any way you can signal students a few minutes before a transition so they can prepare for it?"*

- ✎ **Focus the feedback on just one or two manageable instructional suggestions.** Teachers can be overwhelmed when presented with a laundry list of "to do's." Especially when working to implement a new approach to teaching math, teachers need to experience successes. Sharing one or two points that can be immediately acted upon by teachers is a much more effective approach. A coach might suggest, *"Students' math talk during your small-group lesson shows that they are really engaged in mathematical thinking. Have you considered building on that engagement at the end of the lesson by having them reflect and then share something mathematical they learned or thought about during the lesson? It can help them mentally review the lesson and organize their thinking."*

- ✎ **Recognize and share the successes of the lesson with teachers.** Teachers can use all the positive reinforcement coaches can give them. Even in lessons that need much improvement, it is important to identify and highlight areas of strength that are evident in the lesson. (Adapted from Bean 2009) Comments such as *"Wow! The way you encourage students to respond to each other's comments rather than only responding to you is impressive. In the Math Stretch Huddle today, the class demonstrated a sense of community and seemed to relish their roles as fledgling mathematicians."*

When post-observation sessions are most effective, teachers come away from it with some firm instructional plans they can implement immediately. The process of reflection with coach feedback and support plays a particularly important role as Guided Math is being implemented.

After Peer Observations

As described earlier in this chapter, coaches may arrange for teachers to participate in peer observations of Guided Math lessons. A post-observation conference makes these visits even more valuable. Ideally, the coach visits the classroom along with the teacher. During the pre-observation meeting, the visiting teacher, the visited teacher and the coach will have discussed the plans for the lesson and the visiting teacher's motivation for viewing the lesson. So, the groundwork for the post-observation conversation was put in place.

All three parties to the conference should be asked to bring their Guided Math Peer Observation forms for reference to help focus their reflections. This meeting begins with the host teacher by reflecting on the lesson from his or her perspective—including whether or not there was evidence that students learned what was intended. Both the coach and the visiting teacher may ask any questions they have, but should allow the teacher to complete his or her comments without interjecting any of their own observations. At this point in the conversation, the focus is what the visiting teacher learned. The visiting teacher tells what he or she noticed during the lesson, asks any questions he or she may have, and then reflects on how what was learned will affect his or her future mathematics instruction.

Coaches usually have in mind some teaching or classroom management strategies they hope the visiting teacher will notice. In the event that the teacher fails to mention them, the coach can direct the conversation toward those strategies—perhaps by sharing an observation or by asking the host teacher to explain their use. This is why the attendance of the coach at both the lesson observation and the post-observation conference is crucial. Unless the coach is there to redirect the focus of the conversation, some important professional learning opportunities may be missed.

Finally, the coach encourages the visiting teacher to set realistic goals for using what was learned from the peer observation. The coach should also check with both teachers to see if any additional resources are needed to make the implementation of Guided Math possible.

The Value of Post-Observation Conferences

To make the most of the coaching process, effective coaches rely on post-observation conferences. These discussions between coaches and teachers serve a number of very valuable functions. These rich dialogues provide the following benefits:

- increase collaboration between coaches and teachers

- promote professional collegiality among teachers

- provide models of reflective practice for teachers

- allow teachers to learn what coaches or other teachers had in mind instructionally as they were teaching demonstration lessons

- allow coaches to learn what teachers had in mind instructionally as they were teaching

- focus attention on the intentionality in planning lessons and on the use of specific instructional strategies

- spotlight the importance of identifying evidence of student learning

- allow teachers to receive specific and timely descriptive feedback that they can act on immediately to improve student learning

- give coaches insight into teachers' thinking and coaching needs

The insight coaches gain from these conversations "affords individualized PD...to directly target areas of concern for teachers during lesson observations" (Rapacki and Francis 2014, 559).

Supporting Guided Math Implementation with Group Planning

Coaches usually have little, if any, input in planning the teaching schedule, but they can advocate for schedules with time built in for collaborative planning. Having common planning times encourages collaboration among teachers and, by having a designated time, it makes it easier for coaches to meet with them. In some schools, coaches meet with grade level teams on a regularly scheduled basis.

If a common planning time is not feasible, administrators may opt to schedule grade level planning meetings in lieu of some regularly scheduled staff meetings. Or, if grade level teachers are working together in a PLC, some of their meeting could be devoted to collaborative planning.

When teachers are beginning to implement the Guided Math framework, having a regularly scheduled support session with a coach can be greatly appreciated. Being in on the planning of Guided Math lessons, coaches more easily discover what resources teachers need and can make them available. They can also encourage teachers to share what has worked well in their classrooms as well as what has not been successful. Although teachers are certainly capable of reflecting in this way as they plan collaboratively, in the daily hubbub and rush to complete planning, it may be overlooked. The participation of someone who is one step removed from daily classroom teaching and who spends considerable time learning about the framework and how it works can make the meetings more productive. This is not to discount the knowledge and experience of teachers; coaches are most effective when they are not providing information, but instead asking questions and supporting a collegial atmosphere in which teachers learn from each other.

Having a regularly scheduled grade-level planning period also makes it easier for coaches to provide snippets of professional development as the need arises. If teachers request more information about a topic or if coaches recognize a need when they are working in classroom, it is relatively easy to schedule a time to provide the training.

Furthermore, common planning times can be used for book studies, looking at student work, or brainstorming solutions to instructional problems. A word of warning to coaches, though—remember that teachers need a great deal of unstructured planning time. Too often, when common planning time is scheduled, it is quickly filled with meetings of one kind or another. When this occurs, the productivity and state of mind of teachers is negatively impacted. If coaches are perceived to be adding to this problem, it negatively affects their relationships with teachers. Instead of seeing coaches as collaborators and resources, teachers begin to see them as burdens.

A Differentiated Approach to Coaching

Just as a *one size fits all* approach to teaching does not work with students, neither does it work with coaching teachers. With great wisdom, Marzano et al. (2013) states that "coaching is not a linear process" (62). All teachers are not beginning at the same place, nor will they progress at the same rate in the same areas. Each teacher's professional learning journey is unique.

Math educator Patricia Smith writes, "Every teacher has strengths and interests that math specialists [or coaches] can build on. The challenge is to discover and uncover them" (2006, 116). It is important that the type of support coaches provide match the needs of the teachers with whom they work. Smith adds, "I would have to work with the teachers at their own level and pace, slow down, and nurture and mentor each teacher individually as we traveled the road to reform together" (111). Just as teachers differentiate instruction for their students, "coaches work at differentiating content, process, and product for their staff" (Hansen 2009, 37). Coaches must recognize that to effectively support teachers.

Effective coaches "do not expect teachers to transition in a linear way through any coaching cycle" (Rapacki and Francis 2014, 563). Earlier in this chapter, several steps in the coaching process were described. There is a logical progression in the way they are presented. This does not mean, however, that all teachers will move through them in that manner. Coaches must be closely attuned to teachers' teaching strengths and needs to develop coaching plans that will meet those needs.

Marzano et al. (2013, 213) suggested the following three ways that coaches can differentiate their work with teachers:

- consider teachers' levels of experience
- determine teachers' readiness for change
- use various kinds of coach–teacher conversations

Differentiating by Teacher Experience

Although math coaches should never make assumptions about teachers based on their years of experience, there are definitely differences between working with a rookie teacher and a veteran teacher. A coach's working relationship with teachers should reflect an awareness of these differences. (See Figure 6.5.)

Figure 6.5 Differentiating Coaching for New and Experienced Teachers

Working with New Teachers	Working with Experienced Teachers
• Encourage teacher to share his or her aspirations and goals. • Schedule shorter coaching sessions to avoid overwhelming the teacher. • Provide initial support in getting classroom set up. • Break professional learning into smaller, more easily mastered chunks. • Create opportunities for peer observations and co-teaching. • Share positive, authentic feedback to build confidence. • Realize that new teachers are sometimes reluctant to ask for help for fear of being viewed as incompetent. • More frequently assume role of coach as expert.	• Encourage teacher to share his or her teaching background and philosophy. • Make longer, more intense coaching sessions available. • Ask teacher to share teaching strengths and areas in which he or she would like to improve. • Provide the professional learning big picture, but be willing to break it down into chunks. • Create opportunities to collaborate with teachers across grade levels. • Encourage goal setting and then provide the resources and support needed. • Realize that even experienced teachers may be reluctant to ask for help. • More frequently assume the role of coach as mirror or collaborator.

(Adapted from Marzano et al. 2013, 214)

In spite of the differences due to varying levels of experience, coaches should always be aware of the fact that implementing a new instructional framework or teaching new standards poses challenges for both new and experienced teachers. It may be easier for a new teacher because they have never taught in any other way; while experienced teachers may be wed to the way they have always done things. Both need considerable support.

Differentiation by Readiness for Change

Anyone who has worked in a school can vouch for the fact that teachers vary drastically in both skill and motivation. Coaches find teachers with more experience are not necessarily the ones with greater skill and motivation—especially motivation for change. Coaches are expected to work with new, inexperienced, but highly motivated teachers; inexperienced teachers who lack motivation; highly experienced teachers who are skilled and motivated to excel; experienced teachers who are skilled with no desire to change; experienced teachers with little skill and little motivation; and everything in between.

Teachers who are most receptive to coaching are those who are motivated. Even when they lack important skills to begin, if they are eager to improve, they will usually acquire them over time. Some of the most frustrating teachers with whom coaches work, particularly when new instructional strategies such as Guided Math are being implemented, are those who lack motivation. Some of these teachers will openly voice their intention to continue with their current modes of instruction while others may express a willingness to change, but when they close their classroom doors, totally ignore any new initiative.

In a previous chapter, it was recommended that coaches first work with those motivated and skilled teachers who are willing to try new strategies. Nevertheless, most coaches will find they have to work with unmotivated teachers as well. The following suggestions are useful for coaches when working with these teachers.

- ✎ **Carefully monitor your demeanor.** Maintaining a positive attitude goes a long way in creating a more pleasant working relationship. Be attuned to your nonverbal signals, such as tone of voice and facial expressions.
- ✎ **Maintain the high expectations for reluctant teachers.** As other teachers move forward, these teachers should experience some discomfort if they choose not to engage in the coaching initiative.
- ✎ **Publicly praise reluctant teachers when they have done something good.** Make the praise very specific and offer it without qualifiers.

- ✎ **Give reluctant teachers time.** Some teachers are scared of change. Accept that it will take these teachers longer to open themselves to a coaching relationship.

- ✎ **Consider meeting in a neutral location.** Refrain from asking reluctant teachers to come to the coach's office or meeting them in their classrooms.

- ✎ **Maintain confidentiality.** Reluctant teachers often feel threatened. Make clear what information from the coaching relationship is confidential, and be sure it remains confidential.

- ✎ **Gently probe the teacher's attitude toward coaching with nonthreatening questions.** This is not a time to be direct; instead, it is a time to attempt to understand so the relationship can move forward productively.

- ✎ **Avoid arguments.** Nothing is achieved through confrontation. One method of remaining emotionally objective is to mirror the teacher's comments, paraphrasing them to be sure they are understood.

- ✎ **Call on an administrator for assistance, if needed.** No matter how reluctant a teacher may be, coaches should never have to endure disrespectful behavior. Do not hesitate to involve an administrator should this occur.

- ✎ **Know when to fold 'em.** Some teachers will never enter into a productive relationship with a coach. Ultimately, spending additional time trying to engage some teachers takes coaching time away from teachers who value it. If this situation exists, a coach should make the administrator aware of it and then let it go. (Adapted from Hansen 2009; Marzano et al. 2013) Coaches should pursue this course with caution. There is always the possibility that others may follow suit.

Differentiation through Coaching Conversations in Guided Math

Coaching conversations support and reinforce all other aspects of the coaching process. There are four kinds of strategic conversations that coaches may employ with teachers: reflecting, facilitating, coaching, and directing (Jackson 2008). Each of these has a different desired outcome, so coaches differentiate their coaching as they decide which kind of conversation is appropriate in a given situation. (See Figure 6.6.)

Figure 6.6 Kinds of Strategic Coaching Conversations

Kind of Conversation	Purpose	Coach's Role	Outcome
Reflecting	Help teachers identify factors that impact classroom instruction	Paraphrasing Active Listening	Realization
Facilitating	Clarify teachers' goals	Clarifying questions	Goals
Coaching	Help teachers understand what is hindering progress	Suggest strategies or revisions to strategies being used	Growth
Directing	Give clear instructions as well as possible consequences	Use of specific language	Action

(Adapted from Jackson 2008)

Reflecting Conversations

Engaging teachers in *reflecting* conversations leads them to identify the ways in which what they believe and how they behave impact their classroom instruction. For example, a coach listens as the teacher describes what happens during Math Workshop.

Teacher: *My class will not take responsibility for working independently during Math Workshop. They interrupt my small-group lessons constantly. I have to tell them how to handle everything that happens. Today, three different students interrupted me asking me questions about what to do next.*

Coach: *Your students interrupt your small-group lessons for directions?*

Teacher:	*Yes, they don't know what to do unless I am right there giving them directions.*
Coach:	*So, they don't have a clear idea of the routines and procedures for Math Workshop.*
Teacher:	*That's true. They have to ask me for directions. When the school year began, we worked on routines and procedures for Math Workshop for a couple of weeks. They were pretty good about not interrupting me then. You know, I think I probably need to go back and have students practice those again. Somehow, I have been assuming that they can't work independently without me telling them what to do every step of the way, but at the beginning of the year, they were pretty good at it.*

As the teacher and coach talked, the teacher realized that he had believed that the students were unable to work independently without ongoing directions from him. As he reflected, he realized that this belief kept him from recognizing the fact that his students had worked independently in the past and just needed to be retaught the routines and procedures for Math Workshop.

Facilitating Conversations

Coaches can lead teachers to clarify their goal through the use of facilitating conversations.

Teacher:	*I really think Guided Math will help my students develop a much deeper understanding of math, so I want to try it in my classroom. But, somehow, it just doesn't seem possible.*
Coach:	*Can you tell me what concerns you about implementing Guided Math?*
Teacher:	*Gosh—there are so many parts to it! I just don't know where to begin.*
Coach:	*Do you think it would be more manageable if you focused on one component at a time?*
Teacher:	*I suppose so.*
Coach:	*Thinking about the seven components, which one do you think would be a good starting point for you?*

Teacher:	*Well, I have really wanted to have a Math Word Wall in my room. Maybe I could work on creating an environment of numeracy first.*
Coach:	*That sounds like a reasonable goal. Tell me—what do you plan to do to make your classroom math-rich?*

This conversation helped the teacher identify her concerns about Guided Math implementation which made the process more manageable by focusing on one goal as a start.

Coaching Conversations

Coaches often have to help teachers recognize instructional shortcomings and ways to remedy them. This is particularly true when teachers are attempting to implement new instructional frameworks in which teachers are moving outside their comfort zones.

Coach:	*It is exciting to see you conducting math conferences with your students.*
Teacher:	*Yes, I think I am ready to try conferring. There is so much I can learn by talking one-on-one with these kiddos. But, I noticed that two of the students I talked with sort of shut down as we talked. That wasn't at all what I expected. I thought they would enjoy talking about their ideas.*
Coach:	*When during the conference did you notice this happening?*
Teacher:	*It seemed to be when I got to the teaching points. They were fine telling me about what they were doing. I saw quite a few things that would make their work better and tried to help them.*
Coach:	*When I look at students' work with them, it can be so hard not to overwhelm them with ways to improve their work.*
Teacher:	*I wonder if that was what I was doing.*
Coach:	*In a math conference, it is best to have only one—or at most two— teaching points. That's usually all these young mathematicians can handle at one time.*
Teacher:	*I am going to do a few more conferences tomorrow. I will really focus on just one teaching point and see how it goes.*

Discussing conferring with students about their mathematical work, the teacher described a difficulty. The coach was able to suggest a way to make conferring more effective.

Directing Conversations

While these conversations are not used frequently, most coaches will encounter them at some time or another. While coaches are not supervisors or administrators, they are sometimes expected to directly share expectations and the consequences for not fulfilling those expectations.

Coach: *I wanted to talk with you today about the fifth grade Guided Math implementation goals.*

Teacher: *Yes.*

Coach: *You and your team of teachers decided to focus on Math Warm-Ups this month and set a goal of having students in each class participate in a Math Stretch twice a week.*

Teacher: *I remember, but my class is a little behind where we should be on the curriculum map, so I have had to focus on trying to catch them up. I just didn't have time to do Math Stretches.*

Coach: *Have you considered using Stretches to help reinforce the content you are teaching?*

Teacher: *I just can't do that. There is no way to do all the work in the lesson in the book and something else, too.*

Coach: *The implementation of Guided Math is a school-wide initiative that we decided on as a community. We all play important roles in making it successful. Participation is not optional. Plan on providing a Math Stretch twice a week for your students. I will help you if you need assistance. Our principal has asked me to document the Math Stretches each fifth-grade class is using each week to monitor progress toward meeting your goal. I will be reporting on the progress of each fifth-grade classroom to the principal.*

With this directing conversation, the coach clearly instructed the teacher to follow through with meeting the grade level goal. An offer of help was given, but so were the consequences of failing to meet the goal.

To some extent, the experience of teachers with whom the coach is working and their readiness for change will determine their needs and the type of conversations that will be most effective. Coaches must be willing to flexibly adapt their coaching strategies as circumstances warrant.

Teacher Self-Assessment and Goal Setting to Determine Differentiation

Differentiation of coaching for individual teachers in Guided Math occurs naturally when teachers are encouraged to establish their own professional learning goals. Throughout the year, they monitor their own progress to determine where they are in relation to meeting their goals and identify their own learning needs. This method of formative assessment helps both teachers and coaches focus on those immediate and pressing needs. Research shows that students are more motivated when they have challenging learning goals (Marzano 2007; Davies 2000). It only follows that "teachers are more likely to be motivated to engage with professional learning if it addresses challenging learning goals for themselves" (Timperley 2011, 49).

Another advantage of this approach to professional development is that it gives teachers a voice. They assume responsibility for identifying their needs in order to implement Guided Math effectively. Coaching is then designed to meet those needs, supporting teachers as they work to achieve their personal professional goals. Focusing coaching efforts on teacher–identified needs demonstrates respect for teachers and fosters teacher ownership of the learning process.

Coach or Administration Identified Teacher Needs

Of course, as coaches work directly with teachers, they may notice areas of need that teachers either do not see or would rather not admit. Some of these may not be worth addressing if the teacher is unwilling, but some may be crucial to their success. Focusing on these areas without teacher willingness is a challenge. (See Differentiation by Readiness for Change section on page 175 for suggestions for working with reluctant teachers.) Of course, many teachers appreciate it when coaches make them aware of ways to improve their teaching and are open to amending their goals to reflect additional professional learning goals.

In the long run, administrators carry the burden of ensuring teaching quality and promoting student learning. Coaches should work closely with administrators, keeping them informed of progress. There may come a time when a coach and administrator decide together that the coach's time would be better spent supporting teachers who are more amenable to the coaching process.

Review & Reflect

1. Reflect on a positive learning experience you have had. What about the experience best supported your learning? How can you use that in your work as an educational leader?

2. Now, reflect on a negative learning experience. What are some of the characteristics of that experience? How can you use what you remember about that experience in your role as an educational leader?

3. Consider this scenario: Your school has decided to implement Guided Math to address the learning needs of its very diverse student body. Over half the students are English language learners. By November, the implementation plan called for teachers to teach small-group lessons at least three times a week. While most teachers have met this goal, one teacher has implemented Math Workshop, but not small-group instruction. As a coach, what else would you want to know? How would you handle this situation?

Chapter 7

Guided Math Professional Learning Communities

One way for educational leaders to encourage and support the implementation of the Guided Math framework is by establishing Guided Math Professional Learning Communities (PLCs). By participating in these collaborative study groups, teachers are able to learn about each of the components of Guided Math, plan Guided Math lessons collaboratively, reflect on their own teaching and their students' learning when using the framework, observe their peers as they implement Guided Math, and examine evidence of student learning to gauge the effectiveness of the implementation.

Gulamhussein (2013) writes "research suggests that there's an exceptionally strong relationship between communal learning, collegiality, and collective action (key aspects of Professional Learning Communities) and changes in teacher practice and increasing student learning" (24). Since "teachers learn best by studying, doing, and reflecting; by collaborating with other teachers, by looking closely at students and their work; and by sharing what they see" (Darling-Hammond 1999, 2), it is essential that educational leaders create a climate in which that occurs on a regular basis.

Professional Learning Communities highlight the fact that teaching is a *profession*. A profession can be defined as "a type of job that requires special education, training, or skill" (Merriam-Webster 2015). The inclusion of the words *special education, training, or skill* in the definition is paramount. As a profession, teaching demands ongoing education and training. According to Danielson (2007), "continuing development is the mark of a true professional; it is an ongoing effort that is never completed" (102).

Engagement in PLCs allows educators to further their profession through inquiry, collaboration, and reflection as well as other forms of learning (e.g., book studies, videos, and webinars) to construct shared knowledge that will be applied in the classroom. "It is only when a staff begins to apply new learning that teachers will come to the deeper level of understanding that enables them to adapt new practices to their own setting" (DuFour 2004, 64).

Providing opportunities for teachers to flourish as intellectuals enhances their teaching and demonstrates a respect for them as professionals. PLCs afford teachers the following:

✎   time and resources which will allow them to think through and fashion innovative teaching methods

✎   a support system as they begin to implement them, so that the implementation process results not in frustration, but in continued and refined practice (Gulamhessein 2013, 23)

These learning teams provide a structure of "continuous adult learning, strong collaboration, democratic participation, and consensus about the school environment and culture" (Hord and Sommers 2008, Kindle Locations 257–258). As such, they "serve to sustain change initiatives and empower teachers" (Balka, Hull, and Miles 2010, 108)—exactly what is needed when a new instructional method is being implemented.

There are significant differences between PLCs and other teams of teachers that are created to carry out specific tasks (e.g., creating assessments, revising report cards, developing behavior plans). Those teams may be used to pave the way for PLCs, but should not be mistaken for an effective PLC. Mathematics leaders should be aware of these aspects of Professional Learning Communities that may make their establishment a challenge:

✎   PLCs focus on student achievement and how teaching impacts it, rather than a specific task.

✎   PLCs rely on a level of teacher engagement and trust that is not often established in working teams.

✎   PLCs require a commitment from teachers that often necessitates extra effort on the part of leaders to build because of teachers' lack of understanding or because of previous failed initiatives. (Balka, Hull, and Miles 2010, 112)

Because of these factors, "strong leadership is a critical factor in the success of Professional Learning Communities" (Jones and Vreeman 2008, 153). When leaders work closely with the professional community to empower teachers, identify a shared vision, and develop common goals, the groundwork is laid for effective PLCs.

As Stoll, Fink, and Earl (2003) explain, "being a learning community is also a state of mind, is not linear, is bigger than the sum of its parts, and is about learning as a community" (Kindle Locations 2512–2513). In spite of the efforts needed by leaders to establish efficiently operating PLCs, "Professional Learning Communities have emerged as arguably the best, most agreed-upon means by which to continuously improve instruction and student performance" (Schmoker 2006, Kindle Locations 1569–1571).

Establishing Guided Math Professional Learning Communities

Hord and Sommers (2008) liken the task of establishing of PLCs to that of launching a space capsule. Space engineers expect the lift-off to consume 90 percent of the fuel. The same is true for the process of initiating PLCs. "Overcoming status quo to initiate new ways of interacting requires lots of energy in the beginning phases" (Kindle Locations 945–946). The principal is often the catalyst for this shift in professional learning. Math leaders, however, should not initiate the process in order to "push their own improvement plans" (Balka, Hull, and Miles 2010, 111). Only when the decision to implement Guided Math is part of a vision for school improvement shared by the community should Guided Math PLCs be started.

Planning for Professional Learning Communities

Before beginning the process of establishing Guided Math PLCs, it is important for math leaders to envision how these teams will be organized and will operate. How will the teams be formed? Should teams be made up of teachers from a single grade level or should they be composed of teachers from several grade levels? Each has its advantages. If Guided Math PLCs are made up of teachers of a single grade level, they can engage in common planning and share their experiences teaching the same lessons. Heterogeneous teams, however, give teachers perspectives on vertical alignment of the curriculum that contributes to their overall vision of its progression.

How large will each Guided Math PLC be? Will teams be selected by leaders to ensure a distribution of team leaders and diversity within each group or should they be self-selected? When will they meet? How frequently will they meet? How will the workings of these teams be monitored? What kind of reporting system will they use? Who should teams turn to for support and resources, if needed? These are only a few of the questions leaders face before they implement Guided Math PLCs.

It is also important to remember that while some PLC team members examine data to come up with a focus after teams are formed, the focus of Guided Math PLCs is predetermined—the implementation of the Guided Math framework. Working through the processes described in Part I, the educational community has already developed a shared vision and identified the implementation of Guided Math as a goal to address its needs. Therefore, the work of the PLCs is to make that implementation occur as effectively as possible. To reach this goal, teachers engage in site-based professional learning that is a "focused, coherent effort to develop the collective capacity of school personnel to solve problems and sustain continuous improvement" (DuFour 2004, 63). Teachers build a shared knowledge about Guided Math through their work in PLCs that, when applied in the classroom, leads to comprehensive school improvement.

Teachers collaborate within self-managed teams to improve both teaching and learning. While this occurs, "the principal's job is to monitor, discuss, and support teachers' progress in achieving higher levels of student learning.... This is the best use of his or her valuable time" (Schmoker 2005, 147).

Launching Guided Math Professional Learning Communities

Once the structural and organizational format for PLCs is determined, there are five steps leaders can take to get them up and running.

1. **Educate the professional community about Guided Math PLCs.** The implementation process begins with leaders educating the professional community about Guided Math PLCs. Especially important is educating those individuals who are well respected within the school community. When those educators become enthusiastic about the value of PLCs, they convince others of their worth.

2. **Train teachers how to engage in professional learning through PLCs.** To some, the prospect of working together with other teachers to change their current teaching practices may seem a little threatening. Leaders can allay some of these concerns by providing training on the functioning of PLCs. The success of PLCs is dependent upon teachers having a sense of collective efficacy, "group members' shared perception or belief that they can dramatically enhance the effectiveness of an organization" (Marzano, Waters, and McNulty 2005, Kindle Location 1790). The existence of this sense of being able to collectively make a difference is critical because it has been found to be a better indicator of student success than the socioeconomic status of students. Leaders must champion the belief that teachers' joint efforts really do make a difference and be able to back it up by highlighting examples.

   In addition to having a belief in collective efficacy, teachers must learn how to engage in "meaningful professional conversations within the collegial setting of the PLC" (Balka, Hull, and Miles 2010, 114) for PLCs to function effectively. Most teachers have had little experience with these kinds of conversations, so it should not be assumed that they have these skills. The listening, clarifying, reflecting, and probing skills needed for these professional conversations should be explicitly modeled and discussed during faculty meetings and coach-led meetings, so that teachers learn how to apply them when working together in PLCs. The use of protocols provides structure for the discussions, but before they can be used, teachers have to learn about them and how to use them effectively.

3. **Nurture the development of PLCs.** PLCs need support and resources to flourish. Teams should know to whom they should turn when they need either of those. If PLCs are to implement Guided Math, they require resources to support their initial learning about the framework (e.g., books, overview training, model lessons, and manipulatives). Moreover, occasional release time allows teachers to observe their peers as they implement Guided Math in their classrooms so they can see how others are implementing the components of the framework. They need to have leaders to turn to who will make these observations possible.

   While principals may be responsible for providing some of these resources, coaches are frequently the "go to" people for PLCs. If coaches are not available, an assistant principal, a lead teacher, or a curriculum director may be designated. Whoever serves in this capacity, however, must have a deep understanding of the Guided Math framework and how it can be used in the classroom. As the implementation process continues, PLCs will also require assessment data and time for teachers to analyze it to gauge the impact of this instructional framework on student achievement.

4. **Monitor the work of the PLCs.** Leaders need to be aware of what occurs in PLCs—but, not in an evaluative or secretive way. If PLCs are important enough to be taken seriously by staff members, they are worthy of the close attention of leaders. The extent of a leader's focus and attention to the operation of PLCs signals to the professional community the importance of the work of these teams. Leaders may monitor PLCs by attending meetings, reading meeting minutes, making classroom visits, or analyzing relevant data on student achievement. In most schools, PLCs submit meeting minutes to keep leadership informed of their work and this information can be shared with the entire professional community.

   The task of monitoring is not limited to being aware of what occurs in meetings, but should also include checking to see that this professional learning positively impacts classroom teaching and learning. The expectation is that teachers will apply what they are learning to increase their instructional effectiveness. "Teachers need to understand the process of monitoring and accept feedback as they do other supportive data" (Balka, Hull, and Miles 2010, 114). Additionally, as teacher leaders emerge from the PLCs, administrative and coaching leaders may meet with them as mentors and candidly discuss the functioning of the PLCs.

5. **Celebrate the successes of the PLCs.** To promote a sense of collective efficacy among teachers, it is important to highlight their successes. Celebrations of PLC accomplishments reinforce the belief that their collaborative efforts do, in fact, result in increased student achievement. Moreover, Amabile and Kramer (2011) find that "progress motivates people to accept difficult challenges more readily and to persist longer" (Kindle Location 91). Thus, the celebration of small achievements by leaders motivates PLC teams to continue to take risks and persist in their efforts to increase student learning.

Making Time for Guided Math Professional Learning Communities

Collaborative learning in Guided Math PLCs takes time. And, time is in short supply in schools. But, perhaps the problem is not just a lack of time, but how the time is used. Stoll, Fink, and Earl (2003) share the story of a man struggling to saw trees with a dull saw. When someone suggests that he sharpen the saw, he explains that he has so much to do that he does not have time to sharpen the saw. "If we organize our days and weeks a little better and find time to 'sharpen the saw' then our productivity increases and our mental well-being improves" (Kindle Locations 2393–2396). This is, of course, a problem that educational leaders wrangle with on a regular basis. Yet, leaders have the responsibility of prioritizing and making time for what has the greatest potential for increasing student learning. So, how can time be better organized?

Calling upon the professional community for solutions to the time problem can generate ideas specific to a given school. This kind of brainstorming activity is beneficial because it is inclusive of all members of the community. It leads teachers to not only recognize the problem, but also to be a part of its solution. Hord and Sommers (2008) offer leaders a host of possible ways to make time for PLCs that were proposed by the Southwest Educational Development Laboratory, some of which are listed as follows:

- Bank time by choosing one hour a week before or after school for PLC meetings which would be compensated for by eliminating district-wide professional development days.

- Extend the school day or year to give additional time.

- Have PLCs meet before or after school.

- Pay for Saturday PLC meeting time.

- Handle administrative matters in writing so regular faculty meeting time could be used for PLCs.

- Have teachers from one grade level host "buddy work" with another grade level so that those teachers could meet for PLCs—then trade off the following week.

- Procure grant money to pay stipends for teachers meeting in PLCs after working hours.

- Use state professional development days to create time for PLCs during the school year.

- Provide compensatory time off that can be taken by teachers before or after regular school hours to make up for extra time spent in PLC meetings. (Adapted from Hord and Sommers 2008, Kindle Locations 791–803)

Unless provisions are made for adequate meeting time, Professional Learning Communities will fail to flourish. If teachers feel rushed or severely imposed upon, they may attend, but will only nominally participate. Finding ways to make time for high quality professional learning demonstrates the commitment of leaders to support teachers' professional development and their confidence that when teachers work together, it makes a difference.

School-Wide Support for Guided Math Professional Learning Communities

The success of Guided Math PLCs rests on the entire professional community—leaders, teachers, and support staff. Without whole-hearted commitment from everyone involved, PLCs can become just another ineffective professional development strategy. According to Fullan (2005), "building a PLC is difficult, but it is also unquestionably doable. Educators will be required to act in new ways, to do differently. They will confront decisions regarding what needs to be done and what they need to stop doing" (250). Moving beyond the status quo is never easy. "There are brutal facts regarding the traditional structure and culture of schools that must be brought to the surface, examined, and discussed in the process of building a PLC. Educators who acknowledge and honestly assess their current reality are far more likely to be successful in changing it" (250). When leaders make it a priority to create supportive professional learning environments, teachers are empowered to honestly examine and assess the reality of their teaching and make the efforts necessary to refine and improve their instructional practices.

Establishing Norms for Guided Math Professional Learning Communities

Guided Math PLCs work most effectively when their members are melded into close-knit teams that share visions of educational excellence for students and work together to make those visions a reality. Efforts to build strong and coherent teams should focus on the improvement of individual member's ability to learn and work with others—even those with whom they may disagree. In order to improve communication and build stronger relationships within PLCs, a "primary approach to team learning is improved conversation through dialogue and skillful discussion" (Kaser et al. 2013, Kindle Location 131).

Garmston (2007) suggests seven norms for collaborative conversation and learning. Norms are "the foundation tools with which groups can dialogue, engage productively in conflict, discuss and decide, invent and problem solve" (Garmston 2007, para. 9) all of which are essential for collaborative learning. These norms are:

✎ **"Promote a spirit of inquiry."** Learning results from the questioning of both one's own thinking and that of others. In collaborative ventures, one should expect their thinking to be scrutinized and questioned. One should not only expect it, but value it.

- ✎ **"Pause."** Just as teachers are encouraged to do when teaching a class, PLC members should adopt the habit of pausing before they respond to a comment or ask a question. Pauses provide time for everyone to think before they speak, thus enriching dialogue, discussion, and decision-making.

- ✎ **"Paraphrase."** To ensure accurate understanding of ideas expressed by others, members should paraphrase what was said using starters such as "As you were saying…" or "You are thinking…"

- ✎ **"Probe."** Members of PLCs should probe the thinking and meaning of others by asking them to tell more about their ideas to better understand, but also demonstrate interest in what others in the group have in mind.

- ✎ **"Put ideas on the table."** In productive learning communities, members share their ideas with others. This action indicates a respect for the collaborative process. "Ideas are at the heart of a meaningful dialogue."

- ✎ **"Pay attention to oneself and others."** PLCs are composed of teachers whose perceptions vary greatly. Whenever members share their thoughts, they should be mindful of the way in which they are expressing them and attuned to the way they are being perceived by others. Many times, the way an idea is expressed is as important to listeners as the idea itself.

- ✎ **"Presume positive intentions."** The assumption of the good intentions of others leads to more productive and meaningful dialogue and avoids unintentional slights.

In addition to norms to promote conversational skills, members of learning communities also have to become skillful at working together collaboratively. Teams should begin their work together by establishing norms to govern their meetings and to be adhered to by all members. After these expectations for behaviors are compiled by the PLC, they should be reviewed at the beginning of each meeting to emphasize their importance and to ensure that they are followed. The meeting norms should be simply and clearly stated—and limited in number (i.e., 5–7). Some of the norms most commonly selected by PLCs are as follows:

✎ Begin and end meetings on time.

✎ Turn off all cell phones and other electronic devices during the meeting.

✎ Be respectful of all. Discuss ideas, not people.

✎ Come to each meeting prepared, having completed agreed upon tasks and with the necessary materials.

✎ Listen carefully and with an open mind to everyone's ideas, even if you do not agree.

✎ Invite and encourage the participation of everyone.

✎ All members will share leadership responsibilities according to an agreed upon schedule.

✎ Openly share information you have that is relevant to the conversation.

✎ Remain focused on the goals of the PLC.

Using Protocols in Guided Math Professional Learning Communities

A protocol is a structure to guide professional learning conversations. Its purpose is to "build the skills and promote the culture necessary for ongoing collaborative learning" (Glaude 2005, 2). Although the use of protocols may seem awkward initially, with practice, groups find that they provide valuable structure to conversations and allow meetings to be much more productive. PLCs use protocols for the following reasons:

✎ to keep conversations focused

✎ to encourage all members to offer feedback and insights on a topic

✎ to support less vocal members to enter the conversations

✎ to promote thoughtfulness by allowing time for personal reflection

✎ to encourage lively discussion from multiple perspectives

✎ to focus attention on evidence rather than just opinions

✎ to provide a safe and supportive structure for the examination of teaching and learning (Adapted from Glaude 2005, 2)

With most protocols, a facilitator from the PLC is assigned to keep the conversation moving and to keep time. A few protocols follow, but many others are available.

The "Final Say on Quotes Protocol" (See Figure 7.1) requires members to find evidence to support quotes from reading that the entire group has read. Since an important component of a Guided Math implementation plan is learning about the framework by reading the professional materials available (See Appendix C for a list of Guided Math resource materials), this is an appropriate protocol to use for book studies of these resources.

Figure 7.1 Final Say on Quotes Protocol

---

1. **Introduction (2 minutes):** A facilitator and timekeeper are selected and the protocol procedures are reviewed.
2. **Preparation (5 minutes):** Members read the selected section of the text and choose three quotes for discussion.
3. **Response to a Quote (6 minutes each round):** One member reads a quote and gives its page number, but does not comment on it. In round robin style, each member offers responses (thoughts or experiences related to the quote), building on what has already been said. The person who suggested the quote listens, but remains quiet. When each member has responded, the person who read the quote has the *final say*—explaining the personal significance of the quote and commenting on what was learned by listening to the comments of others. This process is repeated until all members have presented a quote or until no time remains.
4. **Debrief (2 minutes):** PLC members reflect on how the protocol supported their learning and how it might be improved upon.

(Adapted from Glaude 2005, 16)

The "A Change in Practice Protocol" provides a method of analyzing the process team members use to make changes in their teaching practices (See Figure 7.2). This is particularly useful as teachers begin the implementation of the components of the Guided Math framework. It is recommended for groups of three, so larger groups can break down into smaller working teams. This protocol takes approximately 75 minutes to complete.

Figure 7.2 A Change in Practice Protocol

1. **Writing (10 minutes):** Each member of the team writes about a change he or she has made in teaching in as much detail as possible. It should specify what happened, like a snapshot, yet be very succinct. The narrative should answer these questions:
   - What change was made?
   - How did you decide what to do?
   - How do you know whether the change was successful?
   - What are you wondering about now?
2. **Presenting (5–7 minutes):** One member presents, either reading his or her account or telling the story.
3. **Clarifying (5 minutes):** Members of the team ask clarifying questions.
4. **Discussion (10 minutes):** The group discusses what the presenter shared— paying particular attention to evidence presented. The discussion focuses on the process of change and how that process may be applied for future changes. The presenter listens and takes notes.
5. **Reflection (5 minutes):** The presenter reflects on what was discussed and the implications for the teaching practices of the PLC members.
6. **Repeat each round. (27 minutes)**
7. **Debrief (5 minutes):** The group discusses what has occurred and what was learned from the process.

(Adapted from Thompson-Grove 2015)

Figure 7.3 shows a sample of a Change in Practice Protocol.

Figure 7.3 Sample Change in Practice Protocol

1. **Writing (10 minutes):**
   - **What change was made?** *I began conferring with students this month.*
   - **How did you decide what to do?** *After reading* Guided Math Conferences *(Sammons 2014), I made a plan. Every Friday, I identify two students whose work I have wondered about. I try not to seem to talk down to them—to have a real conversation. I am really interested in what they think and hope that they begin to see themselves as mathematicians.*
   - **How do you know whether the change was successful?** *I believe conferences have been beneficial for my students. They seem eager to meet with me. I see how they really try to sound like mathematicians as we talk about their work. They try hard to use the appropriate math vocabulary. For me, these conferences have been extremely helpful. I know so much more about what these students are thinking and how I can help them be more successful in their work. For example, one student stated that he "knew" that in a fraction the denominator was always the greater number. What an eye opener for me! There was nothing in his written math work that indicated that misconception.*
   - **What are you wondering about now?** *Now, I am wondering how often I should confer with these students. Do I need to have conferences with all my students?*

2. **Presenting (5–7 minutes):** One member presents, either reading his or her account or telling the story.

3. **Clarifying (5 minutes):** Members of the team ask these clarifying questions:

How did you find time to confer? I did both conferences as students began working independently in Math Workshop, and then began my small-group lessons.

What in particular made you choose the students you conferred with? One student always seems to have the correct answer but is very quiet during class. He never shares his thinking. Another student makes quite a few errors. I am never sure whether it is because she is in a hurry and is careless or whether she just doesn't understand the concepts.

Did your conferences include teaching points? For the student who is so quiet, I didn't have a math teaching point. I mainly wanted to encourage him and make him more confident so he is willing to share his ideas. For the student with the misconception about fractions, there was definitely a teaching point. We clarified her understanding, and I plan to follow up with her later to be sure she understands now.

Do you feel like you need to confer with all of your students? No, I guess I don't, but I don't want students to feel as if I am neglecting them. I suppose I do want to confer with each one of them at some time during the year, but don't need to do it on a regular basis.

4. **Discussion (10 minutes):** *The discussion focused on the issue of finding time for conferences. Teachers shared ideas for when they may be able to meet one-on-one with students. There was also much interest in how conferences can be used for assessment purposes. Some members of the group wondered how effective teaching points could be given the limited amount of time to deliver them.*

5. **Reflection (5 minutes):** *The presenter thanked the group for helping her come to terms with how frequently to meet with students. The discussion helped her think more about how to effectively decide on and then deliver a teaching point. It also prompted her to consider how to record assessment data obtained during conferences.*

6. **Repeat each round (27 minutes)**

7. **Debrief (5 minutes):** The group discusses what has occurred and what was learned from the process.

The "Carousel Brainstorm Protocol" (See Figure 7.4) is used to generate ideas for solving problems. As PLC members begin to implement Guided Math, they will encounter problems—as occurs with the implementation of any new instructional approach. This protocol encourages members to collaboratively arrive at solutions for the implementation glitches that may arise.

Figure 7.4 Carousel Brainstorm Protocol

1. **Preparation (10 minutes):** At the beginning of the meeting, the PLC identifies several problems to be addressed. Each one is written on a separate piece of chart paper and hung around the room. The PLC is divided into as many groups as there are problems and each group is assigned a problem.

2. **Brainstorming (5 minutes per rotation):** Groups are given time to brainstorm solutions to their assigned problem. They are asked to add their solutions to the chart. Groups move to the next charts and repeat the process until all groups have considered each problem.

3. **Debrief (10 minutes):** Have the group meet as a whole to consider the proposed solutions and determine either a group or individual plan of action.

(Adapted from Stoll, Fink, and Earl 2003, Kindle Locations 2853–2863)

Figure 7.5 shows a sample of the Carousel Brainstorm Protocol.

Figure 7.5 Sample Carousel Brainstorm Protocol

1. **Preparation (10 minutes):** At the beginning of the meeting, the PLC identifies several problems to be addressed. Each one is written on a separate piece of chart paper and hung around the room. The PLC is divided into as many groups as there are problems and each group is assigned a problem. *The group is focusing on Math Workshop during this meeting. Each of these problems is noted on a piece of chart paper and posted:*
   - Finding Worthwhile Workstation Tasks
   - What to Do if the Technology Is Not Working
   - How to Prevent Interruption of Small-Group Lessons
   - Making Students Accountable for their Workstation Work
2. **Brainstorming (5 minutes per rotation):** Groups noted possible solutions to their assigned problem and added their solutions to the chart. Groups moved to the next charts and repeated the process until all groups had considered each problem.
3. **Debrief (10 minutes):** Since the problems presented were individual classroom issues, teachers were given time to determine which of these possible solutions they plan to incorporate into their Math Workshop. Teachers then shared their plans with the group.

Reflection in Guided Math Professional Learning Communities

"The learning in successful learning communities is based on collegial inquiry and on reflection by the participants and their dialogue about their reflection" (Hord and Sommers 2008, Kindle Locations 281–282). This type of reflective process carried out with colleagues has not been common practice in education until recently. Because of the hectic lives of teachers, "if reflection is not practiced during Professional Learning Community meetings, it is likely not to take place at all" (Balka, Hull, and Miles 2010, 116). Yet, it "provides teachers a powerful and much needed feedback mechanism that…enhances their feelings of efficacy" (Conzemius and O'Neill 2001, 70).

Collaborative reflection is especially valuable for teachers who are in the process of implementing the Guided Math framework. Working in PLCs, teachers refine their teaching practices through reflection on the relationships between teaching methods they use and their students' mathematical achievement. Although educational leaders may participate in PLCs, it is imperative that the meetings are "opportunities for teachers to think carefully about their teaching practices and the student learning that is (or is not) happening in their classrooms" (Balka, Hull, and Miles 2010, 117). Teachers should feel safe to share concerns or ways in which they would like to improve their instruction. So, if leaders play a role in the reflection process, they should be mainly listeners. Any questions they pose must be carefully worded so they are open-ended and non-threatening. Teachers should never feel that they are being interrogated or evaluated as they participate in PLCs.

Hord and Sommers (2008) describe four kinds of reflection that may be a part of collaborative professional learning. With all of these reflective practices, teachers share their observations and their thinking, always linked to and supported by evidence of student learning.

Reflection *on* Action

This is the type of reflection that most commonly occurs. It is thinking back on something that has happened to consider what might be done differently in the future to obtain different results, to identify patterns in teaching practices, and to assess their effectiveness. As teachers work together to learn more about the implementation of Guided Math, reflection on action provides motivation for changing their instructional techniques and for refining their attempts at implementation. According to Hord and Sommers (2008), research shows that this type of reflection has a positive impact on both teaching and learning. These questions tend to prompt reflection on action:

✎ How do you think the lesson went? What makes you think so?

✎ What evidence do you have of student learning?

✎ Did you get the results you expected? Why or why not?

✎ How did the actual lesson compare to what you intended?

After implementing Math Warm-Ups, a PLC member who is reflecting on action may share comments like these:

The students were great about following directions and getting the Math Stretch done as they entered the classroom. I had difficulty getting students to engage in math talk during the Huddle. They are much more comfortable having me ask a question they can respond to. Then, they want me to let them know if their answer was right or not. It is going to take some time to change this. They are beginning to think more like mathematicians, though. Several of them noticed patterns in the Math Stretch work and were excited about it. To me, that is evidence of student learning. I just want to see more of it.

Reflection *for* Action

This kind of reflective thinking requires teachers to think forward considering how to improve their teaching. Reflection for action leads PLCs to set goals, plan changes in teaching methods, and explore ways to measure success together as a team. These are all critical steps as teachers implement Guided Math in their classrooms. The following questions encourage reflection for action:

✎ What goals do you have for Guided Math implementation?

✎ How do you plan to meet those goals?

✎ How will you know if the impact of this instructional framework is successful?

✎ What evidence of achievement will you collect to determine effectiveness?

As PLCs implement Guided Math, a member of the group who is reflecting on action may make the following comments:

By the end of the week, my class should be ready to begin Math Workshop. That is my goal. For the rest of the week, we will be practicing routines and procedures. If I have done my work well—teaching these routines and procedures—students should be ready to assume the responsibility of working independently. I have a plan to hold students accountable. They will record their work in a math journal that I will be able to quickly check over at the end of the math class.

Reflection *in* Action

This form of reflection takes place while teachers are actually teaching, so it is not frequently a part of PLC discussions. When reflection in action occurs, teachers are actively involved in adjusting instruction spontaneously to meet student needs and respond to any other factors that are affecting the lesson.

Although this kind of reflection is rarely shared collaboratively, doing so can be beneficial. Members of the PLC may agree to document their *reflections in action* that occur during a lesson and to show how their reflection impacted the lesson. It is best that these thoughts be recorded as soon after the lesson as possible while the reflective experience is still fresh. When the PLC meets, one member is selected to present his or her *reflection in action* experience while the others listen. The other PLC members then respond to the presentation with their thoughts regarding the experience in round robin fashion. Finally, the presenting teacher comments on what was learned from listening to the others. This is repeated until all members have had an opportunity to present or until time runs out.

When sharing a reflection in action, a teacher reported:

As I was teaching a small-group lesson today, I suddenly realized that I was doing most of the talking. One of the things I like most about the small-group lesson format is the opportunity for students to do most of the talking. I just sort of stopped short! What am I doing? Of course, I immediately changed course and shifted the responsibility for math talk to my students.

Reflection Within

This sort of reflection happens when teachers are quiet and have time to think by themselves. Some of the deepest and most insightful reflection that teachers do is *reflection within*. As with reflection in action, it is not often part of PLC discussions—and that is unfortunate. When teachers develop trust for one another and are willing to share, there are ways to include it.

Reflections from within tend to be more personal. Here is an example of what might be shared:

I was so tired when I went home last night. On the drive home, I kept replaying my math lesson in my mind. It just didn't go the way I wanted it to. I realized that instead of allowing my students to struggle productively to solve the math problem we were working on, I got in a hurry. I moved them right along by providing the next steps for them. I know that happens to all of us, but I was disappointed in myself. I know better and will do better.

Leadership for Robust Professional Learning Communities

The quality of ongoing professional learning through PLCs is highly dependent on the ability of leaders to first create and then maintain them. Stoll, Fink, and Earl (2003) contend that educational leaders are challenged to "maintain a school's momentum in creative and exciting ways—'creative continuity'" (Kindle Locations 2429–2430). The actions of leaders "shape a school or school system's structure and culture in ways that promote learning, collaboration, and environments in which all members of the community feel cared for and respected" (Sparks 2005, 157).

Educational leaders who wish to foster robust Professional Learning Communities should:

✎ Understand that teachers can be compelled to engage in collaborative learning, "but only they can volunteer their hearts and minds" (Reeves 2006, 52). Leaders should create an environment where most teachers *choose* to learn as part of a PLC.

✎ Provide structures that require teachers to participate in PLCs and ensure that times are built into the school schedule for this collaborative work. They should create a professional environment that clearly sends a message that collaboration is standard operating procedure for all educators.

✎ Require all PLCs to establish norms and protocols that provide structure for their collaborative work.

- Require that all PLCs have learning goals that are linked to specific and measurable student achievement results.

- Solicit feedback from PLCs about the resources and training they need to meet their goals. It is important to provide those resources, if at all possible.

- Monitor the progress of all PLCs through meeting attendance, meeting minutes, classroom visits, and review of relevant data on student achievement.

- Develop ways for PLCs to share what they are learning and accomplishing with the rest of the professional community. Leaders can establish ways to share PLC minutes regularly. Or, they can ask PLCs to make quarterly presentations. In these ways, everyone benefits from the labors of each team.

- Celebrate the progress PLCs make. Successes tend to yield further success and are proof that teachers working together can make a difference.

- If participation in PLCs is mandated by administrators, confront individuals or teams who fail to participate in this collaborative learning approach. Leaders should make it clear that participation is mandatory for all. Nothing is more demoralizing to hard working PLCs than being aware that others simply opt out of the process with no consequences. (Adapted from DuFour 2004)

Yet, even with strong and effective leadership, difficulties should be expected. Fullan (2005) writes "we know of no faculties that have developed their capacity to create a PLC that did not experience failure and conflict along the way. Those who assume they can completely avoid these problems are either naïve or arrogant" (251). Able leaders acknowledge problems and work through conflicts. They view "an attempt gone awry as a chance to begin again more intelligently" (251).

Being aware of common barriers to collaborative learning communities prepares educational leaders for problems and, in some cases, allows them to avert glitches. Sparks (2005) lists the following as primary barriers to PLCs:

- ✎ failure to clarify values, intentions, and beliefs
- ✎ dependence on outsiders for solutions
- ✎ a sense of resignation among teachers who lack a belief in collective efficacy (162)

Most math leaders are well aware of the fact that what is assessed and monitored by principals or other administrators will be given increased attention by other members of the professional community. This wisdom can be applied to the task of maintaining effective and productive PLCs. "Attending to how well each individual is operating in the PLC and understanding how and why each person is working enables the school leadership to provide assistance to all individuals" (Hord and Sommers 2008, Kindle Locations 1489–1490). Knowing of the level of participation of individuals is of little value in and of itself. Only when that knowledge leads to steps to promote greater engagement is this knowledge beneficial. "Assistance is the essential follow-up to assessment—the two go hand in hand" (Kindle Locations 1488–1489).

The Issue of Guided Math Implementation Fidelity

A word of advice to leaders when PLCs are an integral part of the process of implementing Guided Math: be open to the adaptation of the framework by teachers. Timperley (2011) expressed it well when she wrote "in any professional learning situation, teachers adapt what is learned to their particular contexts. Professional learning facilitators sometimes see these adaptations as problems with implementation…. In reality, if they wish teachers to become responsive to students, then adaptations should be expected" (171).

Of course, it is important that teacher adaptations are consistent with the basic tenets of the framework—particularly its emphasis on small-group lessons targeted to meet students' learning needs—and that they lead to improved student learning. The fidelity to which it is implemented, however, should be to its instructional theory rather than to any specific aspect of the framework itself.

Educational leaders should monitor PLCs and the implementation of the Guided Math framework with the understanding that it is not a "one size fits all" approach to instruction. When teachers collaboratively learn about the Guided Math components and then try them out in their classrooms, they should have the ability to make them fit their own teaching styles and the needs of their students. In fact, teachers should be commended for engaging in a critical examination of the instructional framework and for determining how it can best be applied in their classrooms.

Assessing the Effectiveness of Guided Math Professional Learning Communities

The importance of monitoring the work of PLCs as teachers begin to implement Guided Math has been mentioned several times. How can leaders assess their effectiveness? As leaders review meeting minutes, attend meetings, visit classrooms, and analyze student achievement data, it helps to keep these questions in mind:

- Are the PLCs meeting regularly as scheduled with all members attending?

- Is adequate time allocated for collaborative work?

- Are teachers using the Guided Math resources that are available to them?

- Are teachers discussing Guided Math and how it can be used to improve students' mathematical achievement?

- Are teachers sharing Guided Math instructional strategies that have proved to be effective?

- Are teachers planning Guided Math lessons collaboratively?

- Are teachers engaging in reflection on Guided Math lessons they have planned and taught?

- Are assessment data being analyzed to determine the effectiveness of the strategies being implemented?

- Are teachers examining student work for evidence of understanding of mathematical concepts and skills?

✎ Are teachers engaging in peer observations with debrief sessions?

✎ Is implementation of the components of Guided Math evident in classroom lessons?

✎ Are teachers teaching differentiated small-group lessons to address student learning needs?

✎ Are teachers making use of instructional coaches, if available, to supplement the PLC learning?

These questions encompass the significant functions of PLCs in supporting the implementation of Guided Math. Effective PLCs support the efforts of teachers as they work to improve students' mathematical proficiency.

Review & Reflect

1. Have you ever been a member of a PLC? If so, was it a positive learning experience? What aspects of it made it valuable? If not, what aspects of PLCs do you think are most valuable in promoting professional learning?

2. Choose a short text to read with several colleagues. Use the "Final Say on Quotes Protocol" to discuss the reading. How would you describe the experience? Are there any changes you would make in the protocol? If so, what changes and why?

3. In what ways do you think being a part of a PLC supports teachers when implementing Guided Math? What can you do to support the establishment of a Guided Math PLC at your school?

A Guided Math Learning Plan for Professional Learning Communities

This year-long professional learning plan is designed for use by Professional Learning Communities to support the implementation of Guided Math. Prior to creating PLCs for the implementation of Guided Math, most schools will have analyzed student data and completed a needs assessment leading them to establish Guided Math implementation as a goal in order to increase their students' mathematical achievement. In some cases, however, PLCs are formed before school–wide goals are developed, and then each team is given the responsibility of determining their own professional learning needs. If this is the case, these teams should conduct needs assessments before embarking on any learning plan to ensure that their goals align with school improvement needs.

This comprehensive professional learning plan includes a study of all seven of the Guided Math framework's components as it prepares teachers for successful implementation. The plan suggests activities for each month that provide for inquiry, learning, goal setting, collaborative planning, and reflection. PLCs may pick and choose among these monthly activities to make the plan their own.

Although PLCs are encouraged to select and adapt the suggested tasks to suit their learning needs, it is strongly recommended that all members participate in peer observations as a part of their collaborative learning. Scheduling and arranging release time for peer observations usually needs leadership support, but some observations may be scheduled during an observer's planning period to eliminate the need for release time.

Most PLCs are required by school leadership to keep minutes of their meetings. In addition to these minutes, as a part of this plan, each team member will maintain a *professional learning portfolio* to document evidence of professional learning and a *reflection journal*.

How to Use the Plan

Prior to beginning the learning plan, PLC members should meet to determine leadership responsibilities, agree upon a meeting schedule, and establish norms for the group (See page 191, "Establishing Norms for Guided Math Professional Learning Communities"). Some groups will meet more frequently than others, and the meeting length may vary from group to group. The plan is flexible and can be adjusted so that it works with most PLC schedules. PLCs that meet more frequently or for longer meetings will be able to engage in more of the suggested tasks than others, however.

The plan for each month includes:

- a focus of study for the month
- a reading assignment with discussion questions
- suggested activities that allow teachers to examine the focus in depth and apply what they are learning
- goal setting related to the current topic
- individual journal topics for written reflection

The readings for the learning plan come from the following books by Laney Sammons:

- *Guided Math: A Framework for Mathematics Instruction*
- *Strategies for Implementing Guided Math*

Additional resources include:

- *Math Stretches: Building Conceptual Understanding*
- *Building Mathematical Comprehension: Using Literacy Strategies to Make Meaning*
- *Guided Math Conferences*

Learning Plan for Month 1

Learning Focus: Getting Started

1. Identify the team's learning needs by exploring these questions.

   ✎ What does your current math instruction look like? What about it works well? What evidence do you have to support that? What would you like to improve?

   ✎ What do you hope to accomplish this year through your participation in the PLC focused on Guided Math implementation?

   ✎ What do you already know about Guided Math? How do you think it will help the team improve the mathematics learning of students?

2. Establish team and individual goals for the year.

   ✎ What are the PLC goals for the year? What are the personal goals for each individual?

   ✎ How will the PLC and its individual members measure success? What evidence will be gathered to document the degree of success in meeting established goals?

3. Make a commitment to the learning plan and the goals of the PLC. As a team, review the structure of this learning plan. Establish a method for maintaining portfolios to document learning experiences.

4. Complete the reading assignment and discuss the reflection questions.

5. Select which of the suggested activities for the month the team will undertake and complete them.

6. Record reflections in their personal journals.

Reading Assignment

- *Guided Math: A Framework for Mathematics Instruction,* Chapter 1, pp. 15–31 and/or

- *Strategies for Implementing Guided Math,* Introduction, pp. 7–27

Reading Discussion Questions

✎ Describe the way you were taught mathematics as a student. How does that compare with your current approach to mathematics instruction?

✎ Have you used any of the Guided Math components in your classroom? If so, share your experiences with the team.

✎ What do you consider to be the most valuable aspects of the Guided Math framework in regard to the team's goals for the year? In regard to your personal goals for the year? Why?

Suggested Learning Tasks

The "Final Say on Quotes Protocol"

Use the "Final Say on Quotes Protocol" to structure the discussion of the assigned reading. See Chapter 7, page 194 for a description of the protocol.

Peer Observation

Visit the classroom of another member of the team during a math lesson to observe *current* methods of mathematics instruction. Complete the Month 1 Peer Observation Form (See page 212). Share and discuss these observations during a PLC meeting. Discussion should focus on *what* was observed (e.g., teacher opened the lesson with a review of what was taught the day before, or students completed a worksheet independently as the teacher conferred with a student), not on evaluation of the instruction or expression of value judgments (e.g., the students seemed engaged or a good lesson). Add your observation forms to your portfolio.

Discussion Questions: Were any elements of Guided Math observed? Compare and contrast the current instructional methods and the Guided Math framework described in the reading assignment.

Videotape a Math Lesson

Videotape one of your own mathematics lessons taught using your current instructional techniques, critique it, and add the videotape and the critique to your portfolio to document how instruction is differentiated as the PLC begins.

Goal Setting

Since the focus of the PLC this month is *getting started,* members will not set individual goals for the month.

Journal Reflection

Write a description of your current math instruction. What are its strengths? What do you hope to achieve through participation in this PLC?

Month 1 Peer Observation Form
Mathematics Lesson Observation

Teacher Observing _____   Teacher Observed _____

Date of Observation _____   Lesson Topic _____

In recording observations, be specific. List what is observed without value judgments.

1. What is the teacher doing?

2. What are the students doing?

3. Is differentiation of instruction evident? If so, how is it being differentiated?

4. Do students have opportunities to engage in mathematical practices? If so, in what ways?

Learning Plan for Month 2

Learning Focus: Establishing a Classroom Environment of Numeracy

1. Share PLC members' journal reflections from Month 1.

2. Complete the reading assignment and discuss the reflection questions.

3. Select which of the suggested activities for the month the team will undertake and complete them.

4. Record reflections in their personal journals.

Reading Assignment

- *Guided Math: A Framework for Mathematics Instruction,* Chapter 2, pp. 33–66 and/or

- *Strategies for Implementing Guided Math,* Strategies for Creating a Classroom Environment of Numeracy, pp. 39–76

Reading Discussion Questions

✎ Review the Foundational Principles of Guided Math (page 37 in *Guided Math* or pages 12–14 in *Strategies for Implementing Guided Math).* Which two do you think are most important and why? In what ways does your classroom reflect those principles?

✎ How do your students benefit from learning in an environment of numeracy?

✎ In what ways have you created an environment of numeracy in your classroom? What are some additional ideas for creating an environment of numeracy?

✎ In what ways can you adapt strategies you use to create an environment of literacy to make your classroom mathematically rich?

✎ The focus is often on the physical aspects of a numeracy-rich environment, yet creating a mathematical learning community is equally as important. In what ways can teachers nurture this sense of community?

Suggested Learning Tasks

Peer Observation

At the beginning of the month, visit at least three classrooms looking for evidence of mathematics instruction. Record what you observe on the Month 2 Peer Observation Form (See page 215). Share your observations with the team. Add your observation form to your portfolio.

Discussion Questions: What evidence of mathematics instruction was most frequently visible in classrooms? How does it support student learning?

Focus Walk

As a team, brainstorm what a numeracy-rich classroom looks like. Create a checklist using these ideas. Together, as a team, visit five classrooms (not necessarily PLC team members classrooms) looking for this kind of evidence. Meet as a group to debrief immediately after these visits. What was observed? Were there any surprises? How well do the classrooms in your school exemplify environments of numeracy?

Picture Perfect

Look at your classroom as if through the eyes of a new student. What would he or she see that indicates the importance of mathematics? Take pictures of evidence of mathematics and add them to your portfolio.

Goal Setting

Individually or as a team, establish specific and measurable goals for making your classrooms more mathematically friendly—addressing both the social and physical environments. Record the goals in your portfolio and then document your work toward achieving these goals in your portfolio using written descriptions, photographs, video recordings, and/or examples of student work.

Journal Reflection

In what ways has your classroom environment changed over Month 2? Have these changes positively impacted your students' mathematical work? If so, in what ways? If not, why do you think there has not been an impact? What else can you do to promote an environment of numeracy in your classroom?

Month 2 Peer Observation Form
A Classroom Environment of Numeracy

Teacher Observing _____   Date of Observation _____

List all evidence of mathematics instruction that is observed in the classroom. In recording observations, be specific. List what is observed without value judgments.

Classroom 1:

Classroom 2:

Classroom 3:

Learning Plan for Month 3

Learning Focus: Using Math Warm-Ups

1. Share PLC members' journal reflections from Month 2.

2. Complete the reading assignment and discuss the reflection questions.

3. Select which of the suggested activities for the month the team will undertake and complete them.

4. Record reflections in their personal journals.

Reading Assignment

- *Guided Math: A Framework for Mathematics Instruction,* Chapter 3, pp. 67–103 and/or

- *Strategies for Implementing Guided Math,* Strategies for Math Warm-Ups, pp. 77–139

Optional resources: *Math Stretches: Building Conceptual Understanding K–2, Math Stretches 3–5,* or *Math Stretches 6–8*

Reading Discussion Questions

✎ In what ways can Math Warm-Ups support your mathematics instruction?

✎ How does the use of Math Warm-Ups help students maintain their understanding of previously taught concepts and skills through distributed practice? How can they be used to preview topics to be introduced soon? Why is that important?

✎ Of the Math Warm-Ups suggested in this month's reading, which do you think you will use the most? Why?

✎ How can Math Warm-Ups be used to help students recognize the relevance of math to their own lives?

Suggested Learning Tasks

Peer Observation

Visit a classroom to observe a Math Warm-Up. Record what you observe on the Month 3 Peer Observation Form (See page 218). Share your observations with the team. Add your observation form to your portfolio.

Discussion Questions: Describe the lesson observed. How did the Math Warm-Up support the mathematical learning of students? Are there any changes that you might make in the warm-up in order to use it in your classroom? If so, what changes would you make and why?

Math Warm-Up Wiki

As a team, gather Math Warm-Up ideas, both from the PLC team and from other teachers. Build a wiki of Math Warm-Up information that can be shared with the entire professional community.

Create a Math Stretch

As a team, create a Math Stretch that addresses a learning need for your students. The following books may be used as resources: *Math Stretches: Building Conceptual Understanding K–2, Math Stretches 3–5, or Math Stretches 6–8*. Use this stretch with your students. Then, as a team, discuss its effectiveness. What did students learn from it? Are there any changes you would make if you use it again?

Goal Setting

Team members set a goal of trying at least one kind of Math Warm-Up they have never used before. Record your goal in your portfolio—describing the Math Warm-Up you will use. Use written descriptions, photographs, video recordings, and/or examples of student work. Share your experience with your PLC.

Journal Reflection

Describe a Math Warm-Up that you used with your students. What worked well? What did not go as well as you would have liked? How might you change it to make it more effective? What did you want your students to learn from the warm-up? How successful was the lesson in leading students to that learning? How do you know? What other Math Warm-Ups do you plan to try?

Month 3 Peer Observation Form
Math Warm-Ups

Teacher Observing _____   Teacher Observed _____

Date of Observation _____

Type of Math
Warm-Up _____

List all evidence of mathematics instruction that is observed in the classroom. In recording observations, be specific. List what is observed without value judgments.

1. Describe the Math Warm-Up you observed.

2. How much time did it take?

3. What were students doing during the warm-up?

4. What evidence of student learning did you observe?

Learning Plan for Month 4

Learning Focus: Using Guided Math with the Whole Class

1. Share PLC members' journal reflections from Month 3.

2. Complete the reading assignment and discuss the reflection questions.

3. Select which of the suggested activities for the month the team will undertake and complete them.

4. Record reflections in their personal journals.

Reading Assignment

- *Guided Math: A Framework for Mathematics Instruction,* Chapter 4, pp. 105–132 and/or

- *Strategies for Implementing Guided Math,* Strategies for Whole-Class Instruction, pp. 141–181

Reading Discussion Questions

✎ What are the advantages and disadvantages of using whole-class instruction?

✎ When do you use whole-class instruction? Why? When do you think the use of this type of instruction is most effective?

✎ What are the greatest challenges when using whole-class instruction? How do you differentiate instruction when teaching whole-class lessons?

✎ Sammons recommends the use of whole-class instruction for presenting mini lessons, using activating strategies, reading math-related children's literature, setting the stage for Math Workshop, conducting Math Huddles, providing practice and review, and some kinds of assessment. Are there any other times when you think whole-class instruction is beneficial?

✎ What do you think is the rationale for the four parts included in the architecture of a mathematics mini lesson? Why is each part of the lesson important?

✎ Many teachers using the Guided Math framework only teach mini lessons if there is a compelling reason to do so. Most of their instruction is done in small-group lessons. Do you agree with that practice? Why or why not?

Suggested Learning Tasks
Peer Observation

Visit a classroom to observe a whole-class lesson. Record your observations on the Month 4 Peer Observation Form (See page 222). Share your observations with the team. Ask the observed teacher to share his or her rationale for teaching the lesson as whole-class instruction. Add your observation form to your portfolio.

Discussion Questions: Describe the lesson observed. How did the whole-class format of the lesson affect student learning? Was differentiation of the lesson possible? Were manipulatives used during the lesson? Were students engaged in communicating their mathematical thinking? Who did most of the talking during the lesson?

Whole-class Instruction Data

Document your mathematics instruction for a week to determine how much time is spent doing whole-class instruction. As a team, compute what percentage of mathematics instructional time was spent in whole-class instruction for each teacher as well as for the PLC. Create a graphic display (e.g., bar graph, pie chart) to show what percentage of time each teacher in the PLC spent on whole-class instruction and the average for the entire group. Teachers add a copy of this to their portfolios.

Videotape a Whole-Class Lesson

Videotape one of your whole-class mathematics lessons and write a critique of it. In the critique, answer these questions: Why did you decide to teach this as a whole-class lesson? What worked? What did not work well? How did you assess student learning? Add the videotape and critique to your portfolio.

Goal Setting

Team members set individual goals of trying at least one of the kinds of whole-class lessons suggested by Sammons (mini lessons, activating strategies, math-related children's literature, setting the stage for Math Workshop, Math Huddles, practice and review). Add this lesson plan to your portfolio and document it with photographs, video recordings, and/or examples of student work. Share your experience with your PLC.

Journal Reflection

What do you consider to be the advantages of whole-class instruction in general? How effective do you feel your own whole-class instruction is? What concerns, if any, do you have about limiting the amount of time you spend using whole-class mathematics instruction?

Month 4 Peer Observation Form
Whole-Class Lesson

Teacher Observing _____   Teacher Observed _____

Date of Observation _____   Lesson Topic   _____

List all evidence of mathematics instruction that is observed in the classroom. In recording observations, be specific. List what is observed without value judgments.

1. Describe the whole-class lesson you observed.

         How long was it? _____

2. What was the teacher doing?

3. What were the students doing during the lesson?

4. What evidence of student learning did you observe?

Learning Plan for Month 5

Learning Focus: Supporting Guided Math with Math Workshop

1. Share PLC members' journal reflections from Month 4.

2. Complete the reading assignment and discuss the reflection questions.

3. Select which of the suggested activities for the month the team will undertake and complete them.

4. Record reflections in their personal journals.

Reading Assignment

- *Guided Math: A Framework for Mathematics Instruction,* Chapter 6, pp. 183–205 and/or

- *Strategies for Implementing Guided Math,* Strategies for Math Workshop, pp. 221–276

Reading Discussion Questions

✎ What is your prior knowledge of Math Workshop? What experiences, if any, have you had with it?

✎ For what reasons would you choose to establish Math Workshop in your classroom? What are the benefits to teachers? Students?

✎ What do you think are the greatest challenges in implementing the workshop model?

✎ Why is Math Workshop an essential component of the Guided Math framework?

✎ What routines and procedures for students work best? How should they be taught?

✎ In what ways can students be held accountable when they work independently in Math Workshop?

✎ What types of learning tasks do you think are best for the math workstations? Why?

Suggested Learning Tasks

Carousel Brainstorm Protocol

To find solutions for problems encountered when implementing Math Workshop, conduct a brainstorming session using the "Carousel Brainstorm Protocol" (See Chapter 7, page 197).

Peer Observation

Visit a classroom to observe Math Workshop. Record what you observe on the Month 5 Peer Observation Form (See page 226). Share your observations with the team. Add your observation form to your portfolio.

Discussion Questions: Ask the teacher who was observed to describe the workshop model used. What kinds of tasks were in the math workstations? What did students do if they encountered a problem while working independently?

Math Workshop Wiki

As a team, gather various models for Math Workshop and the students' routines and procedures from colleagues and from Internet research. Compile these to create a Math Workshop Wiki that can be used by the entire professional community.

Workstation Show and Tell

Bring workstation tasks you have used in your classrooms or plan to use to share with the group. Also share the routines and procedures you have developed. Explain how you taught them to your students. These ideas may be added to the Math Workshop Wiki. If time permits, work collaboratively to create math workstation tasks for your classrooms.

Goal Setting

Set a personal goal for creating routines and procedures for Math Workshop and then for implementing the model a certain number of days each week. Share your experiences with your PLC.

Journal Reflection

What are your greatest concerns about Math Workshop in your classroom? How are you addressing those concerns? What is working well for you? How does participation in Math Workshop affect your students' mathematical work? Are there any changes that you plan to make?

Month 5 Peer Observation Form
Math Workshop

Teacher Observing _____ Teacher Observed _____

Date of Observation _____

In recording observations, be specific. List what is observed without value judgments.

1. Describe the Math Workshop model you observed.

2. Describe the tasks at each math workstation.

3. Describe the level of engagement of students while working independently. How were students held accountable?

4. What evidence of student learning did you observe?

Learning Plan for Month 6

Learning Focus: Using Guided Math with Small Groups

1. Share PLC members' journal reflections from Month 5.

2. Complete the reading assignment and discuss the reflection questions.

3. Select which of the suggested activities for the month the team will undertake and complete them.

4. Record reflections in their personal journals.

Reading Assignment

- *Guided Math: A Framework for Mathematics Instruction,* Chapter 5, pp. 133–181 and/or

- *Strategies for Implementing Guided Math,* Strategies for Small-Group Instruction, pp. 183–219

Reading Discussion Questions

✎ Consider pages 133–134 in *Guided Math: A Framework for Mathematics Instruction.* Share your thoughts on the ideas expressed on these two pages. Do you agree? Disagree? Why?

✎ What are the advantages of small-group lessons? What are the challenges in using this instructional model?

✎ How does using flexible, needs-based grouping affect student learning?

✎ What kinds of data can you use to group students by need and plan lessons to meet those needs? How can you determine if students have gaps in the foundational knowledge or skills necessary for them to be successful with a new lesson?

✎ If you are using Guided Reading, how can you adapt its instructional techniques for use with mathematics instruction?

✎ Review the characteristics of effective scaffolding on page 169 of *Guided Math: A Framework for Mathematics Instruction*. Reflect on how teachers using small-group instruction can both provide scaffolding and allow students to experience productive struggle when working with mathematics. Compare and contrast those two learning needs.

Suggested Learning Tasks

Peer Observation

Visit a classroom to observe a small-group lesson. Record what you observe on the Month 6 Peer Observation Form (See page 230). Share your observations with the team. Add your observation form to your portfolio.

Discussion Questions: What are some of the advantages of small-group lessons that you observed? Did you observe any challenges for the teacher? If so, what were they? How might they be resolved? What did the teacher do to differentiate instruction? Who did most of the talking during the lesson? What evidence of student understanding did you notice? Did the teacher record anecdotal notes during the lesson? If so, what method was used?

A Change in Practice Protocol

To examine the instructional changes the team is implementing, discuss your experiences using the "A Change in Practice Protocol" described in Chapter 7, page 195.

Anecdotal Record Keeping Show and Tell

Bring examples of anecdotal notes you maintain from your small-group instruction. During the show and tell, describe the method of record keeping you use.

Small-Group Lesson Planning and Instruction

Read the Sample Grade 4 Small-Group Lesson Plan on page 232 and/or the sample lessons in *Strategies for Implementing Guided Math* on pages 195–219. Work together as a team to plan a small-group lesson using the Small-Group Lesson Planning form on page 231. As you plan, first consider the prerequisite knowledge and skills that students must have to be successful with the lesson. Include in the plan ways to address needs of students who have gaps in their background knowledge (in the section labeled "Rebuilding Foundational Knowledge") as well as ways to provide additional challenge for students who may require it. When planning, adapt your teaching resources to the small-group lesson format by determining which of the learning tasks suggested will be most valuable in helping students learn the content you are teaching and will indicate most effectively whether students master the concepts and skills being taught.

Use the plan to teach small-group lessons in your classrooms. After instruction, meet again to debrief. Add the plan and your critique of the lesson to your portfolio.

Debrief Discussion Questions: Describe your experience teaching this lesson with small groups of students. In what ways were you able to differentiate to meet the needs of your students? Were you able to informally assess students' mathematical understanding? What about the lesson worked best? How would you modify the lesson if you were to use it again? If some teachers were more successful teaching this lesson than others, try to find out what made the difference.

Goal Setting

Set a personal goal for how many days a week you will teach small-group lessons. Share your experiences with your PLC.

Journal Reflection

In what ways does small-group instruction differ from whole-class instruction? What works well for you when you use small-group instruction? Why? What changes might you make? How does the small-group format impact your students' learning? What are your greatest challenges in teaching small groups of students?

Month 6 Peer Observation Form
Small-Group Instruction

Teacher Observing _____   Teacher Observed _____

Date of Observation _____   Lesson Topic _____

In recording observations, be specific. List what is observed without value judgments.

1. Describe the small-group lesson you observed.

2. Describe the teacher's role in the lesson.

3. In what ways did the teacher engage students in the lesson?

4. What evidence of student learning did you observe?

Small-Group Lesson Planning Form

Standard(s) to be Addressed:	
Prerequisite Knowledge and Skills/Informal Assessment:	
Small-Group Lesson	**Additional Challenge**
Connection:	(If students demonstrate mastery, how will they be challenged?)
Teaching Point:	
Active Engagement:	**Rebuilding Foundational Knowledge** (List Common Gaps and Specific Ways to Address Them)
Link:	Vocabulary:

Sample Grade 4 Small-Group Lesson Plan

Standard(s) to be Addressed:

MCC4.NF.7. Compare two decimals to hundredths by reasoning about their size. Recognize that comparisons are valid only when the two decimals refer to the same whole. Record the results of comparisons with the symbols >, =, or <, and justify the conclusions, e.g., by using a visual model.

Prerequisite Knowledge or Skills/Informal Assessment:

- Students can compare whole numbers.
- Students can convert fractions to decimals and decimals to fractions.

Small-Group Lesson	Need for Additional Challenge
Connection: "I understand that you have been learning about fractions and decimals. Turn and tell a partner everything you know about fractions and decimals."	Decimal Sort: Choose a decimal card and place it under the correct heading—near 0, about $\frac{1}{2}$, or close to 1. Explain why.

Small-Group Lesson (continued)

Teaching Point: "Today we are going to learn more about how we can compare the value of decimals."

Active Engagement: Give each pair of students a decimal to represent using an area model and to convert to a fraction. Listen as students work, to identify misconceptions. Have students share their work and ask what they notice about the visual representations. Ask them to compare two of the decimals (emphasize that this can only be done if the whole is the same size). Ask them how they know how the numbers compare. Identify where the numbers fall on the number line. Ask students how using representations helps mathematicians as they work with numbers.

Link: "You have been thinking like mathematicians today—using models to help understand the relationships between numbers. Always remember this strategy when you are comparing numbers. Reflect for a minute and then share something about math that you learned or thought about during this lesson."

Need for Rebuilding Foundational Knowledge

(List common gaps and ways to address them.)

Unable to compare whole numbers: Provide a number line. Have students point out where two numbers fall to determine which is greater, less. Provide additional scaffolding to support understanding.

Unable to convert fractions to decimals and decimals to fractions: Review what $\frac{1}{10}$ represents. Show students an area model of $\frac{1}{10}$ and tell them that 0.1 is just another way of expressing $\frac{1}{10}$. Do the same with $\frac{1}{100}$. Show an area model of $\frac{6}{10}$. Have students write it as a fraction and as a decimal. Show an area model of $\frac{20}{100}$. Have them write it as a fraction and a decimal. Challenge students to convert it to 10ths. Provide additional support as needed.

Vocabulary: fractions, numerator, denominator, decimals, whole numbers, tenths, hundredths, greater than, less than, equal to

Learning Plan for Month 7

Learning Focus: Conferring with Students During Guided Math

1. Share PLC members' journal reflections from Month 6.

2. Complete the reading assignment and discuss the reflection questions.

3. Select which of the suggested activities for the month the team will undertake and complete them.

4. Record reflections in their personal journals.

Reading Assignment

- *Guided Math: A Framework for Mathematics Instruction,* Chapter 7, pp. 207–225 and/or

- *Strategies for Implementing Guided Math,* Strategies for Conferring with Students, pp. 277–300

Optional Resource: *Guided Math Conferences*

Reading Discussion Questions

✎ Have you used one-on-one conferences in any other subject areas? Have you conferred with students in a one-on-one setting about their mathematics work?

✎ What are the benefits of conducting Guided Math Conferences with your students?

✎ Review the architecture for a math conference on page 212 in *Guided Math: A Framework for Mathematics Instruction* and on page 283 in *Strategies for Implementing Guided Math.* How does each of these steps contribute to the overall value of math conferences?

✎ When can you confer with your students during the instructional day? How often do you think you should conduct conferences? Should you plan to confer with every student?

✎ What kind of record keeping system can be used for student conference notes?

Suggested Learning Tasks

Guided Math Conferences Trial Run

Each teacher completes this task and then the PLC meets to discuss the experience. Choose three students randomly from your classroom with whom you will confer. Conduct the conferences and carefully record the research findings, compliment, and teaching point from each. Use the Guided Math Conference Recording Form on page 236. Examine what you learned about your students and their mathematical understanding. Decide how you can use it to more effectively tailor your instruction. Add the recording form to your portfolio.

Discussion Questions: What were you able to learn from the experience that you would not otherwise have known about the mathematical thinking of these students? How did the conference impact the students with whom you conferred? How will it affect your teaching? Do you plan to make conferences a regular part of your mathematics instruction? Why or why not?

Guided Math Conference Role Play

Present a math problem that is appropriate for the grade level(s) of your PLC. Each member of the team solves the problem as a student might and shows his or her work—some of the methods and answers might be incorrect. Work in pairs. First, one teacher plays the role of teacher and the other plays the role of student. The "teacher" confers with the "student" about his or her mathematical work. The conference should include the four parts of the conference structure: Research Student Understanding, Decide What Is Needed, Teacher to Student Needs, and Link to the Future. Once that has been done, the pairs switch roles, so that everyone has an opportunity to act as both teacher and student. Debrief the experience.

Debrief Discussion Questions: What did you notice about the conferring experience? Did the conversation between teacher and student allow greater insight into student thinking? If so, how? As teacher, how did you determine the teaching point for the conference? What was the most difficult role of the conference for you—as either teacher or student?

Videotape a Math Conference

This task can be done in conjunction with the trial run task or completed independently of it. Choose a student with whom you will confer. This task is most beneficial when you are genuinely curious about the student's mathematical thinking. To alleviate student anxiety, explain to the student that you are going to videotape your conversation as a way of helping *you* become a better teacher. Confer with the student about his or her math work, including all four components of the conference structure. Record notes documenting the conference. Later, watch the videotaped conference with your notes at hand and write a critique of it answering these questions: What do you think worked well in the conference conversation? What did not work well? What would you do differently if you could do it over? Did any of your impressions of the conference and what you learned change after watching the videotape? If so, in what ways? Add the videotape and critique to your portfolio.

Goal Setting

Set a personal goal for the use of Guided Math Conferences. Share your experiences with your PLC.

Journal Reflection

During what time of your instructional day did you conduct your conferences? Did that timing work well for you? If not, at what other time could you meet with students? Reflect on one conference. What did you learn about the student's mathematical thinking? Assess the effectiveness of your teaching point. Who do you think learned more from the conference— you or your student? Why?

Month 7 Guided Math Conference Recording Form

Teacher _____

Student Name/ Date	Research Findings	Compliment	Teaching Point

Learning Plan for Month 8

Learning Focus: Assessment in Guided Math

1. Share PLC members' journal reflections from Month 7.

2. Complete the reading assignment and discuss the reflection questions.

3. Select which of the suggested activities for the month the team will undertake and complete them.

4. Record reflections in their personal journals.

Reading Assignment

- *Guided Math: A Framework for Mathematics Instruction,* Chapter 8, pp. 227–244 and/or

- *Strategies for Implementing Guided Math,* Strategies for Assessment, pp. 301–333

Reading Discussion Questions

Why is assessment crucial to Guided Math implementation? What role does it play in teaching and learning?

What kinds of assessment do you use? What kind of assessment is most valuable to you when planning instruction?

Is there a difference between assessment and evaluation? If so, what is the difference?

Why is it important to involve students in the assessment process? How does it help students when they know their learning goals and the criteria for success?

Discuss how you provide descriptive feedback to your students. What are the most effective ways to give students feedback on their mathematical work?

Suggested Learning Tasks

Assessment Analysis

As a group, create a T-chart of the assessments you use in your classrooms. Classify them as formative or summative. Which are most useful to you when you are grouping students and planning instruction? Are there any assessments that can be eliminated? Looking at the list of assessments, discuss how balanced they are. Do they include assessments based on work products, communication, and observation? If not, how can you provide more balance in your assessments? Are students involved in assessing their own work? Do your students have an opportunity to improve their work based on the assessments?

Looking at Student Work

The objective of this task is to improve the ability of teachers to assess the mathematical work of students to identify what the student knows and can do as well as what the next steps in learning should be and to promote consistency in assessment by teachers. The Looking at Student Work Protocol will be used.

Looking at Student Work Protocol:

The PLCs with five or fewer members will work as a whole. A larger PLC should be broken down into working teams of no more than five. Each PLC member brings five copies of a piece of student math work with the names of students removed, but labeled with the teacher name.

1. **Introduction (2 minutes):** The directions for the protocol are shared and copies of the Looking at Student Work Recording Form are distributed. The PLC can be divided into smaller working teams, if needed.

2. **Presentation (2 minutes):** In each working team, a teacher distributes copies of the work sample and then explains the context of the work sample he or she is sharing, including the learning goals for the lesson.

3. **Silent Review of the Work Sample (4 minutes each round):** Members of the working team study the work sample independently to identify evidence of learning and determine learning needs by answering the questions on the Looking at Student Work Recording Form.

4. **Feedback Provided (4 minutes):** The working team members provide feedback by sharing their answers to the questions. The presenting teacher remains silent—only listens.

5. **Discussion (4 minutes):** The presenting teacher discusses the feedback with the team to clarify their comments and explore any issues that were raised. This process is repeated until all members have presented a student work sample or until no time remains.

6. **Debrief (3 minutes):** PLC members reflect on the experience of looking at student work together and what they learned from it. (Adapted from Glaude 2005, 34–35) Include a copy of the student work sample you provided and the Looking at Student Work Recording Forms your working team members completed in your portfolio.

Develop a Self-Assessment Checklist for Students

As a team, create a problem-solving self-assessment checklist for your students. See pages 242–243 for problem-solving checklist templates for both primary grades and upper elementary/middle grades. For additional information, see *Strategies for Implementing Guided Math,* pages 316–320. Develop the criteria for problem solving and list them on the checklist that is appropriate for the grade level.

Introduce the checklist to your students. Explain the importance of the criteria for being a good mathematics problem solver and their ability to assess whether or not they have met the criteria. Have students complete the checklist as they work on problem-solving tasks. If they have not met all of the criteria, encourage them to go back to improve their work.

Come back together as a team to share your experiences.

Discussion Questions: How did you introduce the idea of self-assessment to your students? How did the use of the checklist impact your students' mathematics work? What were the benefits of involving students in self-assessing their work? What challenges did you face? What would you change if you were doing this again?

Goal Setting

Consider your current methods of assessment. Set a personal goal for more effective use of assessment for Guided Math. Share your experiences with your PLC.

Journal Reflection

What assessments give you the best guidance in grouping your students and differentiating their instruction? What system do you use to record anecdotal assessment notes from your small-group lessons? How do you use the notes that you maintain? How can you increase the involvement of your students in assessing their work? What changes, if any, do you plan to make in your assessments?

Month 8 Looking at Student Work
Recording Form

Presenting Teacher _____   Reviewing Teacher _____

Learning Goal(s) and Context of the Student Work Sample:
What evidence is there that the student has met the learning goal(s)?
What are the learning needs of the student as evidenced by this work?
What else would you like to know in order to determine the student's next steps in learning?

Name: _____ Date: _____

Problem-Solving Checklist

Directions: Color the smiley face if you completed each direction.

	Tasks
☺	
☺	
☺	
☺	
☺	

Reprinted with permission from Shell Education from *Strategies for Implementing Guided Math*

Name: _____ Date:_____

Problem-Solving Checklist

Directions: Check the yes or the no box to show whether you met the criteria.

YES	NO	Criteria
		1.
		2.
		3.
		4.
		5.
		6.
		7.
		8.
		9.
		10.

Reprinted with permission from Shell Education from *Strategies for Implementing Guided Math*

Learning Plan for Month 9

Learning Focus: Putting Guided Math Into Practice and Celebrating

1. Share PLC members' journal reflections from Month 8.

2. Complete the reading assignment and discuss the reflection questions.

3. Select which of the suggested activities for the month the team will undertake and complete them.

4. Record reflections in their personal journals.

Reading Assignment

- *Guided Math: A Framework for Mathematics Instruction,* Chapter 9, pp. 245–250 and/or

- *Strategies for Implementing Guided Math,* Introduction, pp. 18–27

Reading Discussion Questions

In what ways can teachers collaborate to make the use of the Guided Math framework more manageable?

If you use Guided Reading in your classroom, can you envision establishing common routines and procedures for both Reading Workshop and Math Workshop? What are some of the common expectations for student behavior in both workshops? How do expectations differ for the two workshops?

What will your next steps in implementing Guided Math be? Are there any additional supports or resources you need to successfully implement it? If so, what are they and what can the PLC do to procure them?

Suggested Learning Tasks

Videotape a Math Lesson

Videotape one of your mathematics lessons while using your current instructional techniques. Critique it and compare it to the lesson you videotaped in Month 1. Answer these questions in your critique: Have your instructional strategies changed over the year? If so, in what ways have they changed? Compare the way you differentiate instruction for your students now with the ways you did it in Month 1. Add the videotape and critique to your portfolio to document how instruction is differentiated now and how your mathematics instruction has changed over the school year.

Implementation Show and Tell

Choose an aspect of the Guided Math framework from your classroom and document it (photographs, videos, student work, teacher notes, or other artifacts) to share with other members of the group.

Whole-Class Instruction Data

Document your mathematics instruction for a week to determine how much time is spent doing whole-class instruction. As a team, compute what percentage of mathematics instructional time was spent in whole-class instruction for each teacher as well as for the PLC. Create a graphic display (e.g., bar graph, pie chart) to show what percentage of time each teacher in the PLC spent on whole-class instruction and the average for the entire group. Teachers add a copy of this to their portfolios. Compare this to the same data collected in Month 4.

Revisit PLC Goals and Celebrate Accomplishments

As a team, review the evidence gathered in portfolios. On chart paper, list: What has the group accomplished? What remains to be accomplished? What will be the next steps (next year)?

Goal Setting

Set individual or group goals for next year. Plan how to proceed.

Journal Reflection

What are the three most important things you learned this year in your PLC? What are two things that you still want to know or do? What is the one most important change you made in your mathematics instruction this year?

References Cited

Aguilar, Elena. 2013. *The Art of Coaching: Effective Strategies for School Transformation.* San Francisco, CA: Josey-Bass. Kindle Edition.

Amabile, Teresa, and Steven Kramer. 2011. *The Progress Principle: Using Small Wins to Ignite Joy, Engagement, and Creativity at Work.* Boston, MA: Harvard Business Review Press. Kindle Edition.

Annenberg Institute for School Reform. 2004. *Instructional Coaching: Professional Development Strategies that Improve Instruction.* Providence, RI: Brown University. annenberginstitute.org/pdf/InstructionalCoaching.pdf.

Azzam, Amy M. 2014. "Motivation to Learn: A Conversation with Daniel Pink." *Educational Leadership* 72 (1): 12–17.

Balka, Don S., Ted H. Hull, and Ruth Harbin Miles. 2010. *A Guide to Mathematics Leadership: Sequencing Instructional Change.* Thousand Lakes, CA: Corwin.

Bean, Rita. 2009. *The Reading Specialist: Leadership for the Classroom, School, and Community.* 2nd ed. New York: Guilford Press. Kindle Edition.

Boreen, Jean, Mary K. Johnson, Donna Niday, and Joe Potts. 2009. *Mentoring Beginning Teachers: Guiding, Reflecting, Coaching.* Portland, ME: Stenhouse. Kindle Edition.

Confer, Chris. 2006. "Being a Successful Math Coach: Ten Guiding Principles." In *The Math Coach Field Guide: Charting Your Course,* edited by Carolyn Felux and Paula Snowdy, 1–18. Sausalito, CA: Math Solutions.

Conzemius, Anne, and Jan O'Neill. 2001. *Building Shared Responsibility for Student Learning.* Alexandria, VA: Association for Supervision and Curriculum Development.

Costa, Arthur L., and Bena Kallick. 2008. *Learning and Leading with Habits of the Mind: 16 Essential Characteristics for Success.* Alexandria, VA: Association for Supervision and Curriculum Development. Kindle Edition.

Couros, George. 2013. "5 Characteristics of a Change Agent." *The Principal of Change: Stories of Learning and Leading.* http://georgecouros.ca/blog/archives/3615.

Covey, Stephen M. R. 2006. *The Speed of Trust: The One Thing that Changes Everything.* With contributions by Rebecca R. Merrill. New York, NY: The Free Press. Kindle Edition.

Danielson, Charlotte. 2007. *Enhancing Professional Practice: A Framework for Teaching.* 2nd ed. Alexandria, VA: Association for Supervision and Curriculum Development.

Darling-Hammond, Linda. 1999. "Teacher Learning that Supports Student Learning: What Teachers Need to Know." *Edutopia.* http://www.edutopia. org/teacher–learning–supports–student–learning.

Davies, Anne. 2000. *Making Classroom Assessment Work.* Courtenay, Canada: Connections Publishing.

Downey, Carolyn J., Betty E. Steffy, Fenwick W. English, Larry E. Frase, and William K. Poston. 2004. *The Three-Minute Classroom Walk-Through: Changing School Supervisory Practice One Teacher at a Time.* Thousand Oaks, CA: Corwin. Kindle Edition.

Drucker, Peter F. 1954. *The Practice of Management.* New York, NY: HarperCollins. Kindle Edition.

———. 1990. *Managing the Non-profit Organization: Practices and Principles.* New York, NY: Routledge.

———. 2015. "Peter F. Drucker Quotes." Goodreads. Accessed April 13 https://www.goodreads.com/author/quotes/12008.Peter_F_Drucker.

DuFour, Rick. 2004. "The Best Staff Development Is in the Workplace, Not in a Workshop." *Journal of Staff Development* 25 (2): 63–64.

———. 2005. "What Is a Professional Learning Community?" In *On Common Ground: The Power of Professional Learning Communities* edited by Richard DuFour, Robert Eaker, and Rebecca DuFour, 31–44. Bloomington, IN: Solution Tree Press.

DuFour, Richard, Robert Eaker, and Rebecca DuFour. 2005. "Recurring Themes of Professional Learning Communities and the Assumptions They Challenge." In *On Common Ground: The Power of Professional Learning Communities,* edited by Richard DuFour, Robert Eaker, and Rebecca DuFour, 7–30. Bloomington, IN: Solution Tree Press.

Dweck, Carol S. 2006. *Mindset: The New Psychology of Success.* New York, NY: Random House. Kindle Edition.

Evered, Roger D., and James C. Selman. 1989. "Coaching and the Art of Management." *Organizational Dynamics* 18: 116–32.

Fisher, Douglas, and Nancy Frey. 2008. "Releasing Responsibility." *Educational Leadership* 66 (3): 32–37.

Fullan, Michael G. 2005. "Professional Learning Communities Writ Large." In *On Common Ground: The Power of Professional Learning Communities,* edited by Richard DuFour, Robert Eaker, and Rebecca DuFour, 209–224. Bloomington, IN: Solution Tree Press.

———. 2014. *The Principal: Three Keys to Maximizing Impact.* San Francisco, CA: Jossey-Bass. Kindle Edition.

Fullan, Michael G., and Matthew B. Miles. 1992. "Getting Reform Right: What Works and What Doesn't." *Phi Delta Kappan* 73: 745–752. http://www.bnaimitzvahrevolution.org/wp-content/uploads/2012/07/Fullan-Miles-Getting-Reform-Right-1-copy.pdf.

Garmston, Robert J. 2007. "Right Way to Begin Depends on Where You Are Right Now." *Journal of Staff Development.* http://www.questia.com/read/1P3-1232437611.

Gawande, Atul. 2011. "Personal Best: Top Athletes and Singers Have Coaches. Should You?" *The New Yorker* 87 (30).

Glaude, Catherine. 2005. *Protocols for Professional Learning Conversations: Cultivating the Art and Discipline.* Courtenay, Canada: Connections Publishing.

Glickman, Carl D. 2002. *Leadership for Learning: How to Help Teachers Succeed.* Alexandria, VA: Association for Supervision and Curriculum Development.

Gulamhussein, Allison. 2013. *Teaching the Teachers: Effective Professional Development in an Era of High Stakes Accountability.* Alexandria, VA: Center for Public Education. http://www.centerforpubliceducation.org/Main-Menu/Staffingstudents/Teaching-the-Teachers-Effective-Professional-Development-in-an-Era-of-High-Stakes-Accountability/Teaching-the-Teachers-Full-Report.pdf.

Hansen, Pia M. 2009. *Mathematics Coaching Handbook: Working with Teachers to Improve Instruction.* Larchmont, NY: Eye On Education.

Hiltabidel, Jessica. 2012. "Instigating Thinking in Math Class." *Educational Leadership* 70 (4).

Hord, Shirley M., and William A. Sommers. 2008. *Leading Professional Learning Communities: Voices from Research and Practice.* Thousand Oaks, CA: Corwin. Kindle Edition.

Huberman, A. Michael, and Matthew B. Miles. 1984. *Innovation Up Close: How School Improvement Works.* New York, NY: Plenum.

Huebner, Tracy A. 2009. "What Research Says About…/Balanced Assessment." *Educational Leadership* 67 (3): 85–86.

Hull, Ted H., Don S. Balka, and Ruth Harbin Miles. 2009. *A Guide to Mathematics Coaching: Processes for Increasing Student Achievement.* Thousand Oaks, CA: Corwin. Kindle Edition.

Jackson, Phil, and Hugh, Delehanty. 2013. *Eleven Rings: The Soul of Success.* New York, NY: The Penguin Press. Kindle Edition.

Jackson, Robyn. 2008. *The Instructional Leader's Guide to Strategic Conversations with Teachers.* Washington, DC: Mindsteps Inc.

Jones, Cheryl, and Mary Vreeman. 2008. *Instructional Coaches and Classroom Teachers: Sharing the Road to Success.* Huntington Beach, CA: Shell Education.

Joyce, Bruce, and Beverley Showers. 2002. *Student Achievement through Staff Development.* 3rd ed. Alexandria, VA: Association for Supervision and Curriculum Development.

Kaser, Joyce, Susan Mundry, Katherine E. Stiles, and Susan Loucks-Horsley. 2013. *Leading Every Day: 124 Actions for Effective Leadership.* 3rd ed. Thousand Oaks, CA: Corwin. Kindle Edition.

Kirtman, Lyle. 2013. *Leadership and Teams: The Missing Piece of the Educational Reform Puzzle.* Boston, MA: Pearson.

Kotter, John P. 2007. "Leading Change: Why Transformation Efforts Fail." *Harvard Business Review* 85 (1): 96–103.

Kruse, Kevin. 2013. "What Is Leadership?" *Forbes.* http://www.forbes.com/sites/kevinkruse/2013/04/09/what-is-leadership.

Kruse, Shawn, Karen Seashore Louis, and Anthony Bryk. 1994. "Building Professional Community in Schools." *Issues in Restructuring Schools* 6: 3–6.

Leithwood, Kenneth, Karen Seashore Louis, Stephen Anderson, and Kyle Walstrom. 2004. *How Leadership Influences Student Learning*. Learning from Leadership Project. New York, NY: The Wallace Foundation. http://www.wallacefoundation.org/knowledge-center/school-leadership/key-research/Documents/How-Leadership-Influences-Student-Learning.pdf.

Marzano, Robert J. 2003. *What Works in Schools: Translating Research into Action*. Alexandria, VA: Association for Supervision and Curriculum Development.

———. 2007. *The Art and Science of Teaching: A Comprehensive Framework for Effective Instruction*. Alexandria, VA: Association for Supervision and Curriculum Development.

Marzano, Robert J., and Julia A. Simms. 2013. *Coaching Classroom Instruction*. The Classroom Strategies Series. With contributions by Tom Roy, Tammy Heflebower, and Phil Warrick. Bloomington, IN: Marzano Research Laboratory.

Marzano, Robert J., Timothy Waters, and Frian McNulty. 2005. *School Leadership that Works: From Research to Results*. Alexandria, VA: Association for Supervision and Curriculum Development. Kindle Edition.

Merriam-Webster. 2015. s.v. "profession." 15th edition.

Moran, Mary Catherine. 2007 *Differentiated Literacy Coaching: Scaffolding for Student and Teacher Success*. Alexandria, VA: Association for Supervision and Curriculum Development.

National Commission on Mathematics and Science Teaching for the 21st Century. 2000. *Before It's Too Late: A Report to the Nation from the National Commission on Mathematics and Science Teaching for the 21st Century*. Washington, DC: US Department of Education.

National Council of Teachers of Mathematics (NCTM). 2000. *Principles and Standards for School Mathematics*. Reston, VA: National Council of Teachers of Mathematics.

National Governors Association for Best Practices (NGA) and Council of Chief State School Officers (CCSSO). 2010. "Common Core State Standards: Mathematics." Washington DC: www.corestandards.org.

National Research Council. 2001. *Adding It Up: Helping Children Learn Mathematics*. Washington, DC: National Academy Press.

Newman, Fred M. 1994. "School-Wide Professional Community." *Issues in Restructuring Schools* 6: 1–2. http://www.wcer.wisc.edu/archive/cors/issues_in_restructuring_schools/issues_no_6_spring_1994.pdf.

Newman, Fred M., M. Bruce King, and Peter Youngs. 2000. "Professional Development that Addresses School Capacity: Lessons from Urban Elementary Schools." *American Journal of Education* 108 (4): 259–299.

Oxford Dictionaries. 2015. "community." http://www.oxforddictionaries.com/us/definition/american_english/community.

Pearson, P. and M. Gallagher. 1983. "The Instruction of Reading Comprehension." *Contemporary Educational Psychology* 8: 317–344.

Quate, Stevi, and John McDermott. 2014. "The Just-Right Challenge." *Educational Leadership* 72 (1): 61–65.

Rapacki, Lauren J., and Dionne I. Cross Francis. 2014. "I Am a Math Coach: Now What?" *Teaching Children Mathematics* 20 (9): 556–563.

Reeves, Douglas B. 2006. *The Learning Leader: How to Focus School Improvement for Better Results*. Alexandria, VA: Association for Supervision and Curriculum Development.

———. 2009. *Leading Change in Your School: How to Conquer Myths, Build Commitment, and Get Results*. Alexandria, VA: Association for Supervision and Curriculum Development. Kindle Edition.

Sammons, Laney. 2010. *Guided Math: A Framework for Mathematics Instruction*. Huntington Beach, CA: Shell Education.

———. 2013. *Strategies for Implementing Guided Math*. Huntington Beach, CA: Shell Education.

Schlechty, Phillip C. 1997. *Inventing Better Schools: An Action Plan for Educational Reform*. San Francisco, CA: Jossey-Bass. Kindle Edition.

Schmoker, Mike. 1999. *Results: The Key to Continuous School Improvement*. 2nd ed. Alexandria, VA: Association for Supervision and Curriculum Development.

———. 2004. "Tipping Point: From Feckless Reform to Substantive Instructional Improvement." *Phi Delta Kappan* 85 (6): 424–432.

———. 2005. "No Turning Back: The Ironclad Case for Professional Learning Communities." In *On Common Ground: The Power of Professional Learning Communities,* edited by Richard DuFour, Robert Eaker, and Rebecca DuFour, 135-152. Bloomington, IN: Solution Tree Press.

———. 2006. *Results Now: How We Can Achieve Unprecedented Improvements in Teaching and Learning.* Alexandria, VA: Association for Supervision & Curriculum Development. Kindle Edition.

Senge, Peter M. 2006. *The Fifth Discipline: The Art and Practice of the Learning Organization.* New York, NY: Doubleday. Kindle Edition.

Short, Paula M., and John T. Greer. 2002. *Leadership in Empowered Schools: Themes from Innovative Efforts.* 2nd ed. Upper Saddle River, NJ: Merrill Prentice Hall.

Smith, Patricia E. 2006. "From the Trenches: Lessons Learned." In *The Math Coach Field Guide: Charting Your Course,* edited by Carolyn Felux and Paula Snowdy, 110–118. Sausalito, CA: Math Solutions.

Sparks, Dennis. 2003. "Change Agent: Interview with Michael Fullan." *Journal of Staff Development* 24 (1): 55-58.

———. 2005. "Leading for Transformation in Teaching, Learning, and Relationships." In *On Common Ground: The Power of Professional Learning Communities,* edited by Richard DuFour, Robert Eaker, and Rebecca DuFour, 155–175. Bloomington, IN: Solution Tree Press.

Stoll, Louise, Dean Fink, and Lorna Earl. 2003. *It's About Learning (and It's About Time): What's in It for Schools.* New York, NY: RoutledgeFalmer. Kindle Edition.

Stronge, James H. 2007. *Qualities of Effective Teachers.* 2nd ed. Alexandria, VA: Association for Supervision and Curriculum Development.

Taylor-Cox, Jennifer. 2008. *Differentiating in Number and Operations and the Other Math Content Standards.* Portsmouth, NH: Heinemann.

Thompson-Grove, Gene. 2015. "A Change in Practice." National School Reform Faculty. Accessed April 14 http://www.nsrfharmony.org/system/files/protocols/change_practice_0.pdf.

Timperley, Helen. 2011. *Realizing the Power of Professional Learning.* New York, NY: McGraw-Hill.

Tracy, Brian. 2008. "The Role of a Leader." *Entrepreneur.* http://www.entrepreneur.com/article/189618.

Van Tassel, Rebecca. 2014. "The Trouble with Top-Down." *Educational Leadership* 71 (8): 76–78.

Vygotsky, L.S. 1978. *Mind in Society: The Development of Higher Psychological Processes.* Cambridge, MA: Harvard University Press.

West, Lucy, and Antonia Cameron. 2013. *Agents of Change: How Content Coaching Transforms Teaching and Learning.* Portsmouth, NH: Heinemann.

Williams, Karolyn, and Chris Confer. 2006. "Coteaching: A Powerful Tool." In *The Math Coach Field Guide: Charting Your Course,* edited by Carolyn Felux and Paula Snowdy, 74–83. Sausalito, CA: Math Solutions.

Zarrow, Joel. 2014. "Five Strategies for Better Teacher Professional Development." TeachThought http://www.teachthought.com/teaching/5-strategies-better-teacher-professional-development/.

Zeller, Erich. 2006. "Making Sense of Arithmetic: Helping Teachers Rethink Their Practice." In *The Math Coach Field Guide: Charting Your Course,* edited by Carolyn Felux and Paula Snowdy, 51–64. Sausalito, CA: Math Solutions.Guided Math Resource Materials

Zepeda, Sally J. 2005. *The Instructional Leader's Guide to Informal Classroom Observations.* Larchmont, NY: Eye on Education.

Guided Math Resource Materials

Sammons, Laney. 2010. *Guided Math: A Framework for Mathematics Instruction.* Huntington Beach, CA: Shell Education.

———. 2010. *Math Stretches: Building Mathematical Understanding, K–2.* Huntington Beach, CA: Shell Education.

Sammons, Laney, and Michelle Windham. 2011. *Math Stretches: Building Conceptual Understanding, 3–5.* Huntington Beach, CA: Shell Education.

Sammons, Laney, and Pamela Dase. 2011. *Math Stretches: Building Conceptual Understanding, 6–8.* Huntington Beach, CA: Shell Education.

———. 2011. *Building Mathematical Comprehension: Using Literacy Strategies to Make Meaning.* Huntington Beach, CA: Shell Education.

———. 2013. *Strategies for Implementing Guided Math.* Huntington Beach, CA: Shell Education.

———. 2014. *Guided Math Conferences.* Huntington Beach, CA: Shell Education.

Other Resources

Bamberger, J. Honi, Christine Oberdorf, and Karen Schultz-Ferrell. 2010. *Math Misconceptions PreK–Grade 5: From Misunderstanding to Deep Understanding.* Portsmouth, NH: Heinemann.

Brummer, Trisha, and Sarah Kartchner Clark. 2008. *Writing Strategies for Mathematics.* Huntington Beach, CA: Shell Education.

Diller, Debboe. 2011. *Math Work Stations: Independent Learning You Can Count On.* Portland, ME: Stenhouse.

Kazemi, Elham, and Allison Hintz. 2014. *Intentional Talk: How to Structure and Lead Mathematical Discussions.* Portland, ME: Stenhouse.

Newton, Nicki. 2013. *Guided Math in Action: Building Each Student's Mathematical Proficiency with Small-Group Instruction.* New York, NY: Routledge.

Parrish, Sherry. 2014. *Number Talks: Helping Children Build Mental Math and Computation Strategies, Grades K–5, Updated with Common Core Connections.* Sausalito, CA: Math Solutions.

Small, Marian. 2013. *Good Questions: Great Ways to Differentiate Mathematics Instruction.* 2nd ed. New York, NY: Teachers College Press and Reston, VA: National Council of Teachers of Mathematics.

Wedekind, Kassia Omohundro. 2011. *Math Exchanges: Guiding Young Mathematicians in Small-Group Meetings.* Portland, ME: Stenhouse.

Mathematics Instruction Observation Form

Teacher Observing _____   Date _____

Characteristic	Evidence to be collected	Evidence Observed
Emphasis on mathematical vocabulary	Math word walls, use of math vocabulary games, or use of math vocabulary journals observed	
Type of instruction	Whole-class Small-group Math Workshop	
Use of concrete/ representational/ abstract continuum of instruction	Use of manipulatives, multiple representations, and scaffolded transitions from one to the other	
Accountable math talk by students	Teacher Talk Student Talk Seat Work	
Differentiation of instruction to meet students learning needs	With small-group lessons or differentiated tasks	
Support for struggling learners	Small-group lessons or one-on-one conferences to provide support for struggling students	
Effective routines and procedures	At least 4 of 5 students asked can describe the routines and procedures they are expected to follow and are observed following them.	

Mathematics Improvement Plan

Shared Vision:

Action Plan:

Process Goals and Measures

Goals	Measures

Results Goals and Measures

Goals	Measures

Guided Math Needs Assessment

1. How comfortable do you feel using Guided Math?

   Not at All   Somewhat   Moderately   Very Comfortable

2. How comfortable do you feel using small groups in math?

   Not at All   Somewhat   Moderately   Very Comfortable

3. How often do you use small groups in math?

   Never   Once a Month   Once a Week   Several Times a Week

4. Circle the things that may help you feel more comfortable using Guided Math.

   Workshops   Book Study   Observing Modeled Lessons   Q & A Session

   Other (please list) _____

5. Please list any barriers you feel may prevent you from using Guided Math in your classroom.

6. Please list any questions you have regarding Guided Math.

(Adapted from Catiia Greene and Laney Sammons, pers. comm.)

Guided Math Implementation
Classroom Visit Checklist

		Evident	Not Evident	Notes
Environment	Table or floor space for small-group lessons			
	Math word wall			
	Math anchor charts			
	Student work displayed			
Instruction: Small Group	Hands-on, active engagement by students			
	Accountable math talk			
	Focused teaching point			
	Differentiation based on needs			
	Lesson uninterrupted by students working independently			
	Informal assessment with method of recording			
Instruction: Math Workshop	Clear routines and procedures			
	Students productively engaged in math tasks or games			
	System of accountability for students			

Guided Math Implementation
Self-Assessment Questionnaire

Please complete this self-assessment to help determine how well the implementation of changes in our school improvement plan is progressing. This reflective tool will aid us as a professional community in perfecting the improvement plan. Rate each item by circling a number with 1 being low and 5 being high.

To what extent...

Have you implemented Guided Math in your classroom/
instruction?   1 2 3 4 5

Has the Guided Math framework positively impacted your
instruction?   1 2 3 4 5

Has it positively impacted your students' learning?   1 2 3 4 5

1. In what ways have you implemented Guided Math? What has worked well? What problems have you encountered?

2. What evidence do you have of any positive impact of the Guided Math framework on your students' learning?

3. What suggestions do you have for making the implementation of Guided Math more effective?

4. What suggestions do you have for adapting the Guided Math framework to make it more effective for teaching and learning?

Mathematics Instruction Observation Form

Date _____   Grade Level _____

1. What is the mode of the instruction?

1	2	3	4	5
Teacher-Centered				Student-Centered

Notes:

2. How engaged are the students in the learning process?

1	2	3	4	5
Passive				Highly Engaged

Notes:

3. What instructional structure is being used?

1	2	3	4	5
Traditional				Constructivist, Inquiry

Notes:

4. What was the curriculum source?

1	2	3	4	5
Textbook				Standards

Notes:

5. What type of assessment is being used?

1	2	3	4	5
Procedural				Performance Task

Notes:

6. What was the level of rigor required of students?

1	2	3	4	5
Rote Learning				Cognitively Complex

Notes:

(Adapted from Hull, Balka, and Miles 2009, Kindle Location 352)

Wows and Wonders

Teacher Visited _____   Date_____

During your classroom visit, jot down what you are most impressed by (wows) and any questions you have about what you are seeing (wonders).

Wows!

I wonder...

Guided Math Demonstration Lesson Observation Form for Teachers

Date _____   Focus of the Lesson _____

Observer_____   Purpose of the Observation_____

What did you notice about the teacher? (Be specific.)	What did you notice about the students? (Be specific.)
What teaching strategies did you observe?	What evidence of student learning did you see?

What do you wonder about?

What did you gain or learn from the observation? What impact will it have on your teaching?

Guided Math Lesson
Observation Form For Coaches

Teacher _____   Observer _____

Date _____ Time _____   Focus of Lesson _____

Requested Area for Feedback _____

Components of Guided Math Being Observed:

_____ Environment of Numeracy   _____ Math Workshop

_____ Math Warm-Ups   _____ Math Conferences

_____ Whole-Class Instruction   _____ Assessment

_____ Small-Group Instruction

Classroom Environment	Classroom Management
What is the teacher doing?	What are the students doing?

Evidence of Learning:

Feedback:

Guided Math Peer Observation

Observing Teacher _____

Observed Teacher _____

Date _____ Time _____ Lesson Topic _____

Pre-Observation Conference

Observing Teacher:

What do you hope to learn from the experience? List at least three take-away goals.

Observed Teacher:

Describe the lesson you will be teaching.

What do you hope your students will learn?

Post-observation Conference

Observing Teacher:

What did you notice?

What did you learn? How will you apply what you learned?

What questions do you have for the teacher you observed?

Observed Teacher:

What are your reflections on the lesson?

Notes